Twu Tanl

Bedwas

Ponty Pant
Nich Price Esqr
Bridge

Pont y Gwindy

Energlyn
John Goodrich Esqr

Gwainy Barth

Iron Works

Piccadilly

Wern y Dommen

Ruddry Heath

Ruddry

eddau

Castle

CAERPHILLY

Van

Coal Pits

Park

Ruperra Col Morgan

Voltvor
Cwm

Meeting House

Warren House

Thorn Hill

Llwyn y Kelin

Ty Maen

Caerphilly Heath

Pen y Bryn

Graig Llisvane

Nant Mooth

Cefn Mabley

Park

J. Kemeys lyme Esqr Park

New House
Wm Lewis Esqr

Malinda

Red House

Llisvane

New Forge

Lanedarne

Wm Lewis Esqr
Green Meadow

Ymount

River

to Newport

Derry
Pentwyn Heath

Wdm Lewis Esqr

Blue House

Lanishan

KIBBOR

Romney

St Me

Whitchurch

Race Course

Kingcoed Mowr

Lanrumney
J Lewis Esqr

Rowldon

Coed y goras

Cardiff Heath

Kingcoed Llwynygrant

Waydell
Red House

Romney

Gabalva
Heath Hurst Esqr

Llystalybont

Penwaine

Renylax

Romney Bridge

ards Esqr
andaff

Landaff Court

Mindean

Roath

Pengam

Penfily

Little Heath

Gallows

Canton

UNDRED

Kings Castle

Cardiff Castle
Mar of Bute

White Friars

Splot

E

Adams Down

D

Canton Moor

Quay

CARDIFF

Leckwith Bridge

marsh

Publications of the South Wales Record Society

No 4

The Diaries of John Bird of Cardiff

Overleaf: **John Bird**

A plaque attached to the gilded frame of this portrait, but of later date than either the portrait or the frame, identifies the sitter as John Bird, mayor of Cardiff in 1862, a nephew of the diarist, but this identification seems to be erroneous, for the costume, hairstyle and general treatment of the sitter all suggest a late eighteenth- to early nineteenth-century date. At the turn of the century the portrait hung in Cardiff Castle and, when reproduced in Volume V of the *Records of the County Borough of Cardiff* (ed. J. Hobson Matthews, 1905), carried the inscription 'Sometime Factor', without any reference to mayoral status. Neither the date at which the portrait left the Castle nor its subsequent history has been established, but the original oil painting has been re-touched and re-varnished, and it seems probable that it was during this refurbishment that the plaque, with its dubious identification, was attached.

The editor is most grateful to Dr Ilid Anthony for her expert advice in helping to date the portrait from details of costume, details which support the hypothesis that the sitter was indeed John Bird the Diarist.

John Bird. Artist unknown. *By kind permission of Mr Ralph Bird and Family.*

The Diaries of John Bird of Cardiff

Clerk to the first Marquess of Bute

1790–1803

Edited by Hilary M. Thomas

Cardiff:
South Wales Record Society
and
Glamorgan Archive Service
1987

Published by the South Wales Record Society
22 Redbrink Crescent, Barry Island, South Glamorgan CF6 8TT.

and the Glamorgan Archive Service
Mid Glamorgan County Hall, Cathays Park, Cardiff CF1 3NE.

First published 1987

ISBN 09508676 3 2

Typeset by Ann Kirwan

Typeset on a Monotype Lasercomp
at Oxford University Computing Centre

Printed by D. Brown and Sons Ltd, Cowbridge and Bridgend.

Contents

List of Illustrations

Acknowledgements

I AM GRATEFUL to the Librarian and staff at the Cardiff Central Library for making the originals of John Bird's diaries available to me in the research room and for allowing me to borrow a microfilm copy of the two volumes transcribed in this edition. The latter facility, coupled with unrestricted use of the general editor's own microfilm reader, enabled my work of editing to progress much less spasmodically than would otherwise have been the case.

I wish to express my thanks to the staff at the Glamorgan Record Office, the National Library of Wales, the National Museum of Wales, the Scottish National Portrait Gallery and the Library of University College, Cardiff, who have helped me to identify events and personalities mentioned in the diaries, and who have allowed me to use items from their collections to illustrate this publication. Dr John Davies of the Department of Welsh History, University College of Wales, Aberystwyth, was kind enough to read the text when it was nearing completion, and to make a number of valuable suggestions which improved both the presentation and content of this work, and I acknowledge his help with gratitude.

My thanks are also due to Mr Ralph Bird of Cowbridge and his family for giving me access to family papers and for drawing my attention to the portrait of John Bird which forms the frontispiece of this volume.

The publication of this volume has been assisted by grants from the Marc Fitch Fund and the South Glamorgan County Council, whose generous support is gratefully acknowledged.

In thanking the officers of the South Wales Record Society for inviting me to undertake the pleasurable task of editing John Bird's diaries, and in acknowledging the help I have received from the general editor, Mr Brian James, I should emphasise that I am solely responsible for any remaining errors and omissions. Finally, I would like to join with the general editor in putting on record our appreciation of the valuable advice and assistance given us by Mr Philip Riden during the course of the publication of this volume.

H.M.T.

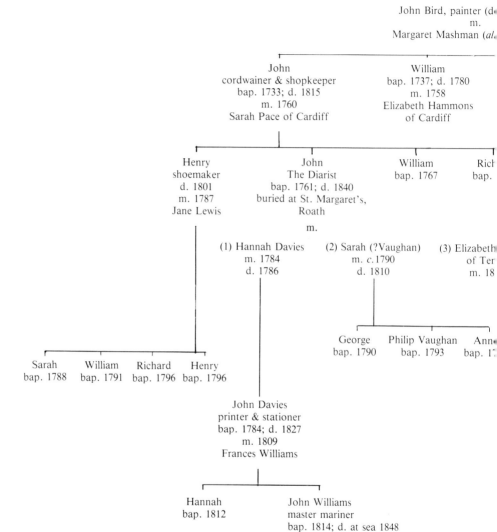

John Bird, painter (d
m.
Margaret Mashman (al

John
cordwainer & shopkeeper
bap. 1733; d. 1815
m. 1760
Sarah Pace of Cardiff

William
bap. 1737; d. 1780
m. 1758
Elizabeth Hammons
of Cardiff

Henry
shoemaker
d. 1801
m. 1787
Jane Lewis

John
The Diarist
bap. 1761; d. 1840
buried at St. Margaret's,
Roath

William
bap. 1767

Rich
bap.

m.

(1) Hannah Davies
m. 1784
d. 1786

(2) Sarah (?Vaughan)
m. c.1790
d. 1810

(3) Elizabeth
of Ter
m. 18

George
bap. 1790

Philip Vaughan
bap. 1793

Ann
bap. 1

Sarah
bap. 1788

William
bap. 1791

Richard
bap. 1796

Henry
bap. 1796

John Davies
printer & stationer
bap. 1784; d. 1827
m. 1809
Frances Williams

Hannah
bap. 1812

John Williams
master mariner
bap. 1814; d. at sea 1848

FAMILY OF CARDIFF

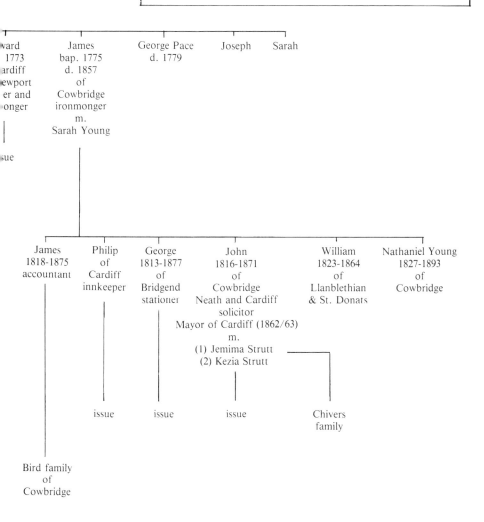

Bird family of the Channel Islands

That the Birds of Cardiff had close connections with the Channel Islands is clear from references in John Bird's diary for 1826 in which there are mentions of members of the family travelling between Cardiff and Guernsey. The diarist's grandson was apparently educated on the island—'paid Le Bert for John's schooling', and a 'nephew', William Knowles Bird, born in Guernsey in 1796 came to Cardiff to assist his kinsman in the Post Office.

Margaret

ward
1773
ardiff
ewport
er and
onger

issue

James
bap. 1775
d. 1857
of
Cowbridge
ironmonger
m.
Sarah Young

George Pace
d. 1779

Joseph

Sarah

James
1818-1875
accountant

Philip
of
Cardiff
innkeeper

George
1813-1877
of
Bridgend
stationer

John
1816-1871
of
Cowbridge
Neath and Cardiff
solicitor
Mayor of Cardiff (1862/63)
m.
(1) Jemima Strutt
(2) Kezia Strutt

William
1823-1864
of
Llanblethian
& St. Donats

Nathaniel Young
1827-1893
of
Cowbridge

issue

issue

issue

Chivers
family

Bird family
of
Cowbridge

BRIEF GENEALOGICAL TABLE SHOWING DESCENT OF BUTE (AND PLYMOUTH) FAMILIES

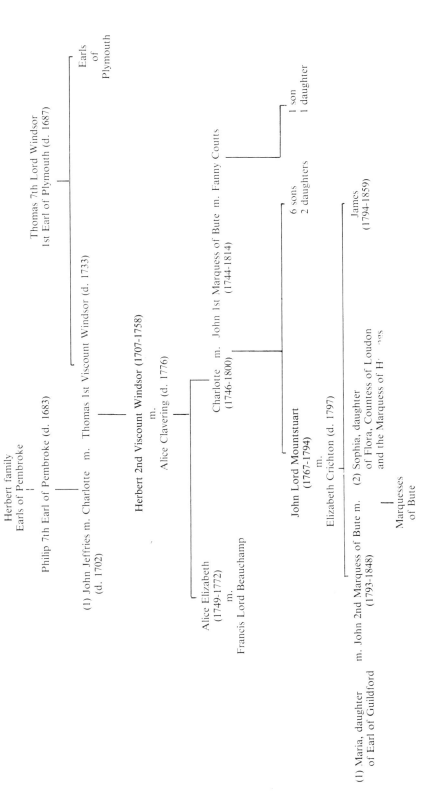

Herbert family
Earls of Pembroke

Philip 7th Earl of Pembroke (d. 1683)

Thomas 7th Lord Windsor
1st Earl of Plymouth (d. 1687)

Earls
of
Plymouth

(1) John Jeffries m. Charlotte m. Thomas 1st Viscount Windsor (d. 1733)
(d. 1702)

Herbert 2nd Viscount Windsor (1707-1758)
m.
Alice Clavering (d. 1776)

Alice Elizabeth
(1749-1772)
m.
Francis Lord Beauchamp

Charlotte m. John 1st Marquess of Bute m. Fanny Coutts
(1746-1800)   (1744-1814)

6 sons
2 daughters

1 son
1 daughter

John Lord Mountstuart
(1767-1794)
m.
Elizabeth Crichton (d. 1797)

(2) Sophia, daughter
of Flora, Countess of Loudon
and the Marquess of H...

James
(1794-1859)

Marquesses
of Bute

(1) Maria, daughter   m. John 2nd Marquess of Bute m.
of Earl of Guildford   (1793-1848)

Abbreviations

CCL	Cardiff Central Library
CP	*Complete Peerage*
DNB	*Dictionary of National Biography*
DWB	*Dictionary of Welsh Biography*
GRO	Glamorgan Record Office, Cardiff
Hist.Parl.	*History of Parliament*
NLW	National Library of Wales

Introduction

THE YEARS spanned by John Bird's life and career — 1761 to 1840 — were years of upheaval in the political, economic and social life of the country, and if great national and international events such as American Independence and French Revolution were remote from the day-to-day life of Glamorgan, the impact of Industrial Revolution was both immediate and profound. During the latter half of the eighteenth century Glamorgan was transformed from a rural backwater into an industrial giant. During Bird's lifetime the mighty ironworks of Merthyr, Dowlais and Aberdare spawned a seething industrial community in the formerly neglected hinterland, the population of the county rose dramatically and both the landscape and economy of Glamorgan were reshaped. Soon after Bird's death the pace of change gathered momentum to engulf and transform the town in which he had lived.

But the Cardiff familiar to John Bird was outwardly little affected by the new industrial order. The town remained what it had been for centuries, a small community of no more than 2,000 inhabitants huddled around the Castle, its trade and commerce dependent upon Bristol and the West Country, its politics and government dominated by the owners of the Castle. Despite the emergence of Merthyr as the largest town in Wales with a population of over 7,700 in 1801, most of the county's population (70,000 in 1801) continued to live in the small towns and villages of the Vale where agriculture predominated. Agricultural produce was the staple of Cardiff's modest trade through its small port, and even when the products of the iron industry began to be transported down the Glamorganshire Canal to Cardiff the traditional links with Bristol were maintained.

John Bird's diaries portray a community and an estate on the verge of change. While the content of the diaries reflects a preoccupation with the past rather than a perception of the future, there are glimpses of a society in turmoil and of developments that would, within a few short years, transform the society and institutions chronicled by the diarist.

John Bird, the author of these diaries, was born in Cardiff on 11 September 1761.[1] In a Directory which he himself published in 1796[2] he is described as a printer and bookseller, clerk to the Marquess of Bute and agent to the Phoenix Fire Office, Bristol Tontines[3] etc, a varied collection of occupations to which can be added those of coach proprietor, tax collector and postmaster, and all of which were complemented by Bird's activities as a bailiff and alderman of Cardiff.

When he died in 1840 John Bird was a substantial citizen, a prominent figure in the life of Cardiff borough. Obituary notices[4] refer to 'the universally respected and esteemed alderman of the borough', a 'gentlemen of much local influence, a kind-hearted, intelligent and useful member of the community'. His funeral was attended by the second Marquess of Bute whose sorrow at losing an old and devoted adherent of his family was apparent to the on-lookers, and it was at the expense of the Marquess that a tablet to the memory of John Bird was set up in the alderman's aisle of St John's church 'as a token of affectionate respect'. The memorial was not unique. When Henry Yeomans, senior alderman of the borough, had died in 1780 a tablet to his memory, dedicated by 'his attached friend' the first Marquess, had been placed in the same church. But between the Bute family and John Bird there were ties beyond the formalities of public service, bonds of loyalty to family, estate and borough forged over more than half a century.

Bird entered the employment of the Bute estate in 1777[5] when, at the age of sixteen, he began work as a clerk in the office of Thomas Edwards, lawyer and estate steward to the dowager Lady Windsor and her heirs and clerk of the peace for Glamorgan. Of his earlier education and employment nothing is known, but his work for the Bute estate continued formally until his retirement in 1824 and informally until his death. In fact he was continuing a tradition of family service, for since the end of the seventeenth century various members of the prolific Bird family had been employed by the lords of Cardiff Castle as craftsmen and minor officials of the estate.[6]

John Bird was descended from a line of gilders and painters whose advent into Glamorgan, in the seventeenth century, was occasioned by the desire of the county nobility and gentry to embellish their residences.[7] By the end of that century members of the family had not only established themselves in trade but had already linked their fortunes to the Cardiff Castle estate.

John Bird senior, a shoemaker by occupation, was baptised at the castle in 1733. His son, the diarist, was born there in 1761. Bird senior became a minor official of the borough, holding the offices of water-bailiff and clerk of the market. His son's career was more intimately connected with the castle and its owners, his involvement in Corporation affairs more significant.

After his apprenticeship in Thomas Edwards's office Bird became clerk or 'factor' to the Bute estate in Glamorgan. By the 1790s he was in receipt of a salary of £40 16s 0d a year, was provided with a house by Lord Bute* and had, by his own business activities, established himself as a substantial citizen of Cardiff.

The so-called diaries are more accurately described as notebooks, aide-mémoires in which Bird recorded items of information to be conveyed to the Marquess of Bute either directly by letter or through the Cardiff steward, Henry Hollier. The entries are spasmodic, reflecting such regular events as estate audits and assize courts, such extraordinary occurrences as the French

---

*John, Lord Mountstuart, fourth Earl of Bute (1792), first Marquess of Bute (1796). Referred to as Lord Bute or the first Marquess in this Introduction.

invasion threat of 1797 and the 'corn riots' at the turn of the century. Some entries were written on the day of the events, others were retrospective compilations, jotted down when Bird could snatch a few moments amid his multifarious activities. When the Marquess was out of the country Bird abandoned his attempts at correspondence altogether, and from March 1795 to March 1797 the sole entry in the diary reads 'LB at Spain', a reference to Lord Bute's undistinguished diplomatic career as British ambassador at Madrid.

It is apparent that communication between Bird and his employer was haphazard and unsatisfactory, the correspondence irregular and one-sided. Neither the diaries nor the estate correspondence[8] of the period indicate that Bird received answers to his letters or any instructions on matters of estate administration. Henry Hollier, nominally the leading figure in the management of the Cardiff Castle estate from 1784 to 1815, and Bird's immediate superior, exercised little authority over the subordinate estate officials and Bird often found it as difficult to communicate directly with him as with the Marquess.

Hollier's pursuit of public office — he was town clerk of Cardiff, collector of customs, receiver general of taxes for Glamorgan, and clerk of the peace for the county — coupled with his efforts to build up his own landed estate evidently left him with little time to concentrate on the active management of the Marquess of Bute's property, and his record as estate agent is best described as lamentable.

Nor did the estate receive guidance from its head. The first Marquess of Bute acquired the Cardiff Castle estate by his marriage, in 1766, with Charlotte Windsor and thereafter neglected it almost entirely. While he cut a dash in London society, dabbled in diplomacy and flirted with politics his estate went to rack and ruin. Contemporary comment suggested that if he applied himself to anything it was to squandering the vast fortune of his second wife Fanny, daughter of the banker Thomas Coutts, whom he married in 1800. 'I never saw an estate in a more neglected condition'[9] wrote David Stewart, land surveyor, in 1818, three years after Henry Hollier had been dismissed from office, and he counselled the second Marquess not to allow an estate of the size and consequence of his Glamorgan property to continue under its 'present' management. Primitive and archaic have been the adjectives employed by a more recent critic[10] to describe that management under which a preoccupation with the collection of manorial rents and dues, a haphazard accounting system, and the demands of the twice-yearly audit absorbed a disproportionate amount of the estate officials' time and laid the estate open to unchecked alienation of rights and resources and encroachment of lands.

'Experience has taught me', wrote the first Marquess to his son, 'that without being excessively attentive, accurate and watchful, an estate must suffer essentially'.[11] Nothing in his life or temperament suggests that he was capable of such application, and the estate suffered still more from its own tangled pattern of descent. After the death of Lord Windsor in 1758 his widow Alice

John, first Marquess of Bute. Engraved by J. R. Smith after J. E. Liotard, 1775. *By courtesy of the National Museum of Wales.*

Charlotte Jane, first wife of the first Marquess of Bute. Engraved by F. Bartolozzi after George Romney, 1783. *By courtesy of the National Library of Wales.*

(née Clavering) held the Cardiff Castle estate[12] as tenant for life. When she died in 1776 her daughter Charlotte, wife of the first Marquess, inherited the estate, her husband enjoying his rights *iure uxoris*. Only after his first wife's death in 1800 did the first Marquess acquire a moiety for life and the administration of the other moiety in trust for his grandson, the future second Marquess.

It is to John Bird's credit that against this background of an absentee land-owner, a lack of any clear policy of estate management, officials left to discharge or neglect their ill-defined duties, he nevertheless emerges as a conscientious and painstaking employee, a servant whose loyalty is sometimes strained by the lack of guidance from his superiors. What was he to make of a remark dropped by Colonel James Capper in January 1801, 'Lord Bute asked for ye Bird, he says he hears from ye *sometimes*'?[13] Should he write more often? Should he send weekly or monthly journals of occurrences to the Marquess? Anxiety over his past conduct underlines his constant dilemma: 'The greatest caution and Secrecy hath ever been observed on my part and I should rejoice at having a line of conduct marked out in that respect'.[14] Neither instructions nor rejoicings were to follow.

The spasmodic entries in the diaries are varied in content, ranging from national events to social gossip, but John Bird's main concern was to chronicle events that had some bearing on the Cardiff Castle estate, and the majority of the entries are concerned with estate management and with the business of the courts. Such matters, often trivial and mundane, are leavened by the inclusion of snippets of local gossip, by eye-witness accounts of extraordinary local happenings, and by pen sketches of personalities known to Bird. The result is a unique view of Cardiff at the time of the Napoleonic Wars.

Manorial business — the collection of chief rents, the claiming of heriots and other manorial dues, and the keeping of accounts — occupied much of John Bird's time and energies. And the importance he attached to these duties is evident in the detailed accounts submitted to the Marquess.

In December 1794 Bird relates how he sped to Llandaff after the death of Thomas Edwards to claim the heriot due to Lord Bute. Having managed to secure a fine saddle horse and mare, Bird's pride in his achievement is evident as he informs his employer that the whole business has been conducted very privately, the only person knowing about it being Mr Edwards's clerk with whom he is on good terms. His efforts to secure the best beast due from the Plymouth estate in August 1799 were less successful, Lady Plymouth having already sold the coach horses and removed the work horses to Hewell Grange before Bird or Hollier could invoke their manorial powers.

The collection of chief rents, cottage rents and burgage rents and the conduct of the twice-yearly audit with Henry Hollier, involved Bird with the minutiae of estate accounting, and the diary entries suggest that he made some attempts to improve the system of account-keeping inherited from previous estate officials. In 1795 he mentions that Hollier has approved his scheme to re-model the estate rental, keeping the 'new' and 'old' estates separate, and that he has prepared a book for the purpose. In 1798, on the appointment of a new bailiff for Senghennydd, he retrieved all books and papers formerly kept at Caerphilly by Thomas Howell, the old bailiff, but found that the chief rent books were twenty years out of date and virtually useless.

The collection of rent arrears was another matter in which Bird was indefat-igable. In January 1801, having spent three days in Cowbridge and neighbour-hood getting in £30 of arrears in the borough, he discovered an old rental made out in 1744 by Thomas Lewis, a Cowbridge attorney. The latter, still alive in 1801, was able to provide Bird with information on the collection of those burgage rents, thereby strengthening his resolve to enforce payment of the oldest arrears from the representatives of such long-standing defaulters as Major Thomas Edmondes and Charles Edwin.

Bird's involvement with book-keeping also cast him, inadvertently, in the role of custodian of the county's records, for as his diary relates, it was he who salvaged the official files and papers from Thomas Edwards's house in Llandaff in 1795, brought them to Cardiff in two carts and 'deposited' them in the drawing room of the Castle.

He readily assumed the role of unofficial custodian of the Castle, a building that had little to recommend itself as a residence. Such improvements as had been carried out by Lord Bute and his son in the 1770s and 1780s were brought

View of Cardiff town and castle from the north-west. Engraved by S. Lacey after Henry Gastineau, c.1830. *By courtesy of University College Cardiff Library.*

to an abrupt end in 1794 on Lord Mountstuart's death, and when visiting his Glamorgan estate the first Marquess stayed either at the *Cardiff Arms* or at Cathays House. While Bird reports occasionally that all is neat and tidy at the Castle, his accounts of sheep grazing the lawns, the use of the gravel walks as promenades by the citizens of Cardiff and the exercising of local troops within the Castle walls underline its neglect by the Stuart family.

The infrequent visits of the first Marquess to Cardiff and his lack of involvement in his Glamorgan inheritance, coupled with the frequent absences of Henry Hollier, not only laid a wide range of responsibilities squarely upon Bird's shoulders but also made him an eager recipient of local intelligence. Hearsay and rumour, if carefully sifted, could be useful tools for the estate clerk. It was gossip heard at the audit in December 1794 that had prompted Bird to make his speedy visit to Llandaff to claim the heriot due on the death of Thomas Edwards. His circle of acquaintances was wide, his ears were finely tuned to the merest hint of events affecting Bute interests, and his access to local intelligence must also have been of inestimable value to his own business enterprises and to his public career.

Scraps of information, rumour and gossip concerning property sales were assiduously collected by Bird, for one of the first Marquess's few active involvements with his Glamorgan estate was in the purchase of land. There is only an oblique reference in the diary to the most significant purchase, that of the Friars estate of William Hurst of Gabalfa and his cousin Calvert Richard Jones of Swansea, a purchase negotiated in 1791 and completed in 1793 for £19,000, but on 6 September 1794 Bird was present at the *Cardiff Arms* where the auction of the Roath estate took place. Bird followed the bidding keenly, and was evidently under the impression that the heavily mortgaged estate had been acquired by Hollier, on behalf of the Marquess, for £5,000. He subsequently learnt that the property had been merely 'bought in' to await future negotiations for sale, and later entries in his diary record the visits of more would-be purchasers to Roath. On the eventual sale of the Roath estate John Bird's diary is silent. The property was not, in fact, added to the Marquess of Bute's property in Roath, but was acquired by the banker and lawyer John Wood, head of that family who were successively supporters and arch-critics of the Bute interest in Cardiff.

In July 1800 Bird received some very dubious information at second hand from a 'gentleman who dined with Robert Jenner at Wenvoe Castle'[15] to the effect that Jenner intended to stand for election as county member at the next election. Such an after-dinner confidence was highly suspect, but Bird dared not ignore it. Any rumour of political aspirations in the county had to be conveyed to his employer, for this was the one sphere of Glamorgan affairs in which the first Marquess showed a determination to exert his influence. He sought to control the parliamentary representation of both county and borough. In Cardiff, where the officials of the Bute estate and the Corporation were often identical — Hollier was regularly a bailiff, Bird was a bailiff and alderman, the Marquess's solicitor, John Wood, was town clerk of Cardiff from 1789 to 1804 — the Castle dominated the Corporation and secured control of the parliamentary seat, the other contributory boroughs[16] succumbing to Bute influence. In the matter of the county representation, the Glamorgan gentry successfully opposed the political influence of Cardiff Castle and it was their nominee, the ineffectual Thomas Wyndham of Dunraven Castle, who represented the county in Parliament from 1789 until 1814.

One of the earliest entries in Bird's diary concerns the parliamentary election of June 1790 when John Lord Mountstuart, eldest son of the first Marquess, was elected for the Glamorgan boroughs, displacing Sir Herbert Mackworth of Neath, whose family had represented the boroughs for over half a century. The following year Mackworth's death, recorded by Bird, left the boroughs firmly under Bute control, and Lord Mountstuart (d. 1794) was succeeded as member by his brothers Evelyn and William. Bird's diary is reticent on one feature of the 1790 election, the fact that over a hundred new burgesses were created to counter any opposition from the disgruntled western boroughs, a fact that would scarcely need to be drawn to the Marquess's attention. He does however record the presence of a Stamp Inspector who examined the admissions of burgesses with Messrs Wood and Hollier, and itemises the expenses of the election, totalling £289 6s. 0d. The election of Thomas Wyndham, the serving county member, whose success was an unwelcome reminder to the Bute family of its failure to impose its own nominee on the county, is also recorded by Bird with suitably scornful remarks upon the indifferent and inaudible nature of Wyndham's speeches and his reluctance to give the customary dinner to his supporters.

Predictably, the diaries record the personal fortunes of members of the Bute family. There were the celebrations in August 1793 when, as Bird relates, the bells of St John's church were rung for three days to celebrate the birth of John Crichton Stuart, son of Lord Mountstuart and Lady Elizabeth Crichton. Six months later, at the age of only twenty-seven, Lord Mountstuart died after a fall from his horse. His widow, who gave birth to a second son later that year, survived her husband by only three years. Where John Bird's diary records such events it does so without comment. In January 1800 Charlotte (née Windsor), wife of the first Marquess, died and was buried alongside her son and his wife in the church of Stanford Rivers, Essex. In September the same year Bird was one of the few observers present at a pre-dawn ceremony 'conducted with the greatest privacy'[17] when the bodies of the Marchioness, her son and daughter-in-law were reinterred in the newly built family vault at St Margaret's church, Roath. In September 1791 John Bird had enjoyed a moment of social triumph when the then unmarried Lord Mountstuart and Lady Eliza Crichton had visited Cardiff. In the absence of Hollier it had been Bird who had shown the young couple around Cardiff Castle, guided them on horseback to Caer-

John, Lord Mountstuart (1767-94). Painting by Mather Brown, 1793. *In a private Scottish collection.*

Lady Mountstuart (Lady Elizabeth Crichton) with her mother, the Countess of Dumfries. Painting by Sir Henry Raeburn, 1793. *In a private Scottish collection.*

philly and proudly conducted them around his bookshop. But no hint of personal feeling colours his factual, eye-witness account of the Roath ceremony.

The premature death of Lord Mountstuart and the first Marquess's lack of interest in his Glamorgan property sealed the fate of the Cardiff Castle estate for another generation. The pattern of neglect by its owners and incompetent management by its stewards continued, antiquated procedures of administration were perpetuated and, inevitably, the estate was exploited to its detriment. Such neglect created many problems. The problems were not of Bird's making, but his diaries show that he was often despatched by Hollier to iron them out.

At Hirwaun encroachments on the common had been condoned to such an extent by the Bute estate officials that illegal takings had been converted into tenancies, to the outrage of other landowners with rights on the common. There were frequent skirmishes among tenants and squatters, disputes between rival landowners, litigation and judgements in the courts, matters with which Bird was involved and on which he kept the Marquess informed.

Particularly vivid are Bird's descriptions of his encounter with the squatters on Cardiff Heath in the summer of 1799. On 30 July 1798 his diary records that he has spent the morning at the Heath selecting twelve persons most eligible to be served with notice of ejectment. Bird assures the Marquess that he will personally deliver the notices 'for safety and regularity' not trusting the sheriff's officers 'who have not the Interest of the Plaintiff properly at heart'. Legal and administrative proceedings dragged on for almost twelve months, and it was June 1799 before a small posse of officials, headed by John Wood senior and John Williams of Cardiff, the deputy sheriff, and accompanied by the indispensable John Bird, rode to the Heath to take down the twelve illegal cots and enclosures. They met with such fierce resistance that Bird was despatched to Cardiff to summon the Volunteer Cavalry. Even after the ringleaders were taken into custody there were fears that the mob would assemble in greater strength in the evening, and Bird was once again sent to enlist military help, this time from the Caerphilly Volunteers. Hastening back with Sheriff Goodrich over Caerphilly Mountain he saw a pall of smoke in the sky and discovered that 'the Cot where the resistance was made had been set on fire as the most effectual method of destroying it.'[18] Ejection of the squatters and the demolition of their cottages proceeded without further incident, but Bird would long remember the confrontation and recall the wrath of the squatters' wives — 'the Women for some time acted the part of the Amazonians, having armed themselves with Pitchforks, etc.' And some of his acquaintances could not resist the temptation to taunt him with reminders of his perilous encounter.

Seldom did Bird become so actively involved in law enforcement. But the administration of justice in the county was a subject on which he kept the Marquess regularly informed, and many of the diary entries relate to the twice-yearly visits of the judges to Cardiff for the holding of the courts of Great

Sessions. Whenever possible Bird attended the proceedings himself, observing and recording the more colourful cases, attentive to any matters affecting the interests of the Castle. When estate or family business made his attendance impossible, he was assiduous in collecting eye-witness reports from friends and acquaintances. The result is an illuminating patchwork of legal personalities and events.

The pageantry of the formalities preceding the judicial business is described by Bird in some detail, with observations on the size and appearance of the shrieval retinue, the procession of the judges and court officials to St John's church, the text of the sermon and the programme of sacred music chosen by the judges. Once the court was in session Bird made notes on those cases both civil and criminal which he deemed newsworthy. His notes are by no means a comprehensive digest of proceedings, but when the diary entries are compared with the formal records of the courts[19] the accuracy and judicious selection of his reports become apparent.

Of particular value are Bird's detailed synopses of the judges' opening addresses to the grand jury, addresses that ranged from recommendations for improving the state of the county gaol and of the county roads to remarks on the progress of the Glamorganshire Canal and the likely benefits for the county, from homilies on correct legal procedures and standards of behaviour expected of court officials to eulogies on the heroic stand taken by the nation and its armed forces against the French and their allies in the Napoleonic Wars.

The state of the county gaol was a perennial problem and this topic figures prominently in Bird's reports. Presentments by the grand jury, inaction by the county magistrates, threats by the judges to remove the Sessions to Cowbridge unless speedy and positive action was taken are all revealed in the entries for 1790 and 1791. There was an abortive attempt by Thomas Wyndham, the county member of Parliament, to get the old gaol demolished and removed to a more central location in the county. Year after year the deplorable state of the building brought censure on the county, and not until 1799 was Judge Hardinge able to voice satisfaction with the improvements carried out there, but within a few years the inadequacies of the gaol were once again apparent.

Cardiff bridge was another burden for the county's administrators. In July 1792 Bird's diary records the decision of the justices in Quarter Sessions to build a new bridge of three arches across the river Taff in Cardiff. In September 1794 he reports progress on the work, but the following January writes that the temporary structure has been swept away by ice and flood while the central arch of the new bridge is still several months away from completion. The fluctuating fortunes of Cardiff bridge are recorded in the formal records of the court of Quarter Sessions.[20] Where Bird's accounts are particularly valuable are in their comments on the hazards of travel occasioned by inadequate roads and bridges — mail coaches overturned, passengers and horses flung into swollen rivers, disruptions and delays to commercial and social life.

In 1794 a new artery of communication linking the industrial centre of Merthyr to the sea at Cardiff was opened — the Glamorganshire Canal. Although Bird's diaries mention the building and opening of the canal and contain the occasional reference to lawsuits involving rival ironmasters and canal proprietors, there is little in their pages to suggest that the activities of the mighty ironworks at Dowlais and Merthyr, exploiting as they were minerals and lands of the Bute estate, were subject to any particular scrutiny by Hollier or Bird. Only once, in fact, does Bird mention the Dowlais Works specifically, on 1 July 1801 when he refers to the Carno lands[21] leased by the Company from the Bute estate. Not until the Cardiff Castle estate's management was put on a more professional footing, particularly after David Stewart's surveys and reports in the 1820s, did the industrial potential of the Marquess of Bute's Glamorgan lands become realised.

The activities of the established ironmasters were beyond Hollier's competence and outside Bird's purview, but neither man could be entirely unaware of the demands of emergent industry. Merthyr might be seen as an alien community, remote in more than geography from Cardiff and the Vale, but the products of Dowlais, Cyfarthfa and Penydarren were transported to the sea within sight of the Castle. Surely other parts of the Bute estate where coal and iron had long been mined on a small scale could be exploited with greater profit and for the immediate benefit of the landowner? Thus it was to the commons of Caerphilly and Rudry, a short ride over the mountain from Cardiff and familiar territory to the estate agents, that Bird accompanied Edward Martin of Llansamlet on his mineral survey in 1799. Delegated by Hollier to accompany the surveyor, Bird wrote enthusiastically in the pages of his notebook, obviously eager to communicate with the Marquess before the despatch of Martin's formal report. The substance of that report, he assures his employer, will be that by proper management and planning the coal and ore resources on Caerphilly Common alone could keep an iron furnace running for a hundred years.[22]

Martin was not the only surveyor to rely on the knowledge and competence of the Bute estate clerk. A year later both Bird and Hollier assisted the Luton surveyor Thomas Brown in his mapping of the Heath lands, a preliminary to the Cardiff Heath Enclosure Act of 1801. Brown stayed with the Bird family and was helped in his work on the Heath by the Bird children as well as by their father. Bird's recollection of the 'Battle of the Heath' was still vivid, but with the squatters evicted and their dwellings demolished the way was now clear for enclosure and the necessary parliamentary procedures were being implemented.

In 1794 Bird had helped to plot the course of the Glamorganshire Canal through Cardiff, his presence occasioned both by the surveyors' need for reliable local information and the Bute estate's concern to forestall encroachments and trespass. When, twenty years later, the advisors to the second Marquess complained that the Glamorganshire Canal had been allowed to usurp land and neglect fences, their censure of the estate's agents should have been directed not so much at Bird as at Hollier who had acted in this, as in so many estate affairs, with characteristic inertia.

For much of the period covered by John Bird's diaries Britain was involved in the Napoleonic Wars. These were momentous years in the country's political and social history, and the military preparations to counter a French invasion threat, the social unrest arising from food shortages and high prices affected most parts of the country. In this context Bird's descriptions of Militia activities, of the drilling of Volunteer forces, of food riots in Swansea and of the distribution of corn to the poor in Cardiff provide unique glimpses of the local community organised for military and civil emergency.

The Glamorgan Militia, raised by ballot in each hundred of the county, were assembled periodically for drills and exercises, and their presence in Cardiff invariably presented Bird with a rich miscellany of local news for the Marquess. On 31 May 1790, after exercises on the gravel walks of Cardiff Castle, officers of the Royal Glamorgan Militia strolled into Bird's shop to purchase books and prints. A local scandal erupted in March 1793 when two young girls were abducted, apparently willingly, by the quarter-master and one of the officers. Lord Mountstuart, as colonel, was reported to be 'much displeased' and threatened dismissals. There were occasions when Bird's musical talents were employed as he joined the bandsmen in playing the Militia out of town. And news of the sudden death of one of the Militia officers, Captain John Richards, a bailiff of Cardiff and a long-standing supporter of the Bute interest in the borough, called for particular mention on 25 March 1793.

The Marquess of Bute, as lord lieutenant, made one of his rare visits to Glamorgan in 1797 to chair the county meeting, thereby giving token leadership at a time of national emergency. The gentry rallied to the call, there was a flurry of military activity in the county, and the services of the Marquess's secretary were heavily engaged. For a few weeks in the spring of 1797 Bird's diary suggests that he had little sleep and that his time was almost totally absorbed by military affairs. The threat of a French invasion led to the Militia forces being hastily assembled, to the raising of a Supplementary Militia and the recruitment of a Volunteer force, the embodiment and training of which Bird describes in detail. By April 1797 over one hundred and thirty men had enrolled in the Cardiff Cavalry Volunteers, supplemented by a contingent from the Melingriffith Works. Led by Captain Wyndham Lewis, with Henry Hollier as lieutenant, they numbered among their ranks John Bird, who not only rode in the Cardiff Troop but also found time to act as its unpaid secretary. The passage of the Supplementary Militia Act brought a load of extra work to Bird — 'I have been writing etc. day and night since the Act came down'[23] — for

A group of local gentry in the keep of Cardiff Castle, from a painting by J.C. Ibbetson, 1789. From left to right: Bloom Williams, surgeon; Captain Sabine, adjutant, Glamorgan Militia; John Richards, senior; the Rev. S. M. Lowder; Lewis Jenkins, lieutenant-colonel, Glamorgan Militia; Henry Hollier, steward to Lord Bute. *By courtesy of South Glamorgan County Libraries.*

the burden of correspondence and communication with the hierarchy of county officials was placed firmly upon his shoulders.

Bird's accounts of military preparations are interspersed with insights into the clashes of personalities among officers, the disagreements among the county gentry as to the relative merits of infantry and cavalry forces, the rash enthusiasms of old military men such as Colonel James Capper who promised to teach the Cardiff Volunteers how to use 'the Great Guns' and to ride with them in an emergency. And as part of the frenzy of activity there were the inevitable muddles and poor communications. Men were sent to the wrong place for muster and drills. Units were disbanded prematurely. There were shortages of arms and equipment.

The progress of the war provided the visiting judges with material for stirring addresses to the grand jury. At the March Sessions at Cardiff in 1797 Judge Hardinge could speak in glowing terms not only of the repulse of the French invaders by Lord Cawdor's Pembrokeshire Yeomanry Cavalry but also of the great naval victories of Cape St Vincent, Camperdown and the Nile. It was the most political address that Bird could remember. In the summer of 1797 the Cardiff Volunteers were congratulated by Judge Hardinge on their smart appearance, a compliment both to the efforts of a drill sergeant from the 18th Light Dragoons and to the activities of John Bird. In the absence of Henry Hollier, Bird had been despatched by John Wood, the clerk of the peace, to collect signatures to a public subscription for the purchase of new arms and uniforms for the Volunteers. It was a task for which he had little time or enthusiasm, his reluctance to undertake yet another duty apparent in his diary entry 'I thought some one of more consequence than I was should go with me as I had done every other part of the business in my power,'[24] but at Wood's insistence he duly and successfully hawked the subscription around Cardiff.

As the threat of invasion receded, so drills and parades became as much social as military occasions. After reviewing the Cardiff Troop of Volunteer Cavalry, John Bird among them, on a frosty January morning in 1799, it was with considerable alacrity that Colonel Richard Aubrey leapt from his horse to join the spectators on the terraces of the Castle. And later that year the Cardiff Volunteers held combined exercises with the Cowbridge Infantry Volunteers 'a grand field day'[25] to celebrate the anniversary of the King's accession.

Against a background of war with France and rumours of mutiny in the Fleet, with the poor hungry and restive and with some bold spirits speaking out against the monarchy, politicians and judges were eloquent in their defence of the constitution. Judge Hardinge, in his address to the grand jury in March 1793, drew attention to societies against Republican and Revolutionary sympathisers, and in his more political discourses vehemently denounced those who sought to undermine the present order of government.

The turmoil in which society was operating[26] is underlined by Bird's accounts of soaring prices, food scarcities, bankruptcies and banking crises.

Prices at Cardiff market were the dearest ever remembered. In October 1799 wheat was sold at 33s. 0d. a Cardiff bushel (20 gallons) and distress in the town was acute. The following spring remarks by the visiting judges on the scarcity of grain and the needs of the poor prompted Bird to tell the Marquess that nothing had yet been done in Cardiff to relieve the distress 'either in making Soup or entering into a Subscription'.[27] He was evidently aware of relief schemes in other counties, accounts of which appeared in the Bristol and Gloucester newspapers, for he was able to inform Herbert Evans of Neath of the activities of the lord lieutenant of Somerset, Lord Poulett, and the trades-people of that county in providing the poor with food. When, in January 1801, a subscription was raised in Cardiff and a shipment of grain brought to the town, one of the prime movers of the scheme — the man who organised the collection of funds and the distribution of provisions — was the ubiquitous John Bird.

Poverty and hunger led to protest and demonstration. Law and order seemed threatened by popular unrest. One pathetic protest, later dubbed a riot, was seen at first hand by Bird in Swansea where, as he and Hollier were collecting taxes in April 1801, a group of starving women and children marched on a corn warehouse in the town. Bird's eye-witness account of the 'rioters' and their ragged procession, of the panic among the Corporation officials that led to the summoning of the military — 'one of the old Ladies of the Corporation (Mr. W. Jeffreys) read the Riot Act' — and his report of the release of the ringleaders by a tolerant local Militia serves to emphasise the volatile situation in the county and to mirror the national unrest.[28]

On this occasion the absence of the lord lieutenant fuelled complaints that the county was without a head, and Herbert Evans of Gnoll, in an intoxicated outburst,[29] voiced the opinions of a large body of discontented gentry. His tongue loosened by alcohol, Evans not only pleaded volubly for the Marquess to give a lead in the county but also attacked the county's largest landowner, Thomas Mansel Talbot, for staying at Penrice and doing nothing, and the county member, Thomas Wyndham, for sitting at home and getting drunk. His indiscreet comments were all noted down by the Marquess's clerk.

Bankruptcies were regular occurrences in this period of economic disruption, and there are several references in the diaries to business failures, debts and rumours of insolvency. Nor were the banks immune from trouble. In 1793 Bird reported that difficulties over payment of bills drawn on the recently opened Cardiff bank of Taitt Wood & Co. would put a stop to any further negotiation of their paper from some time, while in March 1797 Judge Hardinge, in his long 'political' discourse to the grand jury, recommended the utility of the country banks and in particular the Brecon Old Bank of Messrs Wilkins. Public confidence in financial institutions had been undermined, and pronouncements such as that of the learned judge fell reassuringly on the ears of the county gentry and their representatives.

Symptomatic of the need for national reassurance were the loyal addresses from the county and boroughs to Parliament and the Crown. In April 1800 these expressions of local loyalty involved Bird in a rush of activity. The address from the boroughs was sent after him to Llantrisant where he was receiving taxes with Hollier. Having secured the signatures of various members of the Corporation, Bird hastened to Neath where he roused the portreeve from his bed late at night. Early the following morning other members of the Corporation were likewise disturbed from their slumbers to sign the document 'most of the gentlemen signed it in bed and were much pleased at the promptitude displayed on the occasion'[30] before Bird rode to Swansea to gather more signatures. After travelling almost continuously for two days the indefatigable courier arrived back in Cardiff late in the evening but in time to show the document to Wood, pack it up and deliver it to the coach office with strict instructions for its immediate despatch. The following week, as Bird and Hollier continued their collection of taxes, they heard that the address had been received in London. And, while still in the midst of tax-collecting at Pyle, Bird was called upon to fair-copy the agreed text of the county address 'which was done in the midst of Hurry and bustle or I could have done it much better.'[31]

The working day of the estate clerk was often long and arduous. And with such demands upon his time, hard-pressed to find a few moments to make jottings in his diary, Bird's notes degenerate, briefly, into a hotch-potch of jumbled scribblings.

Some of the more colourful incidents described by Bird are also indicative of the unsettled times. Smuggling, long rife in the Bristol Channel, flourished, the task of customs officers made more difficult by the disruptions of war. Barry Island, for centuries a refuge of smugglers, continued to provide a haven for the discharge of contraband and it was a considerable coup for customs officials in 1798 when they seized quantities of brandy and silk handkerchiefs cached on the island, news of which Bird was eager to communicate to the Marquess.

The hated press-gang, its activities intensified during the years of war, also makes an appearance in Bird's diary, providing him with an opportunity to display his journalistic talents in his report of the gang's pursuit of a group of sailors through Cardiff in August 1793. The confrontation between heavily armed sailors and press-gang at Rumney, the intervention of townspeople and the withdrawal of the gang without their intended victims were the ingredients of an exceptional piece of local intelligence for communication to the county's lord lieutenant.

Nor were Bird's talents as a local reporter confined to the pages of his diaries. We learn from an entry of 30 July 1798 that he sent an account of the opening of the Cardiff sea lock of the Glamorganshire Canal to the *Gloucester Journal*, where it was published. By this device Bird tried to ensure that the account was seen by the Marquess, apparently more confident of the

Marquess's reading the columns of the *Journal* than the pages of his letters. However, it was not from the Marquess or from Hollier that Bird was to receive compliments on his report, but from the Merthyr ironmaster, Richard Crawshay.

The occasional entries of births, marriages and deaths within the county families found in the pages of Bird's diaries were noted to refresh his memory when writing subsequently to the Marquess. There are a few discreet comments on family relationships, a few judicious recitals of indiscretions such as Herbert Evans's intoxicated outburst, but no vindictive gossip. Whether these were the county families with whom Bird enjoyed a distant, though cordial relationship, or his professional and business associates, his observations were tempered by the requirements of his role as correspondent to the Marquess. It was a role that demanded a large measure of diplomacy.

Two major personalities emerge from Bird's jottings — Judge George Hardinge and Doctor Richard Griffiths. For the former Bird evidently had not only respect but affection. Towards the latter his feelings were more ambivalent.

Hardinge had first appeared as judge on the Glamorgan circuit in the summer of 1787 when he had sat at the Great Sessions at Cowbridge. The following year Great Sessions had moved to Cardiff, the first time they had been held there for twenty years, and it was at the town hall in High Street,[32] and in rooms in the town's hostelries that the courts were held throughout the period covered by the diaries.

Judge George Hardinge was the 'waggish Welsh judge' of Byron's *Don Juan* and from Bird's observations on his legal pronouncements in court and his social activities in the county, the picture that emerges is of a genial, eloquent and fair-minded man. Not only are Judge Hardinge's addresses to the grand jury at the commencement of each Sessions summarised by Bird, as are his comments upon the individual cases and judgements, but there are some revealing insights into the character of the man beyond the formal image of the courtroom.

Bird's own love of music prompted him to comment on Hardinge's selection of music to be performed at the service in St John's church that preceded the business of each Sessions. He discloses that the judge conducted a regular correspondence with the vicar of St John's, the Reverend Samuel Lowder, for eight years, and that after Lowder's death in 1798 Hardinge arranged for his voluminous correspondence,[33] doubtless revealing of personalities and politics in Cardiff, to be returned to him. And it was the ever useful John Bird who acted as intermediary between the judge and the Lowder family in negotiating the return of those letters.

Urbane, convivial, Judge Hardinge was an unmistakable figure as he travelled around the county by coach, on horseback and occasionally by boat. An excursion to Minehead by boat in 1791, accompanied by Henry Hollier,

Judge George Hardinge. Engraving by an unknown artist. *By courtesy of the National Museum of Wales.*

proved so enjoyable that he engaged the same vessel to take him to Bristol after the next Sessions. In August 1793 there was the unique spectacle of the judge being conducted along a section of the Glamorganshire Canal in a canal boat by Samuel Homfray, with a harper providing a musical background.

Courtroom altercations between the barristers and the judges, complaints by the counsellors over the inadequacy of their accommodation, differences of opinion between the judges, as chronicled by Bird, add a new dimension to the formal records of the courts. After disagreements between the voluble Judge Hardinge and his more taciturn junior colleague, Judge Abel Moysey, over points of law in a property dispute in 1794, Bird heard 'from one who had it from Judge Moysey's clerk'[34] that the judges were in such regular disagreement that Moysey had asked to be removed from the circuit. This was a very confidential piece of gossip, eagerly received and proudly transmitted.

Confronted by protracted litigation over trivial matters, by indolence among jurors or corrupt practice by officials, the judge's customary affability vanished and he became the stern upholder of the dignity and integrity of the court. Nor was he reluctant to impose his own decided views upon the court, as in April 1791 when his declared preference for Cardiff rather than Cowbridge as the meeting place of Great Sessions left the grand jury with no option but to concur.

When only eleven grand jurymen attended the summer Great Sessions in 1793 Hardinge expressed his displeasure forcibly, Henry Hollier's reluctance to be sworn in attracting particular censure. Also empanelled on this occasion to swell the ranks of jurymen was a man well known to the courts and to John Bird — Dr Richard Griffiths.

Born in Llanwonno in 1756 Richard Griffiths was a man of diverse talents whose medical practice as surgeon, apothecary and man-midwife was often subordinated to his role as a businessman, speculator and gambler. Long before his death in 1826 he had, by purchase, speculation and inheritance, acquired extensive mineral-bearing properties in the Taff and Rhondda valleys and had constructed the Doctor's Canal, a waterway that was to carry the bulk of the Rhondda coal trade until the coming of the railways.[35] When he died in 1826 the bulk of his potentially valuable estate passed to his nephews Thomas and George Thomas of Llanbradach and Ystrad Mynach. But it is not his career as doctor of medicine, coroner or industrial entrepreneur that earns Dr Griffiths a place in the pages of John Bird's diaries, but his reputation as a hothead and gambler, his unruly behaviour and predilection for litigation. In the summer of 1790 he was tried at Hereford Assizes for alleged fraud at cards (see Appendix A) and was acquitted. In April the following year he was indicted at the Cardiff Sessions for 'unlawfully, wickedly and maliciously' challenging William Lewis of Whitchurch to a duel, but the case was thrown out of court. In 1792 he was yet again before the court, this time on a charge of assault, accused of beating John Price about the head with the butt-end of a large riding whip. Undeterred and unrepentant after being found guilty and fined £200, Griffiths then influenced the Auditor and Compounder of His Majesty's Land Revenue in Wales to get the major part of his fine remitted. His action, news of which soon reached the judges' ears, earned him a sharp reprimand from Judge Hardinge and he was obliged to pay the fine in full.

The doctor's involvement with non-medical matters could not have enhanced his practice, and in 1797 an action was brought against him in Great Sessions by his partner, Doctor Richard Reece, for a breach of articles of partnership. Bird recounts how, after a seven-hour hearing, damages of 40s. were awarded to the plaintiff, remarking that the action had been occasioned by Griffiths's six-week absence in London on canal business, his visits to Newmarket 'on pleasure', and by his attendance at the Cardiff races and ballroom, all to the neglect of his calls and work as a doctor. Griffiths, for his part, had taken exception to his partner's talking 'politics' to the patients. The case afforded much entertainment to the observers in court, but Bird records the judge's censure of a trial 'founded in malice and brought forward in bitterness.'[36]

While the diaries are essentially rough letter-books of information to be conveyed to the Marquess of Bute they do provide glimpses of Bird's activities outside his role as estate clerk. There are references to his bookshop and to the patronage extended to John Bird, bookseller and stationer, by the nobility and gentry, descriptions of his printing business, mentions of his family and friends.

When he married his first wife, Hannah Davies, in 1784 John Bird's place of residence was in Church Street, Cardiff, but a few years later he was provided with a house next to the Castle gate by his employer. In many ways the property enjoyed an advantageous location, but there were problems of access, for Bird and his family were not the only tenants. When seeking permission, in January 1791, to make a small staircase to enable him to provide the customary lodgings for Counsellor William Nicholl at Great Sessions, Bird reveals that the house had been divided, leaving the front of the property and the main staircase in the possession of William Bew, the other tenant. In this, as in so many other matters, Bird had evidently asked Hollier to speak to Lord Bute but nothing had been done. A year later he announces that Samuel Richardson of Hensol and Robert Curtis of Swansea, following the example of Messrs Taitt, Wood and the Chepstow bankers, intend to open another bank in Cardiff and have agreed with Mr Bew for the use of his front room. The old house, providing as it did family home, office, business premises and lodgings must have been bursting at the seams.

Ambition and the demands of his family led Bird to grasp every opportunity to advance his fortunes. In 1790 he raises the delicate subject of his salary. Anxious not to offend the Marquess, he nevertheless points out that he has given up his coach business (presumably for lack of adequate time to devote to

The Castle entrance and Bird's house (in centre of picture), from a photograph of *c.*1873/4. *By courtesy of South Glamorgan County Libraries.*

it), is unable to expand his shop business and hopes that an increase in salary will be forthcoming. To underline his straitened financial position Bird refers to the loss of some of his belongings, but it appears that his submission fell on deaf ears; his salary remained at £40 16s. 0d. a year and he had to look elsewhere to supplement his income.

In 1791 Bird proudly informs the Marquess that he has purchased the Cowbridge printing press and types 'for the trifling sum of Seventeen Guineas.'[37] Anxious to earn the favour of the Marquess and to justify his purchase he writes, 'Your concerns have frequently met with a delay and inconvenience for the want of a Printing Press being in the Town', and underlines what a bargain he has secured. By August that same year he had acquired new type from London, installed the press in his house against the Castle wall, found a printer to 'put up the apparatus in a proper manner'[38] and was in business.

In 1792 Bird gathered together information for inclusion in the *Universal British Directory*. Four years later, with experience of printing, he produced his own *Complete Directory and Guide to the Town and Castle of Cardiff*, a substantial achievement which has no mention in the pages of his diary. A variety of handbills, booklets and pamphlets rolled off Bird's printing press,[39] increasing both his income and his business and social contacts.

His printing of court calendars and jury lists not only brought in a modest income but also won him invitations to dine with the deputy sheriff and other county officials. His activities as a bookseller were equally rewarding. The to-ings and fro-ings of visitors, Militia officers and townspeople to the Castle brought valued customers to Bird's shop. He enjoyed the patronage of the Bute family and some of the county gentry. Prints of Lord and Lady Mount-stuart were proudly displayed in his shop. A commission from Richard Aubrey of Ash Hall to bind Bishop Watson's *Charge to the Diocese of Llandaff* in morocco leather is singled out for special mention in his diary.

His printing venture was but one means by which Bird sought to augment his income. Later entries in the diaries reflect his abortive efforts to secure a position as collector of customs 'the bringing up my Children etc. makes me feel the pressure of the times.'[40] His disappointment that Hollier had not seen fit to recommend him for earlier vacancies in the customs or tax offices was tempered by the realisation of his usefulness to that gentleman. Not only did Hollier off-load many of his responsibilities as estate steward on to Bird, he also found him an indispensable assistant in his capacity as receiver general of taxes for the county. Bird's boast that his arrangement of the books and his rapport with Hollier enabled the work of tax collecting to proceed so smoothly 'that we absolutely do twice the business that Mr. [Edmund] Traherne and 3 Assistants used to do'[41] was intended to bolster his application for office. The more questionable aspects of Hollier's activities would not emerge for many years, but it was his financial mismanagement both as receiver of taxes and estate steward that led to his prosecution by the Crown, to his dismissal from office and to his public ruin. No opprobrium seems to have attached itself to Bird who continued to prosper as estate clerk and borough dignitary.

In 1802 Bird became postmaster of Cardiff in succession to John Bradley. The eagerness with which he sought the appointment is reflected in the care he took to present his case strongly but diplomatically to the Marquess. His diary entries for April 1802 are spattered with corrections, revisions and amend-ments as he seeks the most felicitous phrase, the right emphasis to assure the Marquess that there will be no 'impropriety' in his applying for the post.

John Bird handed over his printing business in 1807 to his eldest son, John Davies Bird. He held the post of Cardiff postmaster until his death, when he was succeeded by another member of his family, William Bird, for several years his assistant at the Post Office.

By the 1820s Bird wielded considerable influence in the town. He was senior alderman and a bailiff of the Corporation. Although he formally resigned his post as clerk or 'factor' to the Bute estate in 1824 his services were still called upon by the Marquess and his agents, and this despite David Stewart's criti-cisms of the estate's management which were frequently directed at the inadequacies of Bird and his relations. He was a successful businessman, a freemason, magistrate and a member of innumerable local committees. But his

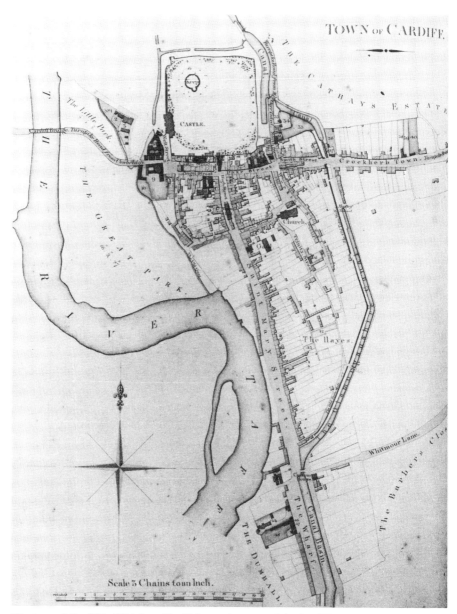

The town of Cardiff in 1824, from David Stewart's survey of the Cardiff Castle Estate. *By courtesy of the Glamorgan Archive Service.*

close connection with the Castle, his dependence upon and allegiance to the Bute family, his long tenure of office on the Corporation and his regular appointment to the influential office of bailiff, made him a target of the anti-Bute faction on the town council headed, after 1817, by the Wood family. Undoubtedly the substance of many of the charges levelled against him was justified, but the impassioned outpourings of the *Cardiff Reporter* and the *Cardiff Recorder*[42] were charged as much with personal invective as objective criticism. These radical short-lived publications, mouthpieces of the Woods and their supporters, portrayed Bird as the tool of the Marquess, the intransigent opponent of reform and the ruler of a narrow oligarchy of power on the Corporation. His regular appearance in the red gown of a bailiff of Cardiff provoked the following diatribe in the *Reporter* on 14 October 1822:

> It appears that Messrs. Charles, Thackwell, Bird, and Pritchard, are the only aldermen possessing sufficient gravity to wear the gown; and this is what we materially object to in the present system of town politicks. Out of twelve respectable aldermen, is it possible that only four are possessed of common discrimination, and that they must therefore succeed each other annually, as regular as a draught of beer out of a dirty pewter pot on the 30th succeeds old Jacob's quart of port and clean glass on the 29th? This cannot be construed into any other than an insult to the whole body corporate... On last Monday fortnight the celebrated male *Talking Bird*, better known by the appellation of *Squire* Jackdaw, took his annual flight to the regions of forgetfulness; where [he] will remain (Cuckoo like) for the cold season, until the reviving rays of the sunshine of power shall kindly warm him to resusitation at the ensuing Michaelmas, when his astonishing sagacity may again be witnessed by the curious. The attributes of this wonderful bird is truly surprising; uniting the gravity of the owl, and imitative powers of the parrot, with the melody of the nightingale. He was discovered in an old ruin near the castle gate, surrounded with Rooks, &c. about six years back, by a gentleman of *legal notoriety*;[43] under whose instructions he has attained the art of repeating short sentences after once hearing, and has even been permitted to echo his master's opinions in the 'judgement hall'. What is most strange is that every alternate year he remains dormant, and is only called into action by the cheering sound of the parish bells on the glorious twenty-ninth. Since he has become so deservedly a favourite the old ruin has been transformed into a comfortable well feathered nest . . .

And the *Reporter* gloated that Bird had, briefly, been deprived 'of the red gown his body filled so well'. In 1825 he was similarly lampooned in the pages of the *Recorder*:

... That he has, like the Irish drummer, made some *noise* in the world, is a well known fact, although we readily admit our own *'sweet Bird'* to have been more musical . . . View him as the faithful servant of his 'approved good master', or the dignified dispenser of justice, or the unequivocating and unembarassed witness, or as a self-taught musical prodigy, and he will be immediately pronounced the very *Phoenix* of the age. How oft have we witnessed him, elate with justassical power, marching, dignified as a monarch, in the van of holiday processions, enveloped in a real crimson gown properly decorated with ermine . . . And although envious wits hath said of his year of glory, *'though thy feathers are so crimson yet they shall become purple'* , we have ever wished him health, happiness, and long continuance of the more glaring plumage; for then does Printing flourish, and edict upon edict are issued forth to the great joy of Lloyd,[44] and to the infinite terrors of publicans, sinners, and evil doers . . . It has been pithily said, that 'He who rules o'er freemen should himself be free.' If therefore, *freedom* be a necessary qualification in a ruler, how can the worthy Alderman . . . for a moment be considered a fit person to hold the Office of Bailiff of the town of Cardiff? . . . is he not compelled by every feeling of *gratitude*, to go any length in support of that *noble*-man who has so long been the sole supporter of the 'Cardiff Aviary' . . . We *take* leave... to make the following observations, by way of advice, to the worthy alderman:- 'Your talents as "Parish Organ"[45] are well known and duly recorded in a *higher* place than this; in fact your fame has been exalted *above* men; be content, therefore, with your present glory, and never attempt to *rule* anything, unless it is music paper or red lines in my Lord's ledger, and you will then be held as an example worthy of imitation. Protect the roost near the castle . . . And sing unto the *lord* even in these words; 'The *lord* my pasture shall prepare,' and he *will* prepare it for you . . .

Prejudiced as are these outpourings they are revealing of the portly, garrulous, somewhat pompous public figure behind the bland features depicted in Bird's portrait.

Bird himself is singularly reticent on the subject of himself and his family. Only incidentally in the pages of his diary does he mention his children, there is not a single reference to his wife, and the compilation of a family tree is fraught with difficulties, not the least of which are the innumerable 'branches' of the Bird clan each with a propensity for the Christian name of John.

But in addition to the two diaries included in this edition there is another volume which provides more personal insights. Compiled during 1826 this is a diary proper, a daily compilation by John Bird of personal, family and social events. Bird was now sixty-five years of age. The successful businessman and public figure had experienced his full share of personal tragedies. His first wife had died after only two years of marriage, leaving a young son. After the death of his second wife, who bore him his only daughter, John Bird married for the third time, but the marriage does not seem to have been a happy one and the couple lived apart for years before Bird's own death in 1840. His eldest son, John Davies Bird, had sold the family printing business in 1817[46] and subsequently traded as a bookseller and stationer in London before ill health brought him back to Cardiff, where he died in October 1827, leaving his young children in the care of their grandfather.

Despite such family tribulations, and despite recurrent attacks of lumbago and rheumatism which confined him to his bed for days on end, John Bird's appetite for work was undiminished and his activities, as recorded in the diary for 1826, are as varied as ever. Although he had retired as clerk to the Cardiff Castle estate two years earlier, Bird's secretarial skills and his long memory of estate affairs continued to be employed by the second Marquess and his agents. In March he assisted Lord James Stuart with his election campaign, noting in his diary that he was writing with Lord Bute until almost midnight. In April he was too busy writing at the Castle to attend the town court. July saw him daily engaged with Lord Bute at the Castle — 'busy in Castle and Record Room'. He assisted the new steward Edward Priest Richards at manorial courts and travelled with him on rent collections, acting not only as adviser but also as interpreter when proceedings were conducted in Welsh.[47] His custodial duties at the Castle also continued — arranging the pictures in the dining room, putting the library in order, guiding visitors around the collection of family portraits. In many ways the pattern of his life over the previous forty years was unchanged.

His public duties as alderman and bailiff absorbed much of his time and energies, and in January 1826 his qualification as a town magistrate brought new responsibilities. But age and office had their compensations. In April 1826 John Bird was among the guests who dined with the visiting judges at their lodgings, and his diary entries reveal his enjoyment of a busy social life.

His life-long love of music was indulged by frequent musical evenings with friends and relations — 'glees, duets, solos, waltzing, quadrilles etc.' There were cherished evenings at the Castle in the company of the nobility and gentry, Bird's enjoyment of the music and conversation enhanced by the social prestige of the occasion. Bird owned and played a variety of musical instruments, and in 1826 he purchased an organ built by Smith of Bristol which appears to have been installed in the Castle, an instrument with evidently gave him great pleasure and which he bequeathed, in his will, to the trustees of the proposed church in St Mary's parish.

In Bristol on his birthday 'enquiring for engine makers' he took the opportunity to engage the cathedral choristers to sing at St John's, Cardiff, the following year, and to attend a performance of *Macbeth*. He gave his support

A group of local worthies, from a lithograph by R. Dighton, *c.*1835. From left to right: Edward Priest Richards, John Bird, the Rev. Thomas Stacey. *By courtesy of South Glamorgan County Libraries.*

to proposals for a theatre in Cardiff and was appointed one of its first trustees. A visit to London provided 'a most delightful evening' in company with fellow freemasons and in the presence of H.R.H. the Duke of Sussex, at the Lodge of Antiquity in Freemasons Tavern. He continued to worship regularly at St John's church and found time to attend the series of Lent lectures given there.

Bird lived until 1840, enjoying an annual pension of £150 from the Marquess of Bute. He had outlived most of his contemporaries and seen many changes in the town that was his home. Glamorgan had been transformed into an industrial county. The growth of Cardiff as a commercial centre was under way. In 1794 he had witnessed the opening of the Glamorganshire Canal. In the year of his death the railway came to Cardiff. In 1826 he records how he walked about the new streets and inspected the new harbour in the town, and by that date he himself had joined the ranks of speculative builders and landlords,[48] with properties at Crockherbtown and the Hayes.

By his will,[49] drawn up in 1839, John Bird bequeathed to his only daughter, Anne, two leasehold houses in Crockherbtown, one subject to a mortgage, the other occupied by the Bute estate solicitor and steward Edward Priest Richards, and seven freehold cottages in Union Buildings at the Hayes. Another nine cottages in the same buildings were bequeathed to Bird's granddaughter and five more to his grandson. John Bird's worldly goods as itemised in his will reveal him as a man of substance. Not all his money had been invested in property. He was part-owner of the schooner *Diana* of Cardiff. He held a

Market day scene at Cardiff, by Thomas Rowlandson, 1799. *By courtesy of University College Cardiff Library.*

debenture in Cardiff Improvement schemes, shares in the Cardiff Theatre, interests in the Cardiff Gas Light and Coke Company and in the Taff Vale Railway.

His household goods included such essential symbols of 'gentility' as a pianoforte, a bureau and bookcase in the parlour, a set of best china, a silver teapot and cream jug and an assortment of solid mahogany furniture. During his lifetime he had assembled a considerable personal library and his will includes the bequest of 'the choice of one hundred volumes' to his daughter, together with manuscript and other music books. Unfortunately the titles of those books are not known. And there are echoes of the printing business in the bequest of 'the letter-press, type and forms now in his possession' to his nephew John Godwin Bird of Bridgend.

There were bequests to his faithful servant Hannah Probert and to his niece Jemima Bird, both of whom cared for him in the latter years of his life. And there was one other bequest that emphasised the life-long association of John Bird with the Bute family — 'I give and bequeath unto my inestimable friend and patron Lord Bute my gold headed cane, which formerly belonged to General Abercrombie of America... as a mark of the feelings of deep gratitude which pervade my bosom for the manifold kindnesses I have received at the hands of his Lordship and of his revered ancestors.'

Throughout his long life John Bird's fortunes had been inextricably linked with those of the Cardiff Castle estate and the town of Cardiff. His surviving diaries and correspondence provide an insight into the estate and the town, an understanding of the man and of the society in which he lived. They provide a unique picture of the bustling, contentious, introspective community that was Cardiff at the turn of the eighteenth century.

The Diaries

Three of John Bird's diaries or notebooks survive among the manuscript collections at Cardiff Central Library (South Glamorgan County Libraries) (Reference: MS 2.716). Each of the volumes measures approximately 8¼in. × 6½in. (21cm × 17cm) and each is in a good state of preservation. The three volumes are bound between parchment-faced boards, only the second volume (1792–1803) retaining its original binding. The original paper cover of the first volume (1790–91) is retained within the rebinding, as are the board covers of 'Marshalls Family Ledger and Housekeeper's Account Book' within which the 1826 diary is written. The volumes for the years 1790–1803 were kept by Bird as an employee of the Bute estate, and are almost exclusively concerned with events and personalities affecting the estate. They have been transcribed in full in this present publication. The volume for 1826 is a diary proper, a compendium of family, social and business activities which provide

Tuesday July 30th 1799.

The High Sheriff Mr Goodrich, and his Deputy Mr Williams,
with Mr Vaughan atty. Mr Bew, the Workmen, Horses, Chains
and Implements for pulling down &c &c went to the Heath,
for the purpose of destroying the 4 Cottages of those who had not
signed the Petition for leave to remain till the 29th of October next.
I attended to Identify the Premises and the four who had not
signed were very glad to come into the same terms with the others.
The best part of a Hedge and Bank was destroyed and Burnt in
the presence of the Sheriff &c, which had been Erected by a Man
not included in the 12, but who had on several Occasions behaved
with insolence. —

    Saturday August 3d ——

The Great Sessions Commenced this Afternoon — Judge Hardinge
in coming from Brecon, dined at Energlyn, but the Sheriff attended
his Dinner at the Cardiff Arms — The Judge was attended by
Mr William Goodrich, and was Met at the 2nd Mile Stone by
a respectable Cavalcade of Gentlemen &c with the Sheriff.

    Sunday Aug. 4th

Judge Hardinge attended Divine Service, as usual this day
and Monday & the Selection of Sacred Music was well performed by Mr
Cook the new Organist with proper assistants. — Judge Morgan
Stoped at Tredegar as usual.

glimpses of John Bird the family man and public figure. It has not been transcribed as part of this edition, but its contents have been drawn upon in the preparation of the introduction and in the compilation of the Bird family tree.

Precisely what happened to the diaries after John Bird's death in 1840 is not known, but they seem to have passed into the hands of his niece Jemima (née Strutt) and from her to the Chivers family, relations by marriage. The three volumes came to light in 1913 during a case in Chancery concerning the will of Mrs R. K. Chivers, and the following year were presented to the Cardiff City Library by C. E. Strong and A. A. Strong, the executors of Mrs Chivers's will. One of those executors, the solicitor A. A. Strong, was keenly interested in the history of Glamorgan (he was a founder-member of the Glamorganshire Society in London) and, recognising the historical value of the diaries, took the necessary action to ensure their future preservation.

His presentation of the volumes to the Library was applauded in the columns of local newspapers, there were the inevitable references to a 'Welsh Pepys', and early in 1914 the *South Wales Daily News* published a series of articles on the Bird diaries with lengthy extracts therefrom. Since that date their contents have provided historians with invaluable sidelights on eighteenth-century Cardiff and Glamorgan. It is hoped that this present publication will enable the diaries to be enjoyed by a much wider audience.

Editorial Method

It has been my objective, in editing these two volumes of John Bird's diaries, to present the text with as few deviations as possible from the original.

The diaries, written in Bird's neat, rounded hand, present few problems of palaeography and only the occasional ambiguity of expression. What they do present, to the modern eye accustomed to standardised spelling and to the regular format of the printed page, is an endearing irregularity that encompasses spelling, punctuation and the use of capital letters. While it is tempting to reduce all such eccentricities to ordered symmetry, and while it can be argued that there is nothing intrinsically meritorious in retaining these anomalies, it seems to me that their total obliteration would destroy both the character and impact of the original, and that the imposition of a spurious consistency would strike a discordant note in an eighteenth-century text. I have therefore retained all Bird's eccentricities of spelling and most of his erratic profusion of capital letters.

Only in a few instances have I sought to regularise the text. In the matter of punctuation I have replaced Bird's dashes and commas with the conventional full stops and commas. As an aid to reference I have rendered the date above each diary entry as day (when stated), month and date (e.g. Monday August

17th), the form most frequently but not exclusively adopted by Bird, and have put the year at the top of each page.

Abbreviations of personal names have been retained as in the text, as have the accepted abbreviations of gent., junr., senr., (also jun. and sen.) etc, but contractions such as wd. and cd. (for would and could) have been expanded. Minor amendments and deletions made in the diaries by John Bird have not been transcribed unless they are revealing of the diarist or his subject matter, in which case they have been retained within parenthesis and the words *crossed through* added. Footnotes have been kept to a minimum and most biographical notes have been incorporated into a separate appendix at the end of the text. Any editorial insertions in the text have been made within square brackets.

Manuscript Sources

The major manuscript sources relevant to the compilation of this edition are listed below. Precise references to individual items are given in the Notes to the Text.

Cardiff Central Library

John Bird's Diaries (MSS 2.716)
Bute Estate records (CCL Bute boxes I-XLI)

Glamorgan Record Office, Cardiff

Bute Estate records (D/DA and D/DB)
Papers of John Wood, Clerk of the Peace (D/D Xeo, D/D Ev and D/D Art/W)
Quarter Sessions records (Q/S)

National Library of Wales, Aberystwyth

Bute Estate records (NLW Bute, especially Box 70, letterbooks)
Records of the Court of Great Sessions for Wales (Wales 22 and Wales 4)

For a comprehensive bibliography of primary and secondary sources relating to the Marquesses of Bute and their Glamorgan estates the reader is referred to John Davies, *Cardiff and the Marquesses of Bute* (Cardiff, 1981).

Notes to the Introduction.

1. GRO Parish register of St John's, Cardiff.

2. *A complete directory and guide to the town and castle of Cardiff* . . . Printed for and sold by J. Bird, adjoining the Castle Gate, Cardiff, 1796.

3. Tontines: annuity schemes. In return for an original investment, participants were guaranteed a yearly income for the life of a nominee chosen by the investor. As the nominees died off the central fund became distributed among fewer and fewer people and the annuity became increasingly valuable. The distinctive feature of a tontine was that the last survivor scooped the pool.

4. *The Cambrian*, 4 and 11 July 1840.

5. Diary, 4 July 1798.

6. NLW Bute Collection, estate rentals and accounts; CCL Cadrawd MSS G; *Cardiff records*, vol. IV, p. 315. Philip Jenkins, *The making of a ruling class: the Glamorgan gentry, 1640–1790* (Cambridge, 1983), p. 279, refers to 'one John Bird' as a great improver of Cardiff in the later eighteenth century, and describes him as being 'from a radical family descended from a much-feared regicide sympathiser'. The relationship of the 'regicide' to the diarist has not been established.

7. *Cardiff records*, vol. III, p. 428.

8. NLW Box 70, letterbooks; GRO D/DA 1-55.

9. CCL Bute IX, 18.

10. John Davies, *Cardiff and the marquesses of Bute* (Cardiff, 1981), pp. 37–8.

11. Ibid., p. 34.

12. A survey of the Cardiff Castle estate compiled after Lord Mountstuart's marriage to Charlotte Windsor in 1766 reveals that it comprised over 11,000 acres, plus extensive rights in common land. NLW Bute 104.

13. Diary, 31 January 1801.

14. Loc. cit.

15. Diary, 31 July 1800.

16. Cowbridge, Llantrisant, Aberavon, Neath, Kenfig, Swansea and Loughor.

17. Diary, 6 September 1800.

18. Diary, 11 June 1799.

19. Records of the Court of Great Sessions for Wales are kept at the National Library of Wales (Wales 4 and Wales 22).

20. Glamorgan Quarter Sessions records are kept at the Glamorgan Record Office, Cardiff (Q/SR and Q/SM).

21. For a detailed account of the Dowlais lease, including the Carno lands, see John Davies, 'The Dowlais lease, 1748–1900', *Morgannwg*, XII (1968), 37–66.

22. Diary, 24 October 1799.

23. Diary, 24 February 1798.

24. Diary, 2 May 1797.

25. Diary, 31 January and 25 October 1799.

26. For the background to this period, see (inter alia), D. J. V. Jones, *Before Rebecca* (London, 1973); Donald Moore (ed.), *Wales in the eighteenth century* (Swansea, 1976).

27. Diary, 26 March 1800.

28. Diary, 20 April 1801.

29. Diary, 22 April 1801.

30. Diary, 30 April 1800.

31. Loc. cit.

32. The old shire hall, within the Castle walls, had been demolished by Lord Mountstuart in 1766 as part of his improvement scheme for the Castle. The town hall, built *c*.1750, stood in the middle of High Street at its junction with Church Street and St Mary Street, and it provided market house, lock-up, assembly room and jury room.

33. The whereabouts of any surviving correspondence with Lowder is not known. One letter from Lowder to Hardinge, concerning the county gaol, was published: *A letter . . . to George Hardinge . . . respecting Cardiff gaol* (London, 1789). Some of Hardinge's letters to political, legal and literary figures of the day are preserved in the British Library (see BL Index to manuscript collections), and some were published in John Nichols, *Literary anecdotes of the eighteenth century* (London, 1812–15), and *Illustrations of the literary history of the eighteenth century* (London, 1817–58). Hardinge's literary works and some of his legal pronouncements were published in *The miscellaneous works in prose and verse of George Hardinge ...* (London, 1818) 3 vols. Included in this work is Hardinge's charge to the grand jury at Cardiff Great Sessions on 6 April 1801, and his address to convicts tried and sentenced at Cardiff on 8 April 1801.

34. Diary, 12 September 1794.

35. For an account of canal developments in South Wales, see Charles Hadfield, *The canals of South Wales and the Border* (Cardiff, 1960).

36. Diary, 7 September 1797.

37. Diary, 6 February 1791.

38. Diary, 4 August 1791.

39. Ifano Jones, *A history of printing and printers in Wales to 1810* (Cardiff, 1925), pp. 92–9.

40. Diary, 18 February 1801.

41. Loc. cit.

42. Quoted in Ifano Jones, op. cit., pp. 97-8.

43. Edward Priest Richards.

44. Richard Lloyd, the Cardiff printer.

45. The inscription on the second bell of St John's church, Cardiff, reads: 'With Watkins, Prichard, Vachell, Morgan, / And Bird who is the Parish Organ'. *Cardiff records*, vol. III, p. 542.

46. Ifano Jones, op. cit., p. 100.

47. It is clear that Bird spoke, read and wrote Welsh. An entry in his unpublished Diary for the week 10–16 July 1826 records the following expenses: 3s. 6d. Plant ym Brawd (my brother's children); 1s. 0d. Ceffyl yw Bontfaen (a horse to Cowbridge); 1s. 0d. Clwyda (gates, i.e. turnpike tolls). In 1818, when the burgesses of Llantrisant pressed for the appointment of a person 'conversant in the Welsh language' to fill the office of town clerk, and some members of the corporation insisted on conducting proceedings in Welsh, Bird's help as interpreter was sought by the steward, Edward Priest Richards (see NLW Bute Box 88, items 2592 and 2501). I am grateful to Mr J. Barry Davies for drawing this incident to my attention.

48. In 1822 when he built two houses on a plot leased from the Marquess of Bute at Crockherbtown (NLW Bute 70, correspondence April 1822). See John Davies, op. cit., pp. 192, 206.

49. NLW Llandaff Probate Records, Will of John Bird, dated 15 March 1839, proved 4 July 1840.

The Diaries of John Bird

1790

February 26th Went to Carphilly relative to Chief Rents[1] due from a Tenant of Captain Richards's[2] in Gellygare. In examining two old Books of Mr. Howell's I discovered that a mistake had crept into that account in 1775, by which the Tenant was overcharged two Shillings per annum, and of course has not paid since that time. Unless he pays the arrears due, which is £2 14s. 0d., the Captain desires a distress[3] may be made, as he is under the necessity of bringing an ejectment against him to get possession for another Tenant. There are two or three others in Gellygare who deserve to be distrained on, but if that should be the case it shall be done very cautiously and in no particular but where a sufficient proof can be produced of the payment of such Rent.

March 1st The Remains of Mrs. Richards[4] was brought from Wenvoe and intered at Cardiff this Evening about 6 o'Clock.

March 6th The Merthyr Canal[5] is the chief topic, and it is rumoured that Mr. Samuel Homfray and Mr. Hill have had a quarrel on that business, and that Mr. Thomas Key and Mr. Hill [have] gone to Lord Plymouth in order to petition his Lordship to oppose it. On the other hand most people wish it may take place [but think it wrong to close the subscription so soon as the 12th Instant *crossed through*]. The elevation from Cardiff to Merthyr is said to be 537 feet, which will cost £40 per foot exclusive of £800 per mile for cutting.

I have it from very good authority that the late Mr. Thomas[6] acted as Deputy Sheriff for three years successively, the first of which he was appointed himself, and the other two his Father and Brother, who is now Agent to Lord Vernon, were named. And I am assured that it might have been done in the present case by having some person of confidence named for that purpose, who could have suffered any one he thought proper to act in his name. And I have since found that it's very often practised to answer particular purposes.

I have been over the Sea Wall[7] this morning and like it very much. It is universally approved of. The length of that which is finished is near three quarters of a Mile, and the Men told me it will be completed by the 1st of August next, the stone work excepted.

The Slaughter House is now converted into a Stable and has been repaired by the present undertenant who is foolish enough to give T. Scandrett[8] eight pounds per annum for that and the Garden behind it.

Molly Powell has removed from the late Mr. Yeoman's House and lives in that lately occupied by Dr. Griffiths and Mrs. Glascott.

The affair between Captain Richards's Son and the Doctor is to come on at Hereford this Sessions.[9]

The large piece of deal which was thrown on shore[10] about two years and a half ago, and which now lies in the Castle, had better be used as soon as wanted, having been exposed to the weather ever since it came on shore.

March 9th Mr. D. Prichard[11] returned to Cardiff from London. The Sessions begins here the 22nd.

An Appointment was made out last Friday for Deputy Constable[12] of Cardiff, but a blank was left for the name.

Carn y Gûst tenement in Glynronthey[13] is fallen in. The Rent was £7 and it is now let for £18.

A small tenement in Aberdare is also fallen in. The Rent was £5; will be let for £14 or £15.

March 13th The general meeting respecting the Canal has been held this day at the Cardiff Arms,[14] at which a very respectable body of Gentlemen etc. attended, and the subscription amounted to about twenty thousand pounds. Amongst the subscribers William Morgan, the Porter of the Castle, has put down his name for four hundred pounds.

The Corporation had a Meeting with a view to have the Canal brought the Westward side of the town, but the Undertaker means to keep at a distance from the River, and they have settled on having it through part of the White Fryars Land,[15] and from thence to enter the town ditch at the East Gate and to be conveyed through part of your Moor land to the mouth of the Great Pill, about a mile below the town, where a large bason is to be errected, from which Vessels of 150 Tons burthen may go every tide, and on Spring tides those that are considerably larger.

The particulars of the subscription I am not at present able to transmit, but presume it will be communicated from another quarter.

March 26th Judge Hardinge delivered a most eloquent address to the Grand Jury[16] on Wednesday last, touching the Gaol, the escape of the Prisoners, the augmentation of the Gaoler's Salary so as to enable him to devote the whole of his time to that business and his residence therein, the present state of the Gaol,[17] and the appointment of a Chaplain with adequate abilities and a sufficient salary. He also spoke in favor and recommendation of the Philanthropic Society, and towards the latter part of his charge reprobated the present practice of the County Courts. But that to which he gave the greatest force and energy, and pointed out in glaring colours many evil consequences arising therefrom, was the practice of continuing a Deputy Sheriff in that Office for more than one year.[18] He observed it was in open defiance of an Act of

Parliament passed in the reign of Henry the 6th[19] and nothing more than a mask made use of for the private emolument of particular individuals, and that he should always set his face against any proceedings of that sort, and that he wished, as it was an office of some benefit, that it should be equally diffused amongst the regular attorneys attending the Courts of Great Sessions.

The Grand Jury that attended were only thirteen in number, notwithstanding near as many more had been summoned, and the Judge expatiated on the impropriety of such conduct and observed that if at any future period there should be so small a number he should be under the necessity of fineing the non-attendants. Their names are as follows: Peter Birt Esqr. foreman, Mr. Price of Landaff, Mr. Tait of Merthir, Mr. Cockshutt, Mr. Price of Watford, Mr. Gibbon of Cowbridge, Mr. Perkins of Cowbridge, Mr. Thomas of Pwlly-wrach, Mr. Llewellin of Stocklon, Mr. Hopkins of Neath, Mr. Lewis of Lan-ishen, Mr. Coffin of Bridgend, Mr. William Price of the Ivy House, Pantgwynlais.

The Grand Jury found a Bill of Indictment against Dr. Griffiths for a fraud at cards with Mr. Homfray, and it will be tryed either at this place or Hereford next Sessions.[20]

March 27th   The affair of the Copyhold at Lantwit[21] was argued last night and supported very ably by Mr. Allen,[22] Mr. Bevan and Mr. Carter. They endeavored to prove by a variety of cases that the title set up by the Lessor of the Plaintiffs was not a sufficient one against the Lord, as the Claimant had never been admitted in the Lord's Court. But I am sorry to say that after an argument which lasted more than an hour the title set up was established as a legal one, and was proved to be equally good in respect to the Copyhold as it was to the Freehold. The Judge declined giving a final descision on the question till the morning, but agreed with the Consel on the part of the Claimant that the title set up was certainly good in Law.

Dr. Griffiths applied in person to five of the Grand Jury (previous to their finding the Bill of Indictment) with the Affidavit of Mr. Blannin in his hand, and I heard the High Sheriff say that Mr. Griffiths had said (after the Bill was found) that the Jury were partial and called them a pack'd Jury. The Sheriff was much displeased at it and threatened to complain to Judge Hardinge on the Subject.

I heard the Resolutions of the High Sheriff and Grand Jury read in Court, which to the best of my recollection were as follows — That they had inspected the present state of the Gaol and found the Debtors' part to be perfectly secure and sufficiently commodious.

That they recommend an addition to the Gaoler's Salary and that the part appropriated for his residence was fully answerable to the purpose.

That if the Gaoler had resided the Prisoners could not have escaped. That the Criminals' part is insufficient and that a part with cells for solitary confinement be built as speedily as possible.

That the Chaplain's Sallary be augmented etc.

There were eleven causes tryed, some for trespass and others in ejectment etc. Mr. Robson,[23] Agent to Sir H. Mackworth, was to have been tryed for perjury, but his Accusers have got it removed to Hereford.

No capital offence this Sessions, only Petit Larceny,[24] Assault etc. Thomas John of Lantrissent who is a Tenant of yours was cast with damages for assaulting a Woman and I am informed he will be almost ruined.

March 28th   The Judges gave their descision on the Copyhold and confirmed what passed on that subject before.

Cardiff 31st April 1790

Sir, In answer to your favor this day, I beg leave to inform you that I am just returned from Landaff and have had a conferrence with Mr. Edwards the Clerk of the Peace for this County, and he assures me that no new Commission[25] can Issue until the Chancellor sends to him for the old one, which has not taken place. He shewed me the last Commission which was dated March in the 23rd year of his present Majesty, and he observed that he did not expect a new one soon, notwithstanding he had been applied to by several Gentlemen on that business. I shall be happy to receive your commands for every exertion in my power and am Sir your much obliged and obedient Humble Servant

P. Deare Esqr.   John Bird

May 13th   The workmen at the Sea Wall discharged.

May 24th   The Chief Rents in the Lordship of Senghenith collected this week. Nothing said at Merthir about Incroachments. The Canal takes all the attention there and soon as the Bill receives the Royal assent the work will commence.

Energlyn estate and John Richards of the Corner House Esqr. are much in arrear for Chief Rents. The accounts have been delivered to them and also to Mr. Morgan of Tredegar, Mr. Lewis of Newhouse etc.

When I cautiously made the necessary enquiry relative to the Commission of the Peace, Mr. Edwards observed that he had heard that R. Morris Esqr. was to be included in the next. Ignorance on my part was the answer. Because, said he 'if he is admitted it will be a Devil of a thing for the whole country'. And Mr. Gabriel Powell told me a little before his death that if he was inserted in the next Commission the Duke of Beaufort was determined to wait on the

Chancellor in order to get him struck out, and if the Chancellor would not do it he would wait on his Majesty in person to prevent his being included in the Commission. Since my answer to Mr. Deare nothing on that head has transpired.

May 27th   A meeting in the Town Hall for granting Licences to the publicans in this place. Ten out of the thirty-one were refused new ones, but 6 are put down, Vizt. the Blue Anchor, the Griffin, the Ship and Dolphin, the Lamb, the Red Lion and the Rose and Crown.

May 31st   The Militia[26] are assembled. They exercise in the Castle on the Gravel Walks. The hay there will be fit to cut in a few days.

June 2nd   Major Jenkins, Captain Gibbon and Captain Gough turned in for some books. The Major asked me if I had not been at Hallingbury,[27] and spoke about the Library there etc.

A Gentleman (who is a Stamp Inspector)[28] is now at Mr. Wood's with Mr. Hollier examining the Admissions of the Burgesses. He is going Westward for the same purpose.

June 4th   A party of the Militia fired three rounds before the Cardiff Arms in honour of his Majesty's birthday. The hay in the Castle will be cut tomorrow.

June 19th   The Honourable Mr. Stuart elected this day. A great number of Gentlemen and Burgesses assembled on the occasion, and the Expence attending the Election as follows:

	£	s.	d.
Bill at the Cardiff Arms for Dinners, Liquor etc. about	160	0	0
Bill at the Angel for 24 Dinners, Liquor etc.	6	9	0
Milliners Bill for Ribbons etc. about	90	0	0
Chairmen, Colourmen, Ringers etc. about	12	12	0
Expences of the Ball, Monday the 21st at which there were 51 Suppers etc. about	15	0	0
	284	1	0
Serjeants at Mace[29] for serving Precepts to the different Boroughs	5	5	0
	289	6	0

The above sums are as near the mark as I can possibly get at. About four

Hundred and thirty dined, including the Cardiff Arms and those at the Angel, with the Castle.

Mr. Edwards and Mr. & Mrs. Richards of Landaff were at the Ball, the Officers of the Core [Corps] and all the Ladies and Gentlemen in this Neighbourhood.

June 26th   Thomas Wyndham Esqr. elected this day. Mr. Edwin and Mr. Talbot attended. The latter Gentleman proposed the Member. After the business was gone through Mr. Wyndham made a short but rather an indifferent speech in which he thanked the Gentlemen for 'This repeated mark of their approbation'. He then paused and began again 'and you may depend upon it Gentlemen, that I shall make it my constant study to deserve such a distinguished mark of your favour'. He spoke rather low and thick, and it was with difficulty I could understand him although I got quite near. Mr. Edwin said a few words by way of thanks which were scarcely heard.

I was informed this morning by Mr. Thomas, who is Steward to Mr. Hurst of Gabalva, that Mr. Wyndham did not intend to have given any Dinner but to have left Cardiff immediately after he had been chaired, had it not been for Mr. Powell of Lanharran who told him a few days since that if he did he would certainly be mob'd. There has been a Dinner at both houses and I have seen many of the Rabble pass by quite intoxicated. Mr. Wyndham is to give a Ball at Cowbridge.

The Canal meeting was held last Wednesday. They are to begin at Merthir and to compleat it to the Quakers yard, and then to proceed in several places.

The approach to Cardiff from the west, by Sir Richard Colt Hoare, 1802. *By courtesy of South Glamorgan County Libraries.*

The Bishop[30] is now at Landaff and is to preach tomorrow. It is expected there will be a strong contest at Monmouth on Monday next. Mr. Kemeys of Newport and Mr. Salisbury of Lanwern mean to oppose.

July 29th   Served the following Tenants with notices to quit at Candlemas[31] next, Vizt. William John Henry on the Heath, Henry Edward for the fields in the forest,[32] John Edward for one small field in Do., Elizabeth Powell for the House by the Bridge in Cardiff, Hopkin Jenkin for the Smith's Shop and House by Do. Also a Notice to Mrs. Lewis of New House and others who have Land adjoining the further Cardiff Moors, relative to its being grazed this Autumn.

July 17th   Made an Assignment from Edmund Lewis of the Derry[33] to Mr. Hollier of the lands and Cots in Forest Cefn y Feed in which Edmund Lewis had an interest for his own life. Consideration money Thirty pounds.

August 2nd   The Gentlemen returned last night from Hereford. The trial between Mr. Homfray and Dr. Griffiths came on on Saturday last at Eleven o'Clock and lasted till near nine at night. The Jury were absent an hour and returned a verdict for the Doctor. Mr. Bridges, Mr. Richards of the Corner House, Young Mr. Hurst, Mr. Lewis of Lanishen and Mr. Lewis of Lanrumney attended there for the purpose of giving the Doctor a Character. I am informed by Mr. Bridges's Servant, who was in Court all the time, that the evidence given by young John Richards was almost diametrically opposite to that advanced by Mr. Wrixen and Mr. Blannin, and that the former Gentleman suffered much from being so severely Browbeaten by Counsellor Plummer on the part of the Defendant, and the Court received considerable amusement upon his Crossexamination.[34]

Parson Lowder and Dr. Williams have been round the Town with a Subscription for putting the Chimes in order, and have just call'd on me for that purpose.

The Races[35] here are to begin on Wednesday next.

Monday August 17th   [Monday 16th or Tuesday 17th Aug. 1790] At Hirwain collecting Cottage Rents and Incroachments. Received there and at Ystrad £33 2s. 7d. Discovered several Receipts for Chief and Cottage Rents received by T. E. which have been returned by him as in arrear, but [he] says he will account for them. Mr. Hollier was indisposed that day and could not come to Hirwain, but came the following day to Ystrad.

A Circumstance transpired about a fortnight back at Hirwain which might have been of serious consequence, and the more so as it was committed by one of your own Tenants. Steps have been taken and the matter is now at an end.

The Case was litterally as follows. Thomas Edward of Ty Newydd, who is Tenant to you for several Incroachments[36] on and near Hirwain, Rents one of them called Twyn Y Brin, which has been enclosed about fifteen years, to a man whose name is Richard Thomas Rowland and who lives very near to Baili Glâs and Hendre fawr. It appeared that this man's cattle frequently trespassed upon Morgan Rees your Tenant of Hendre fawr notwithstanding he had repeated notice from Griffith Rees, son of the said Morgan Rees, to take more care of them. But as they continually trespassed Griffith Rees [by way of retaliation and *crossed through*] in a fit of rage and imprudence took a person with him and broke down the fence of the said Richard Thomas Rowland on Twyn y Brin and turned his father's Cattle into the said Richard's Oats, and then went and informed him the said Richard what he had done and used several improper expressions. The damage done to the Oats was of no consequence as the Cattle were immediately turned out, but the article of breaking down the fence, as being one of your tenants, was looked upon as a dangerous business and was talked of by most of the Tenants who paid their Rents at Hirwain. Griffith Rees attended there amongst the rest, and after the business was over Mr. Davies took him apart and held a conversation with him on the subject of breaking down the fence etc. He declared that he had no view but that of Retaliation, and appeared concerned at the imprudent act he had committed and was willing to make restitution etc. The next morning, in coming from Pont Nedd Vaughan, we called upon this Richard Thomas Rowland and persuaded him to make up the matter with Griffith Rees, upon his personal attendance to replace the fence which only consisted of a few stones, and I believe that has been done, but the matter was much talked of amongst the Tenants and others about Hirwain, and a deal more was made of it than was necessary.

Friday August 20th   Went to Lancarvan in order to look around, and to know from Mrs. Williams[37] if she intended to keep the farm held under you by her late husband per Agreement for 21 years from February 1780, the Rent of which is £70 per annum. Mr. Williams was in arrear, but she intends paying to Michaelmas 1789 next week and will continue the farm for a little while, and says if she finds it will not answer she will give it up in time. A part of it was rented by Mr. Williams to a responsible person who now pays £29 10s. 0d. per annum. Mrs. Williams, I am informed, has property enough to pay all demands. Her Rent per Lease to Mr. Jones of Fonmon is £150 per annum.

Saturday August 21st   Dr. Griffiths spoke to me this morning and told me that as he had employed a short hand writer from London to take down the late trial at Hereford, he intended for his own vindication to have it published, and has made me an offer of purchasing the Copy and will engage to indemnify me if the sale of the publication should be inadequate to the expence of printing. I have declined giving an answer for a few days [and am rather fearfull it would disoblige Captain Richards *crossed through*] and should think myself greatly honoured with your sentiments on that head least I should incur displeasure from any quarter [through the hands of Mr. Hill, as we have written to each other on the score of friendship and relative to a Box which I lost when I came from London *crossed through*].

Saturday August 21st   The Sessions begun this Evening; only Judge Hardinge. Judge Moysey will not be here till Monday.

Sunday August 22nd   Several pieces of Divine Musick selected by Judge Hardinge were performed in church this morning. Sermon by Mr. Williams of Margam[38], Peter 1 chapter 2 verse 17. 'Love the Brotherhood'.

Monday August 23rd   The Grand Jury were 17 in number and consisted of the following Gentlemen, Vizt. John Morris of Clasemont Esqr. foreman., Samuel Homfray of Merthir Esqr., Thomas Guest of Merthir Esqr., Richard Hill of Merthir Esqr., Thomas Edmondes of Landough Esqr., Edward Thomas of Tregrose Esqr., Thomas Williams of Court Herbert Esqr., Rowland Williams of Gwernllwyn Esqr., Daniel Williams of Pertha Glyson Esqr., Reynold Thomas Deere Esqr., Thomas Thomas of Lanbradach Esqr., Llewellin Traherne of Coedriglan Esqr., John Popkin of Talygarn Esqr., Richard Aubrey of Ash Hall Esqr.

Judge Hardinge, in addressing the Grand Jury, made several very pleasing observations. He said he was happy to see so handsome an attendance, and began with congratulating them on the state of the Roads[39] which enabled the Gentlemen on the Circuit to pursue the Route from Brecon to Cardiff through the village of Merthir. And that he enjoyed the opportunity while there of visiting the different Works. He spoke much in praise of the Proprietors and conductors of them, and then adverted to the Canal, on which he expatiated for some time and pointed out the advantages thereof with considerable force. And [he] reprobated the vulgar idea that the Canal would be prejudicial to the road from Merthir to Cardiff, which he was sorry to find was in a bad state,[40] and strongly recommended Bills of Indictment as the only mode to cause the Repairation of them, though at the same time he expressed himself extremely averse to their incurring any expence of that sort if it could be effected any other way.

But what he dwelt longest upon, and to which he gave the greatest force [and energy *crossed through*] was the present state of Police at Merthir. He pointed out the evil consequence arising from the want of Justices of the Peace in that place,[41] a place he observed which stood in greater need of them than any other in the County, and he strongly recommended the Body of Grand Jurymen to present a formal petition to the Lord Lieutenant[42] praying him to use the greatest dispatch in completing the new Commission, which he understood was either preparing or prepared, and to request his Lordship to insert therein all the respectable names he could find in that place and neighbourhood, as the sure method of preserving peace and good order amongst a set of people which he understood were naturally turbulent etc. etc. He then proceeded to recommend the encouragement of Matrimony in that quarter, and while on that subject he read some very pertinent remarks from a Pamphlet of the Reverend Mr. Paleys,[43] on which he bestowed great encomiums. He said he was exceeding proud to be honoured with such a foreman and such a High Sheriff, and spoke much in the praise of both for the material service they were of to the parts of the County in which they resided. Compliment paid Mr. Lewis.

He complained that nothing had been done to the Gaol although the Grand Jury of last Sessions delivered in a string of Presentments on that subject. He lamented their want of activity and observed that it was a foible to which the Gentlemen of this Country were much addicted etc. etc.

Twenty seven Alehouses, Playing [*Illegible*], County Court fees etc.

Tuesday August 24th   Only four Criminal prisoners to be tryed, 2 of whom are condemned for Execution, Vizt. Griffith Lloyd for Horse Stealing and Thomas John for Felony [Burglary *crossed through*]. Ten Causes entered and tryed, the most material of which was between Lord Vernon, Plaintiff, and the Corporation of Swansea, Defendants. The Action was brought to recover a piece of [waste *crossed through*] ground lying between the Pottery at Swansea and a farm of Lord Vernon's. It is of material consequence to Mr. Morris of Clasemont because he has a Waggon way over it. After a long tryal a verdict was given for the Plaintiff. Councellor Morris on the part of the Defendants made a very long speech, and Judge Moysey observed that that was not the first time that Mr. Morris had entangled much better heads than his. Judge Hardinge made it appear that Mr. Morris had done more service to the Case of the Plaintiff than to the Defendant. Mr. Morris made the Court laugh very heartily once in the course of his speech by observing to the Jury that the Plaintiff had produced four old women who had all sworn heartily but, says he, I trust Gentlemen we shall produce you one old Woman who will beat their four old Women put together etc. etc.

Disfranchisement of Dr. Collins.[44]

August 25th and 26th   Transcribed the Charter of the Town of Cowbridge which Mr. John Thomas of that place lent to Mr. Hollier.

1790

August 27th   The Judges left Town this Morning.

August 28th   Mrs. Williams of Lancarvan paid £70 full Michaelmas 1789. The Proprietors of the Vessels on the Cardiff Trade to Bristol have just had a large Sloop which is called the Cardiff Castle. Mr. Dadford and his son are now here, and there has been a Canal meeting this day. Mr. Cockshutt and Mr. Hill have just left Town.

September 8th   Mr. Lowder[45] has received a Letter from Judge Hardinge in which were some strong hints that unless such things were carried into execution as he noticed in his last address to the Grand Jury, that he should remove the Sessions to Cowbridge. But what he particularly alluded to was the Gaol and the Alehouses.

September 10th   The Pictures[46] are arrived safe.

It did not occur to me in time to mention that the Reverend Mr. Rickards was indicted at the last Assizes for a Riot and the Bill found, and of his being put in the Crown office. And next Assizes Mr. Popkin of Talygarn will bring an action of Trover[47] against him for detaining his hat, which was the cause of the above proceedings.

Received the intimation wished for relative to the late Trial at Hereford.[48]

September 14th   Prodigious quantities of Salmon are continually caught in this River which are all sent off either to Glocester or Bristol. And last week upwards of half a Ton was conveyed away, while the inhabitants are murmouring because they can get none of it under 6d. per 1b. and that very rarely. The fishermen who have your slime catch little or no Salmon. The only two caught there for some time was bought this day by Dr. Williams[49] to send off with a quantity, and an hour after a large fish was brought to Town from Cogan Pill for sale which weighed about 30lbs. And the Doctor absolutely wanted that, but the man would not hear him when he called after him. The above I was an eye witness to.

The Inhabitants have just reason for complaint, for Mr. Williams has been known to order his fishermen to throw salmon into a ditch rather than sell them under 6d. per 1b. Formerly whole fish were sold at 1½d.–2d. per 1b. and I have heard some Freemen say that they would join in petitioning you to remedy the evil, as they understand the lease is given up and at your disposal. The inhabitants would reap great benefit from the fish being sold here at a reasonable rate, suppose 3d. per 1b., which would reduce the price of Shambles[50] meat and be a blessing to the poor instead of a scourge.

September 17th   A Curious trial took place in the Town Court this day Between John Purcel, Plaintiff, and Margt. Howell, Executrix of the late

Hezekiah Hopkins, Defendant. The action was brought to recover eight Guineas which was lent 29 years ago to Margt. Howel, and which she promised to pay with interest for as long time as she should keep it. Dr. Williams has had the whole management of the late Mr. Hopkins's effects for this woman, and, though a sitting magistrate on the trial, gave the strongest marks of partiality for the Defendant, and was once in the course of the proceedings sharply reproved by Mr. Wood who was employed for the Plaintiff, but procured Mr. Prichard to plead for him. The Jury found a verdict for the Plaintiff, Twenty pounds damages, which is the amount of the principal and interest for the 29 years.

September 18th   I have just declined an offer which was this day made me of superintending the Partnership Books between Mr. Harford of Melin Griffith and others who are concerned for the sloops on this trade to Bristol. Captain Prichard[51] does not intend being concerned any longer in that business but to attend to the building line. [Mr. Bradley told me just now this morning that he was going to London in a week or 10 days and should wait on you *crossed through*].

[I trust I shall not offend by asking whether it was not your intention to raise my Sallary, as my discontinuing the coach business has reduced my income. Allow me an equivalent for discontinuing the coach business. *crossed through*]

The present occupier of the late George Williams's farm in Lanishen, Rent £16, is to give £20 per annum for it and to enter on a new agreement. The Tenement of lands near Dowlais furnace, Rent £3 10s. 0d., which fell in about a fortnight past, will let for about £10 per annum.

The Magazine[52] in the Castle is nearly finished and is a good imitation of the old work. The job will cost about thirty pounds. Mr. Bridges' kitchen is enlarging etc. I suppose that job will cost between twenty and thirty pounds.

Lord Portarlington[53] and family have passed through this place. They stoped a day and two nights here.

I trust I shall not offend in asking if it was your pleasure [to] allow me something more than my present Sallary, as the deficiency of what I received for doing the Coach business is felt by myself and family. I have not had it in my power to do anything more in the Shop way [than I did before *crossed through*] and when I came from London I was so unfortunate as to loose a Box which contained about eight pounds worth of things, and although I can prove the delivery of it there I understand the proprietors will defend an action was I to bring one against them for the recovery of it.

September 27th   The Workmen began again on the Sea Wall.

1790

September 28th Mr. Crawshay called on me and appointed a day to look at Howell's farm.

September 29th Francis Minnit, William Prichard, Samuel Sabine and Henry Hollier Esquires were returned for Bailiffs[54] for the year ensuing. Three others and myself were returned for Serjiants at Mace. The Dinner was at the Angel. The whole number that dined were 138. John Richards of the Corner House Esqr. received the Return in the Castle. The day went off as usual.

September 30th Went to Hirwain and made a distress on Carn y Grist farm as the under Tenant for this year had sold part of his corn and sent all the Cattle he had into Brecknockshire. The distress will not amount to half the Rent, which is Eighteen pounds, but the man will be liable to the Remainder. I go there on Friday to have the things Appraised.

October 1st Left Mr. Hollier at Merthyr. He went to look over Edward Edwards's land lately fallen in. Mr. Tate is in treaty for it.
The Canal goes on rapidly. Nothing is yet done to the Bason.

October 4th Went to New House. Mrs. Lewis[55] is to settle her Chief Rents etc. this week.

October 5th Mr. Hollier is gone with Mr. Crawshay to look over the Commons of Caerphilly and Rudry.
Mr. Richards of the Corner House has been bit in the leg by a cat and Dr. Williams has laid it open and applied causticks etc.
Morrice of St. Melons[56] has nearly finished a Map of all the lands in the Parishes of St. John's and Saint Mary's. I was with him on the Moors etc.

October 7th Went to Hirwain to appraise the things at Carn y Grist. Appraised the amount £9 11s. 6d.
Mr. Crawshay and Mr. Homfray are looking out for a place near the Town to errect a manufactory for nails and Hardware.
Mr. Prichard has begun to remove from the House by the Castle Gate.
The Mail Coach was overturned on Roath Bridge owing to the Tide being all over the road from Rumney Bridge to the former. It was with difficulty the passengers and Horses were saved from being drowned. The Mail bag was in the water for two Hours. The Bridge has been indicted, for it was entirely owing to the side walls not being extended a sufficient length.

December 9th Thomas Edward having given Notice to several of the Tenants on Hirwain to pay their Cottage Rents, Mr. H[ollier] sent me to attend the Collection, which proved to be very trifling as the Tenants had but a few days notice. But those that I saw and conversed with seemed very willing to pay, though most of them asked Questions relative to Hirwain to which I made such replys as were consistent and satisfactory.

About 3 weeks back Mr. Walter Wilkins of Brecon, at the instigation of his Tenants, accompanied by his Brothers Thomas and Jeffrey, together with Mr. Gwyn of Buckland, were on Hirwain and inspected the Incroachments etc. And after some enquiries Mr. Walter Wilkins asked some of them what they would have if there was Common enough for them all and enough to spare, and that he would never lay out a farthing towards carrying on any law suits nor would suffer any of his Tenants to do so.

It is said at and about Hirwain that Mr. Walter Wilkins and his Brothers are going to build a furnace[57] on land of theirs joining your farms occupied by Morgan Rees called Hendre Fawr etc., but they must have your consent before they can get water.

George Williams, the old man whose fence was torn down 3 years back and whom you saw at Hirwain, was an old Tenant of Mr. Wilkins's and when the latter was on Hirwain he promised George that he would sign a presentment himself and would use his influence to get the freeholders to sign also, that George might keep what he began to enclose which was about 15 or 20 Acres.

I am told that Mr. Wilkins is very well-disposed to your Interest, but the reason is obvious, for if the Neath Canal[58] takes place they certainly mean to erect a furnace, and the object of Water and a supply of Ore (of which there is enough on Carn y Grist farm) will be of material consequence. They have Ore on their own land but will probably want much more.

The Chief Rents in Ruthin are £3 14s. 2½d. per annum. They have not been collected these many years. Mr. Davies has the Survey of that Lordship, but he says that he can get no Account of the lands. There is no Rental of them that I have ever seen either at Landaff or here. I asked Mr. H[ollier]'s permission to speak to Mr. Edwards on that Subject, which I did lately, and he says that we might easily get at the particulars by comparing the Survey with the Parish Books and Rates which may be obtained at any time. I wish to receive orders to accompany Mr. Davies on that business that we may have a Rental of those Rents, and if it should be at first imperfect it can be amended on every opportunity. The sooner this is done the better, otherwise those Chief Rents will be lost.

1791

January 4th   Last Paragraph. I am exceedingly thankfull for the part of the House[59] which I have [being that next the Castle Gate *crossed through*]. May I beg permision to make a small stair case of about 10 or 12 Steps in a more convenient part of the House than the present one? My reason for this application is that Councellor Nicholl has constantly had a bed room of me at the Great Sessions and would wish to have the same accomodation at the ensuing one, but I am incapable of obliging him unless you will please to permit the above. Mr. Bew has it in his power to accomodate a Gentleman at those times, for in Dividing the House the Front and principal stair case are in his possession.

When I represented the matter to Mr. H[ollier] he told me he would speak to you on the Subject.

February 4th   Went to Castle Town[60] in order to settle Chief Rents with Mr. Phillips and to bring back the Deeds of Exchange between you and Mr. Morgan. That Gentleman has been so indisposed lately as not to have been able to go to his Steward's for that purpose.

February 5th   Mr. Morgan attended and signed the Deeds. I was near him at the time; he complained of a violent headach[e]. Mr. Phillips settled the Chief Rents with me. Mrs. Morgan of Tredegar is 4 or 5 months advanced in pregnancy.

Dr. Griffiths has had the trial printed at Bristol. He gives them away. Mr. H[ollier] has one for you.[61]

February 6th   Mr. H[ollier] will have possession of Mr. Morgan's field opposite Cathays Garden immediately; the Tenant has consented to give it up. The Pocket Rental is done and the Chief Rent Book also. The Recruiting Accounts are made out in another way.

Young Mr. Hurst of Gabalva has agreed to sell the whole of his Estates to his Cousin, Mr. Jones of Swansea, who has taken a Mortgage on that and his own for Eighty thousand pounds, which Sum has been advanced by John Morris Esqr. & Co. for 5 years certain. Mr. Hurst has sold all but Gabalva, and he will have, after paying his Debts, about Twenty six thousand pounds and a Moiety of five hundred Guineas per annum from the Collieries at Swansea. They have seen a deal of Company at Gabalva for these three weeks past and are to have many more visitors this week as it is said on the strength of the Sale. Mr. Thomas, who is now agent to Mr. Jones, told me that he had asked him if he would sell the Fryars. Mr. Jones Reply'd 'not Immediately', but Mr. Thomas thinks he will sell it.[62]

For the trifling sum of Seventeen Guineas (for which I have given my note to pay in six months), I have bought the Printing Press and Types that was at Cowbridge.[63] I asked Mr. H[ollier] his opinion previous to the purchase. Captain Richards and Dr. Williams express'd their approbation of such a thing being in the Town as it was much wanted; for nothing of that sort could be had here but at an extravagant rate for Carriage etc. either from Bristol or Swansea. Your concerns here have frequently met with a delay and inconvenience for the want of a Printing Press being in the Town. The greatest Temptation to me was that offered by the owner of letting me have it and to pay as above.

March 13th Set off Post for Hirwain. Got to Baili Glaes[64] just as Thomas Edward and part of the Witnesses were coming away. Procured all David John's Receipts etc. for the spot in litigation, and assisted in Subpeonaing Witnesses and got back to Cardiff about 12 at night in company with 7 of them.

March 14th With the Witnesses all day. Two of them subpeona'd by Mr. Prichard on the part of the Plaintiffs. To one of them Mr. Prichard gave two Guineas.

March 15th Mr. Edwards of Landaff[65] came here early and was in the Castle examining sundry Books and Records.[66] They all set off about 11 o'Clock for Hereford.

March 16th Began Colonel Capper's business.

March 21st Much concerned at the Verdict given at Hereford.[67]

April 4th Several of the Hirwain Tenants came here. Their plea for coming down was that they were afraid to sow or any thing. I assured them that they need not be alarmed at what had happened at Hereford, but go on in their business as usual, and if any attempts were made to pull down fences recommended it to put to repel the assailants with force of Arms. And in order to strengthen them I thought it prudent to take them to Mr. Wood who was pleased to corroborate what I had before advanced, and directed them what to do, and so far quieted their minds that they returned home next day. Except one Man who was determined to wait till Mr. Hollier came home, which he accordingly did and returned to Hirwain with a degree of satisfaction, and promised to satisfy the Tenantry in that Quarter.

April 5th The Judges came to Town this Evening.

April 6th All at Church in Magisterial order. A Selection of Sacred Musick sent down by Judge Hardinge. A good Sermon preached by Mr. Lowder from 'Swear not at all'. After Church they proceeded to Court. The following Gentlemen were the Grand Jury:

1. John Price of Landaff Esqr. Foreman
   William Lewis Esqr.
2. Robert Rouse of Michaelston le Pit
3. Richard Aubrey Esqr.
4. Wyndham Lewis Esqr.
5. Herbert Hurst Esqr.
6. Wm. Tate Esqr.
7. Wm. Landeg Esqr.
8. Lewis Jenkins of Caercady Esqr.
9. John Richards Junr. Esqr.
10. William Price Esqr.
11. Jno. Williams Landaff Esqr.
12. Ed. Turberville Esqr.
13. Jno. Hopkins Esqr.
14. Thomas Thomas Esqr.
15. Thomas Bridges Esqr.
16. John Bassett Esqr.
17. William Jones Esqr.
18. David Thomas Esqr.
19. John Bennet Esqr.
20. John Williams Esqr.

In addressing the Grand Jury the first thing Judge Hardinge touched upon was the present state of the Commission of the Peace and of the dangerous situation in which that oppulent and Populous place called Merthyr Tydvil stood in for want of the due administration of Justice, and lamented very much the want of a new Commission and recommended to them in the strongest terms to address the Chancellor, and made it appear that the delay in issuing the new Commission rested with him. He observed that all party recommendations of Justices ought to be entirely out of the question, and those only admitted who were likely to be of service in the active Administration of it.

The present State of the Gaol was the next subject, and beg'd their endeavours to put that in a proper state etc. etc. with all speed.

The last thing (except the Calendar)[68] was a request that they would let him know their sentiments respecting the situation of the Assizes,[69] and whether they thought it of more essential service to the County to have it held at Cowbridge. He dwelt a considerable time on the subject, and after handling it in a most eloquent and masterly manner he concluded with giving his decided opinion and exercising his official right in favor of *'This place that we are now in.'*

The next day Mr. Williams of Landaff, who was on the Grand Jury, came to me for a Book. He asked me if I had heard the Judge's speech. I told him I had, and he smilingly said 'He asked us for our Sentiments relative to the Assizes, and then took away the power of our giving any by his determination to continue them here, so that puts an end to the matter, and I am glad of it as the Gentleman in the West will now be quiet'.

April 9th Mr. Price of Landaff called upon me about 5 o'Clock, and asked me to make two fair Copies of what he then produced — one of them intended for The Honourable John Stuart and the other for Thomas Wyndham Esqr. — and were as follows:

Cardiff 6th April 1791

Sir, We the High Sheriff and Grand Jury of the County of Glamorgan at the Great Sessions held at Cardiff the sixth day of April 1791, having taken into Consideration the many dangers and inconveniences that daily arise from the great number of Dogs[70] kept in this County, and understanding it is in contemplation to bring a Bill into parliament to impose a Tax upon Dogs in aid of the Poor rates, do earnestly recommend it to you to give your support to that measure. We are, Sir, etc.

Signed by the Sheriff and Grand Jury

Eight Causes were tryed but none of them of any material Consequence. A Bill of Indictment was brought before the Grand Jury against Richard Griffiths, Surgeon, for sending a Challenge to Wm. Lewis Esqr. the day after the fracas at the Cardiff Arms, but was not found. Mr. Griffiths had worded his letter to Mr. Lewis in the following manner: 'Sir, You said you would meet me, attended by a proper Gentleman, in order to give me satisfaction for the insult I received last night. I therefore beg your determination by the Bearer'. etc. etc. Mr. Thomas of Lanbradach, Brother in law to Mr. Griffiths, carried the Letter to Green Meadow but received no answer from Mr. Lewis.

April 9th The last thing in Court this Sessions was Affidavits of Wm. Lewis Esqr., John Price Esqr., John Richards of the Corner House Esqr., John Richards Junr. Esqr., Edward Thomas of the Cardiff Arms and Elizabeth his wife, and John Morgan, Door Keeper, stating the whole transaction of the Ball and the affair [Riot *crossed through*] that night. An hour's Pleading took place on this business between Councellor Caldecot on the part of Mr. Lewis etc. and Councellor Bevan on the part of Mr. Griffiths. The Judge heard the whole with a deal of Patience till half past 10 o'Clock and then observed that it was treating the Court in a very unbecoming manner and compelling them to sit as

Jurors on a [Petty *crossed through*] transaction at a Ball, which silenced the Attorney General and put an end to the business for this time.

April 12th   No more work to be done here on the Canal till Michaelmas next. The Stopping your Pill by Mr. Dadford's men is far from being done properly [and has been attended with a great expence *crossed through*]. The man who took your Sea Wall assured me he would have done it completely for Sixty pounds, whereas it has cost the Proprietors *One hundred and fifty* and must have a better foundation than it has at present or it will not do.

April 18th   Mr. Blannin's Brig launched this afternoon, rigged upon the stocks and immediately loaded with Iron for London. Owing to the neglect of the Ship Carpenters in leaving a Post Hole open the Vessel filled in the Night and Sunk, but was freed the next day. A Man who lay on board was nearly drowned.

April 22nd   Mr. Traherne of Castella told me that Mr. Tate of Merthyr[72] had taken his House by the Town Hall [lately occupied by his Sister *crossed through*] and that he was going to build Stables etc., and that Mr. Tate removes her[e] next October.

[The following two entries, dated 7th and 3rd June, were crossed through by Bird and an abbreviated account incorporated in the entry for 4th August.]

[**June 7th**   Mr Rothley was at the Flat Holmes[73] last Saturday and asked Mrs Taylor if she could accomodate the Miners,[74] but she said she had no room for any of them till the Masons were come and had finished the Repairs of the light House.[75] Mrs Taylor told me on the Island this day that there was work enough for 6 or 8 Masons 12 Weeks, as the Crown of the light House must be entirely new. I was there with a party from [Cardiff *crossed through*] this place. The Crack in the building extends from the Top to within 8 feet of the bottom. The new Grate I saw. It is much stronger than the old one and is upon a better principle. They are at present very short of Water, and the grass begins to burn, having had no rain there of any consequence since March last *crossed through*].

[**June 3rd**   The Remains of Peter Birt Esqr. were interred at Wenvoe this day *crossed through*].

August 4th   Thomas Llewellin Rees, your Tenant who is employed at Hirwain Furnace, came here this morning and brought an Account that Yesterday Samuel Rees, his two Brothers, Griffith Rees of Hendre Fawr and a gang from Aberdare to the number of Twenty or more, assembled on Hirwain. They were attended by D. Prichard, Attorney at Law. They proceeded from Aberdare to the further end of Hirwain, and in their way invited people to Join them. They had *no tools* of any sort in their hands, except some of them who had walking sticks. Thomas Edward met them at that end of Hirwain next Baili Glâs, and some altercation took place. Mr. Prichard remained on the Road and did not come within an hundred yards of the [Rioters *crossed through*] people, two of whom, *by the direction of* Samuel Rees, Griffith Rees, etc. etc. began [with seeming deliberation *crossed through*] to push and pull down with their hands and sticks, sufficient Gaps for Men and Horses to enter into the enclosures, which several of them did and walk'd and rode through them. They began on a Taking of T. Ed[ward] called Tyr Jenkin David Hafard, on which a lease was signed by Lady Windsor in 1763, and I trust they have burnt their fingers. They then proceeded deliberately through those takings that have been granted within twenty years. Some trifling altercation ensued and a few blows passed at one place, but the business was conducted more peaceably than otherwise. Griffith Rees of Hendra Fawr was one of the foremost and Thomas [Edward *crossed through*] Llewellin tells me that he gave frequent orders to the two men who pulled down, where to begin etc. etc. and that he in particular has behaved in the most impudent and insulting manner.

In going to Cathays with Thomas Llewellin, saw Mr. Wood. He smiled at the transaction and said he was very glad to find they had begun. I observed that I thought they had left it late. He said 'O, we shall have time enough to tickle them yet'.[76] Mr. Hollier came to Town immediately, and went to Mr. Wood with T. Llewellin [but the latter returning I wish'd to know the result of their interview, but Thomas Llewellin, hurrying off, put it out of my power *crossed through*]. Thomas Edward came to town soon afterwards.

I trust that [something will be done this time *crossed through*] the utmost rigour of the law will take place this Sessions against them at Cardiff [Hereford *crossed through*] in order to quash any future attempts and make them smart for what has been done.

I am informed that the Honourable Mr. Stuart and Robert Rouse Esqr. are appointed Stewards of the Races at Cardiff for the next year.

I am very happy to hear of the purchase of the Friars[77] etc. etc. Old Mr. Hurst told me a few days ago that he intended waiting upon you when he returned to Town (which he will do in a few days) in order to give you the refusal of all the property he has in this Town and Neighbourhood. Twenty seven years purchase is what he means to ask [and he said that Mr. Crawshay offered him a thousand pounds for Listalybont, which has been rented by Mr. Blannin at £28 per annum. Mr. Crawshay considered the bargain as struck, and is not pleased with Mr. Hurst for receding *crossed through*].

My grateful thanks are due for the Press. Have just had the new type from

London and have met with a printer who has put up the Apparatus in a proper manner. Several small Jobs are waiting, hope next week [to enclose a hand bill *crossed through*].[78]

I am Copying the General Chief Rent Book, the one containing the Customs of the Manors has been done some time. I have spoked to Mr. Davies relative to some customs he informed you of. He says that he knows of no other Customs than what are inserted in that Book, and says he does not recollect having said any thing about Customs of Leases except that for Felin Fawr.

Flat Holm. Engraving by an unknown artist. Early 19th century. *By courtesy of the National Museum of Wales.*

It is said that you are going to turn the road round Cathays and the Friars. Miss Pigot (who has property by the North Gate) told me that in Justice to herself and Mr. Priest's Children, her wards, she should oppose such a measure.

The Light house on Flat Holmes must undergo a thorough repair. The Crack in the building extends from the Top to within 8 feet of the Bottom, and the Crown of the Light house must be entirely new. I was there lately with a party from hence, and Mrs. Taylor was then in expectation of 8 Masons for 12 weeks, for which reason she said she could not accomodate any Miners. I told Mr. H[ollier] of it when I returned.

The Bailiffs and Corporation had a meeting in the hall last Tuesday relative to the money you have advanced to pay Mr. Edwards and other matters. Mr. Edwards did not attend.

Old John Lewis of the North Turnpike is dead.

September 2nd   A Vestry was held in our Church to take into consideration the proceedings of the Reverend Mr. Lowder, who, without any application to the Church Wardens or Inhabitants, took down the old Pulpit and errected a simple deal one in its stead. The Gentlemen present at the Vestry were Mr. Wood, Mr. Hollier, Mr. D. Prichard, Mr. James Williams, and 12 or 14 Inhabitants with the Church Wardens (Messrs. Thomas and Bew) and myself. After some Conversation an order was drawn up and signed, the purport of which was, that unless the Reverend Mr. Lowder should make a proper appology for his conduct in taking down the pulpit without the consent of a Vestry, that an Action should be commenced against him by the present Church Wardens. Whilst the Vestry was holding, the Carpenters brought the new Pulpit into Church and set to work in fixing it, as if done in defiance of the Vestry.

September 3rd   The Great Sessions commenced this Evening.

Sunday September 4th   At Church in Magisterial order. The whole Service by Mr. Lowder.

September 5th   The Grand Jury as follows: Thomas Wyndham Esqr., Thomas Edmondes Esqr., Hen. Knight Esqr., Jno. Llewellin Esqr., Saml. Richardson Esqr., Edward Thomas Esqr., Reynold Deere Esqr., Hugh Lord Esqr., Mathew Gwynn Esqr., T. Eaton Esqr., Ed. Snead Esqr., Walter Coffin Gent., Jno. Prichard Gent., Davd. Samuel Gent.

In Addressing the Grand Jury the first and general part of Judge Hardinge's Speech was a full explanation of the oath taken by that body collectively and individually, in which he displayed very great abilities. His Address this time was shorter than at any former Sessions, as he took notice of nothing more than the Offences in the Calendar.

September 9th   Cardiff Assizes ended this day when four prisoners received Sentence of death, but two of them are ordered for execution on Friday the 7th of October next, Vizt. Henry James and Cathrine Griffiths for a Burglary in the House of Mrs. Price of Park and carrying away a great quantity of plate and some wearing apparel. Sarah Birt, concerned in the above Burglary, is ordered for transportation with Rees Hopkin for Robbing a Smugler in Lougher of goods to the value of £4 9s. 0d.

Joseph John of Lantrissent, Carrier[79], for an Assault on Thomas Jones, Constable, was fined £10, and in consequence of articles of the peace exhibited against him by the Reverend Mr. Rickards he was bound in a Recognizance of £400, but as he could not find Security he was committed to Jail where he now remains.

At the *Nisi Prius*[80] bar there were 16 Causes tryed. The most material was between Messrs. Guest and Tait, Plaintiffs, and Homfray and Co., Defendants, being an Action of Trespass for placing Cinders, Rubbish etc. out of Pendarran Works, upon land belonging to the Plaintiffs. After a trial of 6 hours the Jury found a Verdict for the Plaintiffs 40s. damages, contrary to the Opinion of the Judge. And a Motion being made for a New trial it was granted, and will be tryed next Assizes by a Special Jury. This Affair has sown the seeds of enmity between the Pendarran and Dowlais Companys, and Saml.Homfray has been heard to say that he will try what he can do towards taking down the Dowlais Furnaces, but that can be nothing more than the effect of a gust of passion. The spot of ground in Question was worth about 30s. per annum.

September 10th   This morning Judge Hardinge and Mr. Hollier went over to Minehead in that Boat that Mr. Stuart and the Miss Powells had to go to the Holmes. His Lordship and Mr. Hollier went forward to Exeter. When the Boat returned I was informed that the Judge was so much pleased with the excursion that he has engaged the same Boat to take him to Bristol after next Assizes.

September 16th   The Earl of Dumfries[81] arrived here this evening.

September 17th   In Consequence of Mr. Hollier's being from home, and understanding that Lady Mountstuart had written to Mr. Hollier to pay his Lordship every respect, I thought it necessary to put myself in his way, which I did, and was with him and Lady Eliza Creighton round the Castle. They were afterwards in my shop, and I shewed them the print of the Castle which Yates[82] did and which was shown to you at Cardiff. Her Ladyship liked it very much and had the use of it to Copy from. His Lordship [Lady Eliza and Lady Loudon *crossed through*] talked of going to Carphilly. I offered my service as an Escort, which was accepted of, as they took their own Horses and the Servants were Strangers to the Road. Lady Eliza and Lady Loudon[83] accompanied his Lordship to Carphilly. The Countess was indisposed and did not go. They were mightily pleased with the Journey, and Lady Eliza made a drawing of part of the Castle there and took a View of the Holmes, Penarth etc. from the Hill above New House.

September 18th   His Lordship and family left Cardiff this morning.

September 23rd   Your Tenant Mr. Morgan of Pengam dyed this morning. He has left his fortune to his Daughter who, with the assistance of her Cousin, will continue the farming business.

Several applications are made for the Adams Down and part of the Moors.

Sir Herbert Mackworth. Painting by John Russell RA, c.1780. *By courtesy of the National Museum of Wales.*

Mr. Vernon of Dynaspowis[84] who now lives in old Mr. Hurst's farm would take the greatest part of it, if not the whole.

September 26th   Certain News was brought to Cardiff this morning of the death of Sir H. Mackworth at Gnoll. It was occasioned by a thorn in his thumb which turned into such a Mortification that could not be stopped.

Mr. Cockshutt is no further concerned in the Cyfarthfa Works.

September 27th   I was at Landaff this Morning to invite Mr. Edwards to the Dinner on Thursday next. He told me he believed he should come.

They have begun, at the expence of the County, to put down Cribbs[85] and to use proper means to prevent the River from making further incroachments at Place Turton.

Mr. Hollier will return tonight.

1792

March 27th   Cardiff Assizes commenced this Evening. Judge Hardinge too much engaged in London to attend at Cardiff, but is to meet Judge Moysey at Brecon.

The appearance with the Sheriff, J. Llewellin Esqr., was a very thin one, and as it rained hard when the Judge came in, no form could be kept up by the Magistrates, Serjeants at Mace and Constables, as the whole body came in at a brisk trot.

March 28th   The Judge etc. etc. went to Church in the usual form. Mr. Lowder Chaplain to the Sheriff.

In called [sic] the Commission over, the Earl of Bute and Lord Mountstuart were named by their new titles.[86]

The Grand Jury were: Rd. Aubrey Esqr., J. Richards Senr. Esqr., D. Thomas Esqr., Reynold Thomas Deere Esqr., William Thomas Esqr., Llewellin Traherne Esqr., Nicholas Price Esqr., William Price Esqr., John Bassett Esqr., Thomas Thomas Esqr., Samuel Richardson Esqr., Anthony Mathew Gent., and John Robotham Gent.

Judge Moysey's speech was a very short one. He said that he was well convinced of their integrity and abilities to determine what was brought before them, and should not take up much of their time. He then referred to the Calendar, and made some observations thereon as to the nature of the offences, and then proceeded to business.

A Great Number of Notices for debt called over, and affidavits of service in Ejectment.

March 29th   An Ejectment Cause was tried this morning between William Hurst Esqr. and Thomas Hughes Vernon Esqr. which was given in favor of the former, and Mr. Vernon is to quit Dynaspowis immediately, for his Agreement, being on unstamped paper, was of no avail. Mr. Vernon has agreed for Duffryn Frood and removes there immediately [but can't say whether he can have possession of it immediately or not *crossed through*].

A Bill of Indictment found against Richard Griffiths, Surgeon, for an Assault on John Price Esqr. to which he pleaded guilty, and by that means he has put it out of Mr. Price's power to remove the cause to any other Court. He entered into a Recognizance for his appearance at the next Sesssions, himself in £100, Mr. Thomas of Lanbradach in £50, and Mr. John Thomas of Cowbridge in £50.

A Bill of Indictment was found against Mr. Robson of Neath, Agent to the late Sir H. M[ackworth] for Perjury, and another against the same person for an Assault on Mr. Elias Jenkins, Attorney of Neath. Bail was given for his appearance at the next Sessions.

A Bill of Indictment was also found against Joseph John of Lantrissent for Perjury, who has given Bail.

At the Instigation of Wyndham Lewis Esqr. the Inclosed paper has been this day stuck up in several parts of this Town by the Cryer.

March 30th   The Prisoners tryed this day, one of them to be transported for a break of Prison and escape.

March 31st   Fifteen causes were tryed, referred and made up, but none of them of material consequence.

April 1st   Rained all day, which prevented the Judge from going to Church.

April 2nd   This morning the first Pier of Cardiff Bridge on the side next the Black Friars fell down [and it is likely that part of the two arches will follow *crossed through*]. The Mail Coach has since gone through Landaff, but Chaises, Horses [and foot passenger *crossed through*] pass over. It is supposed that the Repairs of it will cost about £500, and as the [County *crossed through*] Gaol is to be enlarged this [summer *crossed through*] year, the County Rates must of course be considerable.

The Judge etc. left Town this morning.

A Meeting of the Creditors of Wm. Prichard, Builder, and William Lewis Junr., Cornfactor etc., was held this day. Mr. Prichard proposes to pay 13s. 6d. and William Lewis 5s. 6d. in the pound. Jonathan Davy and Phillip Davy are also Bankrupts; the former has proposed to pay 12s. and the latter 4s. in the pound. It is thought the Statute will not be worked against either of them.

Mr. Willet[87] of this Town and myself have foolishly and unthinkingly lent our names to Phillip Davy[88] in some transactions in the Bill way, and we both stand at this time in an awkward situation, but hope we shall be able to extricate ourselves with credit. P. Davy has behaved very ill in taking his friends in, and I am exceedingly hurt at his having bought some Moor Hay from Mr. Bew and for which he had agreed to pay £40. I did not know that he had not paid for it till the day after the Commission was sent for [the Docket was struck against him. He was a Bankrupt *crossed through*] or I would have insisted on his paying for it while it was in his power. Mr. Willet and myself are bound for his payment of £26 for the Rent of Blackfriars Land.

Mr. Hollier having heard that the Canal was to go through the *meadow lands* of Tyn y Wern and not through the Wood, he sent me to Mr. Dadford's about 3 weeks back on that Business. The Levellers assured me that the report was false and supposed that as they in general take one level on the lowest ground, as a guide to finding the true one, it must have originated from that.

There are 13 small trees on the side of the Road near Newbridge[89] and which I had some time ago delivered to Mr. Dadford as belonging to you, and upon your Waste. Captain Richards has laid some claim to them from the Representation of his Tenant, and some conversation has taken place between him [and] Mr. Hollier, but have heard nothing of it lately. The Cut of the Canal is exactly under them, and the value is trifling. Mr. Howell can prove their having been cut for Lady Windsor's use.

Mr. Aubrey of Ashall turned in to my shop several times, and once while Mrs. Traherne of Castella and some Ladies were looking at the prints of Lord and Lady Mountstuart which I had got framed and glazed by Mr. Traherne's request. They talked about the likenesses, and after the Ladies were gone Mr. A[ubrey] said he should like to have the prints, but that he never thought of asking his Lordship for them, and he supposed it was too delicate a thing for his Lordship to offer him the prints of himself and Lady. He gave me an order for the B[ishop] of Landaff's last Charge to be bound in Morrocco.

Having been applied to by Mr. Wilkes, the Patentee of the British Directory[90] now publishing for the names of the Inhabitants and the Particulars of this Town and Carphilly, I have sent him such an Account of both Towns, Castles etc. as it was in my power to collect.

April 6th   Mr. Reynolds of this Town is removed to Cogan Pill.

I have got Thomas Lewis of Whitchurch and John Owen of the Heath to deliver up their Grants, and they have been given to Mr. Hollier. Mr. Vaughan of Melin Griffith, who has three Grants on Cots in Whitchurch, will be particularly careful that no person shall see them.

1792

April 11th At the High Market this day 4 of your fat oxen were sold for £63.

Mr. Harford of Melin Griffith has declined having any further connection in the Cardiff Sloops.

Surrenders in the name of J.E. of B.

Mr. Tait is removed to Mr. Traherne's House.

April 16th The Creditors of Wm. Prichard, Builder, met at the Angel this day. He has preferred having the Statute worked against him than to pay 13s. in the pound to which Composition his Creditors had acceded.

This morning arrived from London Thomas Wyndham Esqr. on his way to the Quarter Sessions at Cowbridge. I was informed by his Vallet that he had not given up the Idea of having the Jail removed to Bridge-end, and that [if when that measure should be adopted *crossed through*] Mr. Talbot had empowered him to put his name down for £500 if any business of that sort could be accomplished.

April 17th This Evening at Cowbridge the state of the Jail at Cardiff and plans for repairing the Bridge were laid before the bench when Mr. Wyndham, as Chairman, proposed that no more money should be laid out in repairing the County Gaol at Cardiff, and that it ought to be totally taken down [and Rebuilt *crossed through*]. And [he] threw out several hints of Removing it to a centrical situation, when a long conversation took place, but he was not supported in the article of Removing it. At last they agreed to appoint a Committee of Justices to attend at Cardiff the 9th of May to take that matter into consideration. Mr. Lewis of Green Meadow, Mr. Price of Landaff and Mr. Lewis of Lanishen are named to form that Committee.

The Collection of Chief Rents in Senghenith will begin at Merthyr on Monday the 1st of May next.

May 2nd Last Monday at Merthyr, in looking over the Chief Rent Book, discovered that the late Mr. Gwinnet of Cottrel was in possession of a small Tenement of Land in Eglwsylan Parish and for which an anual Chief Rent of $4\frac{1}{2}$ has been regularly paid, for which reason there is a Heriot[91] of the best due in Senghenith as well as the one had for Miskin. On my return from Gellygare last night I informed Mr. Hollier of it and he consented to my waiting on Miss Gwinnet at Cottrel, from whence I am just returned, and have satisfied her as to its being due, when she said that Mr. Franklin should settle the matter with Mr. Hollier as soon as she could conveniently see the former. She conversed with me some time and appeared to be in perfect good humour, asked me if you was gone from Bath and said that she meant to ask the favour of your inserting a particular friend of hers in the new Commission of the Peace which she understood was soon to come out. She told me that the person she alluded to had an Estate of £500 per annum and that he would act as Justice and Deputy Lieutenant, for as her Brother had acted in the latter capacity she hoped, that upon proper application to you, her friend would be deemed eligible to fill the vacancy occasioned by her Brother's death. Just as I was coming away she told me that the person for whom she meant to solicit was her neighbour Mr. David Samuel of Bonvilstone.

There was a Canal meeting at Merthyr last Monday and the Comittee dined with Mr. Crawshay. Mr. Wood attended. Iron is now brought down the Canal from Merthyr to within half a Mile of Newbridge.

Messrs. Tait, Wood and some of the Chepstow Bankers opened a Bank here last Monday, but have not yet fixed on the House it is to be kept in. Mr. Richardson of Hensol and a Mr. Curtis of Swansea are to open another Bank here in a few days. They have agreed with Mr. Bew for his fore Room.

The keep of Cardiff Castle. Engraved by W. Woolnoth after H. Gastineau and F. Stockdale, c.1825. *By courtesy of South Glamorgan County Libraries.*

1792

May 9th   The Justices that attended at the Meeting this day at the Angel Inn were David Thomas Esqr., Reynold Thomas Deere Esqr., Robert Jones Esqr., John Bassett Esqr., [and] Wyndham Lewis Esqr.

There was nothing done at this meeting relative to the Gaol, but a proposition was made to build a New Bridge about 80 yards below the present one. Mr. Wyndham Lewis was the only one that objected to it, as he was for repairing the present Bridge, but the Committee have adjourned to Wednesday the 30th Instant when they will meet to receive plans of the Gaol and Bridge and determine thereon.

May 10th   A Meeting of the Bailiffs, Aldermen and Burgesses was held this morning relative to the Corporation land held by Captain Richards on the side of the little Heath. His Lease thereon is expired some time since. It is to be let to the best bidder, and the Timber thereon is to be sold.

May 11th   [A Coroner's Inquisition was held by the Bailiffs etc. this morning on the Body of a Poor Man who dyed suddenly at the Black Wears. Verdict, dyed by the Visitation of God *crossed through*].

The Castle is Hurdled round and the Sheep are turned in which will greatly improve the [Lawn *crossed through*] Herbage.

A Gentleman from Barnstable, of the name of Knight, with a large family, is come here and lives in the house lately occupied by Mrs. Llewellin near Mr. Wood's.

Sent Account of the Death of Mr. Morgan of Tredegar and of Proceedings Relative to the Bridge and impounding Cattle at Hirwain.

July 9th   Yesterday, the Remains of Mr. Morgan of Tredegar were interred in the family Vault at Machen. A Hearse and two Mourning Coaches from London attended. Judge Gould and his Son the Colonel were present and the whole of the Tenantry in that Neighbourhood, and a large Body of the respectable part of the Country.

It is said that Judge Gould is to reside at Tredegar, and Colonel Gould at Ruperra, and that Mrs. Morgan is left four thousand pounds per annum and all the Chattels. Mrs. Ball is to live with her Father, Judge Gould at Tredegar, and Mrs. Morgan is to live at the Friars, near Newport, at which place she now is with Mrs. Ball.

The Justices have this day determined on having a New Bridge of three Arches which is to be built considerably below the present Bridge, and the Road to lead through the Cardiff Arms Yard. The Contract is to be signed on Wednesday next at the Quarter Sessions at Neath. A Person from Brecon of the name of Parry[92] is to contract for the building of it at Three Thousand pounds, and to give three hundred for the materials of the old Bridge.

I have delivered Bills for Chief Rents in Senghenith to the following persons, and it is expected they will settle shortly. I spoke to Mr. Thomas of Landaff this day and he said he would settle his arrears before the end of this month.

	£	s.	d.
J. Richards Junr. Esqr.	31	3	0
J. Richards Senr. Esqr.	22	18	2
Mr. Wm. Key	10	8	0
Wm. Price Gent., Ivy House	6	4	10
Edwd. Morgan Esqr.	5	9	2
Edmund Lewis, Whitchurch	5	9	0
	£81	12	2

August 18th Cardiff Assizes began this Evening, Judge Hardinge came in on Horseback from Merthyr. He spent part of two days there and in the Neighbourhood.

August 19th The Judges etc. at Church as usual. Mr. Lowder officiated.

August 20th Do. Do.

The Gentlemen of the Grand Jury were: Thomas Wyndham Esqr., Robert Rouse Esqr., John Price Esqr., Edwd. Morgan Esqr., Saml. Homfray Esqr., John Bennet Esqr., Thomas Hopkins Esqr., John Nicholl Esqr., etc., in all 13. The Judge complained of the non-attendance of John Morris Esqr., Wm. Gibbon Esqr., Wm. Tait Esqr., etc., and declared that he would fine the absentees £20 each unless very substantial reasons could be assigned.

In his address to the Grand Jury he began with the state of the County Gaol, and was quite warm in his animadversions thereon, complaining of the inattention of the Justices etc. etc. He then came to the Commission of the Peace, and in a short time work'd himself up to a degree of vehemence and said that if something was not done he would [go] to the King himself and lay the lamentable state of the County before him etc. etc. When his Lordship concluded, Mr. Wyndham spoke to him and said that he had the pleasure of informing him that he had seen the Lord Lieutenant a few days before he left Town, and was told that the List was made out, on which his Lordship said he was very happy to hear it and hoped it would shortly be Issued.

August 21st The Will etc. of Rd. David Deceased was argued last night and this morning the Judge read a long account and cited various cases relative to Marshalling Assets, payment of debts etc., and it was at last decreed that the Creditors should be paid out of the real estate, and that the Charity business should be open for further investigation, and directed that proper enquiry should be made whether such Charity existed etc.

August 22nd   The Criminals Tryed this day: Margaret Hopkin for setting fire to a Barn and Beasthouse at New Castle, Bridge-end, Sentenced to die. Two others to be whipp'd and imprisoned for 12 months, and four others were acquitted. Special Pleadings on the Affidavits in the matter of John Price and R. Griffiths, Surgeon, this Evening; Judgment to pass tomorrow.

August 23rd   A Cause in which Edmund David of Black Brook, near the Quakers Yard, was Plaintiff and Thomas Dadford Defendant. The action was brought for the recovery of £42 13s. 8d. for work and labour on the Merthyr Canal. After a tryal of 5 Hours a verdict was given for the Plaintiff for the whole amount with Costs.

[Joseph John *crossed through*]

In passing Judgment on Mr. Griffiths, the Judge represented in glaring colours the Brutal act Mr. G. had committed in so violently Assaulting Mr. Price, and declared that was it not for his profession as a Surgeon and Midwife that he should commit him to Prison for six months. And after giving him a severe reprimand he ordered that he should immediately pay a fine of £200 and enter into a Recognizance himself in £300 and two Sureties in £150 each on condition of his keeping the peace etc. towards John Price Esqr. for three years.

His Sureties were John Thomas Gent. of Cowbridge and Mr. James Williams of Cardiff. A smart altercation took place between the Attorney General and Mr. Allen relative to the Bail, which caused Judge Hardinge to tell Mr. Allen that he was over warm and zealous in the Business, which expression of his Lordship's threw Mr. Allen into a very great Passion, in the course of which he told his Lordship that warmth in a Barrister was excusable but warmth in a Judge was inexcusable. It was some time before the matter was cleared up, and Judge Hardinge said that it was one particular reason that prevented him from making it a serious business, and Judge Moysey was under the necessity of acting as Mediator between them, when a suitable apology on Mr. Allen's part induced Judge Hardinge to say that he should think no more of it.

Joseph John of Lantrissent was fully convicted of Perjury. Mr. Powell of Lanharran attended and gave him a Character.

August 24th   Sentence was this morning passed on Joseph John, and he is to stand in the Pillory on three successive Market days at Cardiff and to be Transported for seven years.

Judge Hardinge is gone to Ireland, and Rides on Horseback with one Servant to Milford Haven.

August 25th This day there was a meeting to have been held at the Cardiff Arms to contract with Parry for Building the Bridge, but neither he nor the Justices attended. Mr. Edwards and Mr. Thomas of Landaff were there but no others.

Mr. Edwards was to have laid your letter with the offer of £500 before the Committee. Robert Jones Esqr., who now lives at Barry, sent to Town yesterday to know when the meeting was to be held.

It is said that Colonel Gordon[93] intends suing T. Mathews Esqr. for *Crim.Con.*[94] with Mrs. G. Mr. Mathews has sent the principal Evidence out of the way.

August 26th Mr. Hollier set out for the West.

August 27th Called on Captain Richards and Mr. Edward Morgan about the Chief Rent. They said they would settle any day that Mr. Richards of the Corner House would. Saw him in the afternoon, and after some talk he said that after he had had a further search over some old papers that perhaps he would settle this week. Mr. Thomas of Landaff promised to settle tomorrow or next day.

1793

January 15th Epiphany Quarter Sessions at Cardiff.

The only Justices that attended this day were: John Price Esqr. Chairman, Wyndham Lewis Esqr., and Edward Morgan Esqr.

The Bridge business was expected to come on the first thing, for which reason I endeavoured to place myself behind D. Prichard and Hopkin Llewellin, when I found they were prepared to bring it forward as I observed the Case in Mr. Llewellin's hands, but on some account or other they thought proper to decline bringing it forward this day.

Mrs. Hollier having requested me to watch the different motions on this business, I informed her of all that passed.

In the morning Court nothing of consequence took place, nor in the Evening, except the last thing which was an Address from Mr. Elias Jenkins to the Bench stating that he was requested by the Gentlemen of the Law in this

County to observe that at the last Quarter Sessions at Swansea he understood Mr. Aubrey and Mr. Calvert Jones, or one of them, had influenced Mr. Wyndham to join them in declining to dine with the Attorneys, and from the present appearance of things he was induced to imagine that their Worships meant to Sanction their proceedings rather than accomodate them, and that if they were determined to proceed in that manner he was directed to say that they would have no Lawyers to attend their Courts. Mr. Price said a few words in reply, but Mr. Wyndham Lewis entered into the matter with some warmth. He said that 'We should have been glad to have associated with the Attorneys as at other times, but we did not think ourselves obliged to ask them to come to us. If they had come we should have been glad to see them as usual'. Mr. Jenkins said that when a matter takes place at one Court and is not done away by any order, it must be understood to continue. Mr. Morgan thought the Assertion unfounded and Mr. Lewis said it was an illiberal attack upon the present Bench. Several replys were made which seemed rather to aggravate than palliate this business.

The foregoing not sent at all. Mr. Wood going off the next day.

March 25th   The Royal Glamorgan Militia marched this morning at 6 o'Clock for Newport. I assisted the Band in playing them out of Town, and on my return found that Captain Richards had died about half past 6. He dined with Lord Mountstuart and the Officers yesterday at the Cardiff Arms, and was taken ill last night. A New Bailiff must be sworn in in his stead. About three months back he admitted Mr. Tait a Burgess of the Town. He promised me that he would settle all his Chief Rents last Christmas, but it has not been done.

Yesterday morning Mr. Bevan[95] the new Quarter Master set off for Newport, and in the afternoon about 5 o'Clock, while the Militia were on Parade in the Castle, a Daughter of Wm. Lewis's the Cornfactor, and a Daughter of Mrs. Stewart's who formerly lived at the Angel, met Mr. Bevan about half a mile out of the Town where he was in waiting with a Chaise and four which he had got at Newport [and into which he put the young women *crossed through*] and took them off. Dr. Griffiths was the first that brought the News to Town, and the Father and Mother of the Girls went after them but did not go further than Newport, as they had been gone forward more than an hour, and concluded that they should not overtake them. It seems that Mr. Quin,[96] a new Officer, was in league with Mr. Bevan in this business, and when it was publickly known Mr. Quin shewed several letters that he had received from Lewis's Daughter to Lord Mountstuart and the Officers. It is said that his Lordship is much displeased at Mr. Bevan's conduct, and has hinted that he shall be dismissed the service. Mr. Bevan is a married man and has a family.

10 o'Clock at night. It is now said that Lord Mountstuart has insisted on Mr. Bevan's restoring the Girls and that they are on the road home.

A Letter from the War Office reached Lord Mountstuart last night, desiring the Militia might remain here till further orders, but as the Sessions begin Tomorrow they were obliged to be removed.

March 26th The Judges did not come in till 9 o'Clock at Night.

March 27th Church as usual.
The new Commission of the Peace read in Court.

The Grand Jury were: David Thomas of Pwllywrach Esqr., Herbert Hurst Esqr., Nicholas Price Esqr., William Jones Esqr., Jean Baptiste Mon. De Choiseul, Robert Wrixon Esqr., Wyndham Lewis Esqr., Rowland Williams Esqr., David Williams of Pendoylan Gent. and others.

The Judge in his Address began with an explanation of the Different Societies against Republicans and Levellers,[97] and mentioned Judge Ashurst's Speech[98] etc. He then described the present situation of the War, the Paper credit of the Kingdom and the manner in which it had been strained. He congratulated the Gentlemen of the County on the valuable acquisition of the new Commission of the Peace, and said that as far as he could hear or find out, it was a very impartial one, and earnestly requested that the Gentlemen named therein would take out their Dedimus[99] with all speed.

March 28th Among the Bills of Indictment one was found against the Old Bridge at Cardiff. It was brought by Elias Jenkins, Attorney.

Very little business of consequence this Sessions. Two Prisoners found guilty of Felony, and sentences of death were passed on them, but they are to be Transported for 7 years.

March 29th Captain Richards interred this Morning at 6 o'Clock. Went to Newport by Lord Mountstuart's desire. Two Soldiers who had absented themselves for two days were sentenced to be flogg'd and were tyed up, but just as they were going to begin his Lordship pardon'd them.

March 30th The Militia left Newport this Morning at 6 o'Clock and marched for Chepstow.

March 31st The Judges at Church. Judge Hardinge dined at Gabalva.

April 1st The Judges left Town.

April 2nd D. Prichard and J. Bradley were returning home from Glocester, where Bradley had had a trial with a Man from Bristol, about 11 at night. Just at the Long Cross[100] they met two men who are Smuglers and had two kegs of Gin. Prichard pretended to call out to Mr. Phillips the Supervisor and Bridgewater an Exciseman, and then seized the Liquor and carried it to Prichard's House.

April 4th   Mr. Blannin and John Waters, Sadler, has failed, and others in the Town are talked of. Mr. Bradley's name was mentioned but I think without foundation. I heard that he borrowed a thousand pounds on his buildings a few days ago. He lost a fine Stallion and two Colts last week, and he told me himself that it would be three hundred pounds out of his way.

April 5th and 6th   Several of the Bills drawn by the Cardiff Bank and payable at Bristol have been returned, but they have paid them here. This circumstance will put a stop to any further Negociation of their paper for some time.

April 8th   Mr. Minnet was this day sworn in as Bailiff and John Hussey Assistant.

April 10th   The man from whom Prichard and Bradley took the Liquor was in my shop this morning. He told me he should prosecute Prichard.

The next payment to the Glamorganshire Canal will be on Saturday next when the Subscribers will have paid the Sixty thousand pounds as contracted for. Mr. Vaughan of the Melin Griffith told me it would cost near thirty thousand more to complete it.

April 11th   At the Quarter Sessions at Cowbridge no business of any consequence was done, and no Attorneys attended but D. Prichard and Hopkin Llewellin. The former made a motion for some money to repair the old Bridge and was seconded by the latter, but the Justices turned a deaf ear to them.

There were three Appeals heard, and the Overseers etc. were suffered to plead their own causes.

Prichard wanted five hundred pounds, but when he found they would agree to nothing he beg'd hard for even five pounds. This I find was nothing but a motion grounded on the Bill of Indictment found at the Great Sessions.

April 18th   This morning at 2 o'Clock Old Franky died.[101] She was out last Sunday. Mr. Hollier desired me to tell her Daughter and Son in law, to let her be decently interred etc.

John Richards Junr. Esqr., Son to the late Captain, was in with me this morning, and being in a good humour and rather familiar he gave me an opportunity of telling him that his Father had told me about two months back that he would settle the Chief Rents very soon, and that he intended doing so last Christmas. He ask'd 'What Chief Rents, there's nothing due is there?'. 'Yes, a considerable sum in arrears for the Energlyn Estate'.[102] 'The devil there is?'. I wish'd to explain further to him but he went out.

A group of local gentry and others, from a painting by J. C. Ibbetson, 1789. From left to right: Old Franky, aged 94; William Morgan, porter; the Hon. Thomas Windsor; John, Lord Mountstuart; John, Marquess of Bute; Lord Herbert Windsor Stuart; John Richards, junior; John Wood, town clerk. *By courtesy of South Glamorgan County Libraries.*

The Walls of the new Stable at Cathays[103] will be up to their Square tomorow, and on Monday they will begin to pull down the old Stable and Brewhouse. The new Brewhouse is done.

August 12th to 15th   The news arrived of Lady Mountstuart's being safely delivered of a son,[104] on which account the Bells have been ringing these three days.

August 15th   This day David Prichard had Two Writs of Enquiry at the Angel.

The Sheriff's Clerk requested me to be upon the Jury and I happened to be Foreman. The first was brought by a Man of Ystradyfodwg against Thomas John Meredith, one of the Hirwain Tenants, for Damages sustained by Meredith's having impounded his Cattle from Hirwain in May 1791. The Evidence produced was the lamest I ever heard, but as the Plaintiff was entitled to Damages the Jury gave him one penny only.

The other Writ was brought by Prichard in the name of Philip Davy only, against a Man at Merthyr for Twenty pounds. This was wrong, as Davy is not in the Kingdom, and the Action should have been brought in the name of Davy's Assignees, but it was done by Prichard himself without their knowledge for the purpose of applying the money to his own use. The Jury were obliged to find a Verdict for the Twenty pounds.

August 17th   Cardiff Assizes began this Evening. Being known to the Deputy Sherriff on Account of Printing the Calendar and Pannels[105] for the Jury, he ask'd me to dine with him. Mr. Hollier was not there.

Judge Hardinge Rode from Newbridge on Horseback. He came from Merthyr to Newbridge in one of the Canal Boats, accompanied by Mr. Samuel Homfray, with a Harper.

Sunday August 18th   The Judges at Church as usual. Judge Hardinge's Selection of Church Music was performed.

August 19th   At Church till 2 o'Clock. And after the introductory business the Grand Jury were called over, when there was found to be eight of them deficient and only 11 attended, on which there was a sad Rumpus by the Judges. And they both declared that they would fine every Absentee Ten pounds, and a strict examination of the Bailiffs who summoned them immediately took place. The Gentlemen to pay the fines are John Richards Corner House, Edward Morgan, John Price, Richard Aubrey and Robert Rouse Esquires.

As there were but Eleven Gentlemen present, Mr. Hollier was applied to but declined, on which Judge Hardinge said 'It is extremely wrong in Mr. Hollier to refuse. He is an Honorable Man, and in Office, and certainly ought on a case of this sort to give his assistance', when Mr. Hollier immediately consented and was sworn in with Doctor Griffiths. The Grand Jury then stood as follows: Thomas Wyndham, R.T. Deere, Thomas Bridges, John Llewellin, John Bennet, Thomas Thomas, John Bevan, Edward Thomas and Henry Hollier Esquires, and Walter Coffin, Anthony Mathews, Thomas Maddox and Richard Griffiths Gentlemen. Judge Moysey addressed them and only said 'Gentlemen of the Jury, the Calendar is rather small, and you see that the crimes are only common occurrences, therefore you will proceed to expedite the business before you'.

This being the day for trying the Old Issues, there was only one tryed, which was brought by a farmer of Penlline against Miss Gwinnet's Game Keeper for going into two fields of standing Barley on the first day of September last, and wantonly beating about for Game therein. The Trial lasted five hours, and it was proved that 3 Bushels of Barley at 10s. per Bushel was spoiled. The Attorney General exerted himself to prove that the Action was maliciously brought, but the Judges were convinced to the contrary, and Judge Hardinge told the Jury that if they found Thirty Shillings damages, and the Consel on the part of the Plaintiff would Certify, that they should be entitled to Costs. On which the Jury, after some deliberation, found a Verdict of thirty shillings damages. This will cost Miss Gwinnet from Fifty to Sixty pounds.

August 21st   The Prisoners were tryed this day as per Calendar.

August 22nd   New Issue day. The first Tryal was between William Lewis and William Tait Esquires against Saml. Homfray Esqr. and Co. for the recovery of a small spot of ground at Peny Darran Works claimed by the Dowlais Company and not worth 6d. a year to any persons but themselves. The Trial lasted some time when a Verdict was given for the Dowlais Co., on which an Arrest of Judgement was moved and it is now thrown into Chancery. This was disputed two years ago.

The next were two Actions for Defamation and Scandal between two Butchers at Neath. Each of them obtained a Verdict under 40s. therefore they must pay their own Costs. Some other trifling matters were tryed, and then came on the Replevin *Bail Cause*[106] between Wm. Hurst Esqr., Plaintiff, and George Phillpotts of Roath and Wm. Westmacutt of Cardiff, Defendants, who were Bail for Thomas Hughes Vernon Esqr. who has absconded some time since and is now at Edingburgh. Mr. Hurst obtained a Verdict and the Defendants are liable to pay the whole money due to Mr. Hurst from Vernon. Westmacutt and Phillpott are obliged to keep out of sight, but they expect that Vernon will exonerate them shortly. Mr. Wood, who was concerned for Phillpotts, has made a nominal distress at Roath for Lady Mackworth and sent Geo. Phillpotts out of the way to prevent the Sheriff from levying the Execution.

The Validity of the late Richard David's Will was again argued this Evening, and it came out in the Course of Business that Mr. Bold has paid and Expended all the money except about five pounds which were in his hands for Ty yn y Wern, and it is fully proved that you will be entitled to the Bond Debt due to the late R. David from the Executors of the late Robert Jones Esqr.

Some of the Councellors have complained to the Judges that they are not well accommodated with appartments, and Judge Hardinge wrote to Mr. Hollier on the Subject. The Complaint arises chiefly from the Counsel at Mr. Verity's who have only one Room each. I have waited on Miss Gwinnet (who has been in Town during the Sessions) relative to the Heriot due in Senghenith. She has promised that Mr. Franklen should pay a Composition of Five Guineas before he leaves Town. I have made out the Particulars of Lord Plymouth's Chief Rents, and Mr. Key has promised to settle them. His Lordship pays Chief Rent to you for 153 Tenements.

August 23rd   The Judges left Town this morning.

August 24th   A Party of Sailors, 45 in number, passed through Town about 3 o'Clock this afternoon, armed with Cutlasses, Bludgeons etc. They had landed at Barry to avoid being Pressed at Pennarth, and a Quarter of an hour after they went through a Press Gang consisting of 14 men well armed came up and went in pursuit of the Sailors and overtook them at Rumney. Fifty or 60 of the Towns-people went with the Gang, and had it not been for their Interference the Gang would all have been killed as the Sailors were drawn up ready for Action, and were determined not to be Impressed. The Gang very prudently declined the attack [abandoned the pursuit *crossed through*] and the Towns-people treated the Sailors with a pint of ale each at Rumney.

Sunday August 25th   Copying Release from Edward Deere of Crayford in the County of Kent, Grocer, Digby Mackworth of Holywell in the County of Oxford, Esquire and Jane his wife, to Henry Jones of Penmark in the County of Glamorgan, Clerk, of premises in Lanblethian on which Surrenders have lately passed.

August 26th 1793   Do. Do.

[Colonel *crossed through*] Capper turns in often for Books. Thomas Wilson who now lives in this Town has this work and I believe would sell them. I am told there were but two Copies of them in England twenty years ago, and that Lord Delaraine has one Copy and this is the other. Histoire Metallique des 17

Provinces Pays-Bas, de Monsieur Gerard Van Loon, 1732. 5 Vols. in good preservation.

Roath Farm without your sheep walk called James's Farm would be a very bad Estate.

1794

September 6th Went to Mr. Llewellin at Keven Mably for the particulars and different amounts of your Land through which the Canal has passed and Trespassed, the surveying and valuing of which by Mr. Morris and Mr. Llewellin I have constantly attended. And as there was a Canal Meeting this day Mr. Hollier wanted the amount. The Moors cannot be valued and surveyed on the part of the proprietors until the Bason and Lock are finished, but the amount of the whole, from Ty yn y Wern to the East Gate at Cardiff due to you is £386.

Cardiff Assizes began this Evening. Judge Hardinge rode from Brecon.

The Sale of Roath Estate[107] and several Houses in Cardiff was at the Cardiff Arms this Afternoon. Mr. Hollier attended, as did Merchant Jones of Bristol who owns the Longcross and several Gentlemen. They were some time before any one would begin to bid, when Dr. Williams in a Jocular but Ironical manner said 'Why doesn't the Affrican Merchant begin?'. Upon which Mr. Jones said 'Three Thousand Guineas', and after many biddings it was knock'd down as I thought to Mr. Hollier at £5000. I found myself extremely happy supposing it was intended to be annexed to your Estates in Roath and conceiving it to be very cheap being not 21 years purchase,[108] but found afterwards it was only bought in, as was all the rest.

September 7th The Judges etc. at Church as usual.

September 8th The Gentlemen who formed the Grand Jury were: John Morris Esqr., Rd. Bevan, C.R. Jones, Ed. Thomas, Jno. Goodrich Esquires, and several Gentlemen from the West, in all Seventeen. Judge Hardinge, in addressing them began by noticing the political state of these Kingdoms both at home and abroad and made it appear that our prosecuting the war abroad was the sure means of keeping peace at home. He then said that he found himself compelled to Trespass greatly on their time, but as he had by the greatest exertions and indefatigable Labor got rid of a shameful and scandalous abuse in the Offices of Auditor, Deputy Auditor and Receiver of His Majesty's Land Revenue in Wales he trusted they would pardon him for entering fully into that business, the substance of which was that Dr. Griffiths had, by the application of some of his friends to Thomas Johnes Esqr. the Auditor and Compounder, got £175 of the Fine of £200 for Assaulting John Price Esqr. remitted. The Judge went through the whole business which took up near an Hour in stating particulars, reading part of Acts of Parliament, Certificates, Declarations etc. by which it appears that no such right does exist in any Auditor or Compounder, and the Doctor was obliged to pay the £175 back again to the Deputy Auditor. And in future no fine of a similar nature, or laid on by way of punishment, will be mitigated by Mr. Johnes or his Deputies. I was told by Dr. Reece, who is in partnership with Dr. Griffiths, that it was a friend of his in the West (to use his own words) that let the cat out of the bag, or Judge Hardinge would not have heard of it.

His Lordship then proceeded to the State of the Gaol, and recommended the Gentlemen to view it and to adopt a plan for Penetentiary Cells and a proper place for the sick, and gave them Plans and regulations of the Gaol at Dorchester which, he said, was the best kept in this Kingdom, perhaps in the world. He then took up the Calendar, made several observations thereon and proceeded to business.

September 9th   Several Old Issues tried and accomodated this day, but nothing very material.

September 10th   The Prisoners tried this day as per Calendar.

The Grand Jury delivered in a Presentment stating that the County Gaol was in good repair but deficient in a place for the sick and for penetentiary confinement.

September 11th   A Cause came on between John Goodrich Esqr., Plaintiff, and Evan Thomas of the Aber near Energlyn, Defendant, to recover the Ruins of a small Mill on the Aber Estate. Several respectable Witnesses proved the property to belong to the Energlyn Estate, but in examining the Will of the late Mr. Powell it was found that the attesting Witnesses were Edward Morgan Esqr., George Williams who was at that time servant to Mr. Morgan, and Mr. Henry Williams Attorney of Cardiff, Deceased. A Son of Mr. Williams's proved his Father's hand writing, but Mr. Morgan said he had no sort of recolection of his having been a Witness to Mr. Powell's Will, and it was the more extraordinary to him as he had told Mr. Powell that if he left the Estate from him and Mr. Richards of the Corner House he ought to be Crucified. This declaration threw the Court into amazement, for five Minnits before Mr. Goodrich had made good his claim to the Mill, but as George Williams could not be found and from Mr. Morgan's declaration the validity of Mr. Powell's Will was disputable Mr. Goodrich was inevitably nonsuited. Judge Hardinge was for letting it go to the Jury, but Judge Moysey opposed it for the foregoing reasons, and some considerable Debates ensued. Judge Moysey observed that if Mr. Morgan could prove that he saw the Will duly executed, and the other two Witnesses attest it, the Plaintiff would certainly be entitled to a Verdict, but as it was he must suffer a nonsuit. Mr. Goodrich must find George Williams, if alive, for as the matter stands Mr. Powell's Will is invalid.

Mr. Jenner sued Mr. Hurst for property in Dynas Powis and got possession of it.

There were several petty causes tryed, but no other of consequence.

September 12th   The Judges left Town this morning.

I have heard from one who had it from Judge Moysey's Clerk, that the Judges do not agree, that Judge Moysey had applied to be removed and that the learned Brothers had differed no less than eight times before this, and the matters have been constantly laid before the twelve Judges who have as constantly given it against Judge Hardinge. I am persuaded that this article is not known but by a very few individuals.

September 13th   David John, the present Tenant of Ty yn y Wern, has this day agreed to give £45 per annum for it and to have a Lease for 14 years.

The new Stables and Coach Houses at the Cardiff Arms[110] are up to the Square and the Carpenters are framing the Roof, which is 90 feet long, in the Castle yard.

September 15th   Two of the Arches of the new Bridge are turned and the other is in great forwardness.

Henry Cunniff Esqr., a West Indian, has lately married Merchant Jones's daughter of Bristol and is coming to live at the Long Cross. Part of their goods are come.

September 16th   A Vessell arrived this morning from London with Deals and Mr. Howdon's furniture.

News is just arrived of the Death of Sir Robert Mackworth.[111]

I have lately pick'd up several arrears of Chief Rent and have had the Burgage Book from Mr. Bew by Mr. Holliers desire to collect those Rents.

September 17th   I have just heard that two strange Gentlemen were yesterday looking over the Roath Estate, but did not like the House nor lands, though at going away they said they should call again in a few days.

Miss Jenkins, the tenant of St. Quintin's Castle and Land, offered to pay £25 in part of her arrears, but as there is £55 due Mr. Hollier would not take it.

December 6th Mr. Edwards of Llandaff having been very ill for this fortnight past his Dissolution was daily expected. His Son, Mr. Powell Edwards, arrived at Landaff at 10 o'Clock last night. His Father had not spoke since

Llandaff House, from a survey of the estate of Thomas Edwards, 1776. *By courtesy of Mr J. B. Hilling.*

Thursday night last and died this day at 2 in the afternoon. He refused to see Mrs. Richards during the whole of his Illness.[112]

The news arrived here exactly as Mr. Hollier and your Tenants sat down to Dinner (being Audit day), and some observations having passed in the morning relative to Heriots due to Mr. Aubrey of Lantrithyd, Mr. White of Miskin, Mr. Jones of Clytha, etc. I proposed to Mr. Hollier that I would go over to Landaff as soon as the event should take place to prevent others from taking the best Cattle Mr. Edwards had. He immediately consented and I went to Landaff and secured a fine Saddle Horse and Mare. This was done in as private a manner as possible, as no one knows of it but Mr. Edwards's Clerk with whom I am very intimate.

In talking with him on this business and the Office of Clerk of the Peace, he told me that about a month ago his Master told him that Mr. Wood had asked him to resign that Office [of Clerk of the Peace *crossed through*] to him, but that Mr. Edwards had refused, saying that he would not resign it during his life. It is publickly said that Mr. Hollier is to succeed him in that Office. And it is also said that Mr. Wood will not act as Deputy under Mr. Hollier. Mr. John Thomas of Cowbridge asked me an hour back who was to be Mr. Hollier's Deputy. I said I knew nothing of the matter.

1795

January 27th In Consequence of the sudden thaw last night the oldest Inhabitant in Cardiff does not remember to have seen so great a quantity of Ice as appeared in the River Taff this morning; which being driven by the Rapidity of a very strong Flood has unfortunately carried away the Temporary Bridge, and from the great quantity of Ice in the River it was impossible to prevent the smallest part of it from driving out to sea. The Mail Coach etc. must now go through Landaff until the Center Arch of the new Bridge can be turned, which in all probability cannot be effected this four months.

The inclosed Statement is to be sent to each of the Justices.

This Account has been collected from the Records by Mr. Hollier and myself. All the Acts of Parliament, Files and Papers belonging to the County are deposited in the Drawing Room in the Castle. I brought them from Landaff in two large carts.

[I some time back proposed to Mr. Hollier to let me new-model the Rental by keeping the new things apart from the old, which he approved of and I have prepared a Book for the purpose of a rough Rental *crossed through*.]

I have lately delivered a Bill to John Richards Junr. Esqr. for Chief Rents in Senghenith and Burgage Rents in Cardiff to Michaelmas 1794 amounting to £68 9s. 10d. I have not seen him since, as he went to Bath and it was said that he was to be married to Miss Jones of Fonmon. But the match is now off as Mr. Mathews has refused to settle any thing.

I have also delivered a Bill for Burgage Rents in Cardiff to John Richards Senr. Esqr. amounting to £26 15s. 8d. and he told me he would order the Tenants to pay. I have lately made a new Book of the Burgage Rents in Cardiff and Chief and Cot Rents in Roath, Lystalybont, Lequeth, Cosmestone, Landough and Cogan, and Kibbor or Friars, on a better plan than heretofore, and as I have now the collecting of those Rents I will use my best endeavours to get in [the] arrears.

March 24th The Sessions began this day. A large Cavalcade with the Sheriff, Wyndham Lewis Esq. He has sixteen Javalin-men.

Judge Hardinge rode on Horseback.

March 25th The Judges at Church as usual.

The Grand Jury were: John Price Esq., John Llewellin Esq., John Knight Esq., John Bassett Esq., John Landeg Esq., Roger Landeg Esq., etc. etc., in all sixteen.

Judge Hardinge, in Addressing the Grand Jury, lamented as usual that nothing had been done to the County Gaol, and recommended the Gentlemen to adopt a plan for solitary confinement, which had been found to have the desired effect in other places.

L.B. at Spain[113]

1797

March 7th   Mr. Wood did not return from the Meeting at Pyle till last night as he stopped at Dunravon with Mr. Rous, who dines at the Corner House today, and this Morning ordered the second form for a Meeting at Cowbridge next Tuesday. I wished very much to have got a Copy of the Resolutions entered into at Pyle, but Mr. Wood told me he was going to send a Copy of them to Mr. Hollier by Tomorrow's Post, and that the only Resolution of any consequence was that every Hundred[114] in the County shall be considered as a separate District and shall Subscribe for Arms and Accoutrements for a Body of Cavalry to be exercised in each Hundred.

The Sussex Fencibles Cavalry [being about 130 men and Horses *crossed through*] went from hence last Wednesday night at 9 o'Clock in consequence of the 2nd Alarm from Pembrokeshire, and travelled all Night till they got to Neath and were there informed that every thing remained quiet.

It is said that Colonel Aubrey and Mr. Llewellin of Penllergare had some high words at the Meeting at Pyle, in consequence of their difference in opinion relative to Cavalry or Infantry, and Mr. Talbot said he would raise a Thousand Men[115] for his own protection [Cavalry men at his own expense *crossed through*] and keep them at Penrice. He did not stop at Pyle to dinner with the other Gentlemen.

Dr. Collins of Swansea wanted the County to Reimburse the Swansea people for the Expences they had been at on the late Alarms, but was strongly opposed, which was the means of introducing the Resolution for every Hundred to be kept separate.

As Mr. Hollier was absent, I seized the Horse Mr. Thomas of the Aber rode on as a Heriot. The Jury brought in a verdict of 'Suffocation in consequence of falling into the Ditch near Cathays'. Therefore no Deodand[116] can be claimed.

Mr. Howell of Caerphilly is much better.

March 28th   Robert Rouse Esq., Sheriff, and a very respectable party dined at the Cardiff Arms previous to their Escorting the Judges who came in about 6 o'Clock.

March 29th   The Judges at Church as usual. A selection of Sacred Music by Judge Hardinge. The Assize Sermon by Mr. Lowder, the text 'Fear God, Honour the King'.

The Grand Jury were: Thomas Wyndham Esq., John Richards Senr. and J. Richards Junr. Esquires, Mr. Taitt, Mr. Wrixon, Mr. Calvert Jones, Mr. Jere. Homfray, Mr. Bassett, Mr. Richardson of Merthir Mawr, Mr. Knight of Tythegstone and many others, in all 18 which I believe was gratifying to Judge Hardinge as he is always pleased at seeing a large Body of Grand Jury Men.

His address to them was more political this time than ever I remember to have heard. He began with the State of things in general, and painted in lively colours the nature of the Plan that had been adopted relative to the Bank of England,[117] and then mentioned the Country Banks and explained their utility under certain restrictions, recommending very strongly the support of the Bank at Brecon,[118] and pointed out the infinite service that Bank was of to this part of the Country as well as the place in which it was situated, from the respectability of its firm.

In the Course of his Charge he mentioned the repulse met with by the Enemy in Pembrokeshire, and paid the highest compliment to the prompt exertions of the Welch, and said he was convinced that the spirit of the ancient

Swansea Castle. Engraved by Richard Godfrey after Paul Sandby, 1786. *By courtesy of University College Cardiff Library.*

Britons would be ever alive to resist the common enemy and to ward off the impending blow.

He noticed the state of the Jail and was proud to say that it was what he wished and [thanked the foreman for the Presentment that had formerly been made by him and his colleagues *crossed through*] was happy to see it nearly ready for solitary confinement.

The Prison at Swansea[119] was next mentioned and he said that he had received a polite answer from the Duke of Beaufort saying that it should be immediately attended to, and said he had seen a plan which fully met his approbation.

April 5th The number of Signatures for the Cardiff Volunteers are 134. I was over the parish of Whitchurch and Melingriffith yesterday. Mr. Vaughan, the Agent at those Works, proposed to me that they would form a Company of 60 or 80 men, to be exercised there but to be subject to the Commanding Officer at Cardiff and to co-operate with the Cardiff Volunteers when called upon. They agree to spare four Musicians from thence to fill our Band.

Mr. Wood has just had from me a fair Copy of the Resolutions and sends them to you by this post. The Supplementary Militia are now Exercising in the Castle. We have here near 300. The men for the Hundred of Ogmore went to Swansea by mistake, but are to come here as soon as possible. We have clothing but for two hundred. The letters to the Clerks of the Subdivision Meetings of the Western Hundreds I have just given to Captain Gough Aubrey[120] who goes to Swansea by this Evening's Mail. Mr. Hollier went to Bristol this morning at 5 o'Clock by the Coach.

The following Copies of letters will explain the reason of Captain Aubrey's Journey from Swansea:

To H. H. Esq.

Sir, Captain Aubrey came here this morning by the Coach and lamented his having missed you as he wanted directions how to act on the Circumstances of there having been a mistake at Swansea in dismissing two thirds of the Men. Mr. Wood advised me to write by Captain Aubrey in your name to the Clerks of the Subdivision meetings. A Copy of those letters I now transmit. Should there be any thing improper in what I have done I must rely on your goodness for excuse, and at the same time observe that every exertion on my part shall be devoted to your commands on this and every other occasion.

I beg leave to subscribe etc. etc.

J.B.

Captain Aubrey begs you will forward the Arms and Clothing from Bristol to Swansea with all speed.

Sir, Captain Aubrey having represented that a mistake had arisen at Swansea in dismissing two thirds of the men belonging to the Supplementary Militia for the Western Hundreds of the County of Glamorgan, I am directed to request you will use the utmost Exertions in causing the men so dismissed belonging to your Hundred to assemble at Swansea immediately in order to join those who are now training there. I refer you to Captain Aubrey for further particulars on this business and am, Sir, for H.H. Esq. your most obedient etc.

J.B.

May 2nd At length, after three several adjournments, a Meeting of the Cardiff Volunteers was held in the Town Hall this day, John Richards Senr. Esq. in the Chair, when it was at first intended to select a Committee to nominate Officers. But after some deliberation the following Gentlemen were voted for and agreed to, Vizt.

Wyndham Lewis Esq. to be Captain
Henry Hollier Esq. Lieutenant
John Williams Gent. Ensign

Colonel Capper had the particulars of last Saturday's meeting of me, and he has this instant sent for me to give him the particulars of this day's business.

On Tuesday last, just before Mr. Wood went to the Quarter Sessions at Cowbridge, he gave me the Subscription paper to hand about and told me I must do it for Mr. Hollier as he was absent. I observed that I thought some one of more consequence than I was should go with me as I had done every other part of the business in my power, but he said there was no one else and I must do what I could.

At that time

Wyndham Lewis Esq. had put down his name for	£21	0s.	0d.
Wm. Tait Esq.	£10	10s.	0d.
Bloom Williams Esq.	£10	10s.	0d.

The Volunteers agree to take what Government allows, and the Subscription is in order to defray the Expences of having better Arms and Clothing.

Colonel Capper told me he would Subscribe the same that Mr. Richards did, but I have been unable to get Mr. Richards's name to the Subscription, as he talks of consulting the Colonel, who has not been able to come to Town.

Mr. Wood has not signed the Resolutions and for some private reason has been extremely flat ever since the first meeting. Mr. Tait told me his reason was because the Troops of Cavalry had not been accepted, as they wanted more allowances from Government that it could afford to give. How far that conjecture may be well founded I am at a loss to determine. Mr. Wyndham Lewis and Mr. Tait have been very anxious on the business, and Mr. Richards was much enclined at this meeting [but did not attend on Saturday last *crossed through*]. Mr. Wood did nothing but propose John Williams.

Colonel Capper seemed pleased at what had been done this morning, and desired me to inform them that he would give every assistance in teaching their Exercise and the use of the Great Guns, should any be sent down, and that when any Meeting was called he would attend and march with them on any immergency.

The difficulty of selecting Officers seems now to be got over, and I hope there will be no impediment to its being carried into Execution. I believe Mr. Hollier will soon finish at Bristol, as on his return his assistance will be necessary.

I presume it now lies with Mr. Wood to transmit the names of the Officers for approbation etc., but Colonel Capper told me just now that there should be two Ensigns.

The Annual Meeting of the Cardiff Sympathetic Society was held at the Angel yesterday and attended by all the persons of any respectability in the Town and Neighbourhood. It now consists of 104 Members who attended divine service on the occasion. It is intended for the benefit of widows, who are to have from £15 to £30 per annum after the decease of their Husbands. Mr. Richards of the Corner House, Colonel Capper, Mr. Hollier, Mr. Tait, Mr. Wyndham Lewis, etc. etc. are Members. Mr. Lowder is President and was one of the first to set it on foot. It has been established three years and the present fund is more than £300. The annual Expence to each Member is about £1 8s. 0d.

Militia Reviewed 21st April — Colonel Aubrey.

May 15th A Parish Meeting was held at the Workhouse this morning for the purpose of appointing New Overseers and settling accounts.

Colonel Capper rode to Town a little before 12 o'Clock. He told me he had heard from you and that another Lieutenant must be appointed in stead of Mr. Hollier, and that a meeting should be held as soon as the Parish Meeting was over. In coming from the Parish Meeting Mr. Bailiff Williams told me he would attend at the Hall and propose Mr. Wood for Lieutenant. I told him it was what most of the Volunteers particularly wished, and I hoped it would take place. He seemed quite sanguine, but while I went to inform some of the Volunteers [send the Bellman round *crossed through*] Colonel Capper, Mr. Wood, Mr. Williams and Mr. Richards had some conversation on the business and I presume Mr. Wood objected to it, for on my return, finding the Gentlemen going into the Hall and Mr. Williams by his own door, I told him that the Gentlemen were going up, when he answered in a pet 'I don't care, I wont go

The old Guildhall, Cardiff. Engraved by J. H. Lekeux after W. H. Bartlett, 1841. *By courtesy of South Glamorgan County Libraries.*

a-near them'. I directly went to the Hall, and the Gentlemen were coming out, having gone no further than the door. Mr. Wood told me the Meeting was adjourned to this day fortnight as no notice could be given to call the Inhabitants together.

Mrs. Hollier writes to Mr. Hollier tonight on the business, and I presume it is Colonel Capper's wish that Mr. Hollier should still accept the Lieutenancy. I have just heard that many of the Volunteers do not approve of Mr. John Williams's being an Ensign, he not being of sufficient consequence.

I saw Mr. Hollier on Saturday last at Bristol. He told me he should be home in Ten days.

Mrs. Jones of Fonmon is getting better. She is still at Landaff.

Mr. Cunniffe of the Longcross sells his furniture etc. by Auction on Monday next. He is going to Lodgings at Bristol. He is a West Indian and very much given to inebriety. The House is to be let.

Saturday September 2nd   Cardiff Assizes began this Evening. Judge Hardinge left Judge Moysey at Tredegar where he is to stop till Monday next as he chuses to be out of the way till the Court opens on Monday, and particularly as Dr. Small of Bristol is now here and is to Preach a Charity Sermon on account of the Sunday School Tomorrow when a Collection will be made at the Church door.

September 3rd   The Judge etc. at Church. The Collection amounted to £13. A Selection of Music by Judge Hardinge appropriate to the occasion was performed. He dined with Mr. Rouse the High Sheriff at Court'r Alla.

September 4th   Mr. Hollier desired me to pay particular attention to Judge Hardinge's Address lest he should notice something relative to the Heath business, but not a sylable on that subject escaped him.

The Gentlemen of the Grand Jury were: John Llewellin of Penllergare Esq., John Morris of Clasemont Esq., John Price of Wenvoe Esq., John Llewellin of Welch St. Donats Esq., Samuel Richardson of Hensol Castle Esq., Thomas Thomas of Lanbradach Esq., John Landeg of Swansea Esq., Wm. Jeffreys of Swansea Esq., Edward Nicholl of Lanblethian Esq., Thomas Morgan of Aburthin Esq., Edward Thomas of Tregroes Esq., John Rees of Wick Gentleman and John Richards of Barry Gentleman.

In addressing the Grand Jury, he made a long preface relative to the Roads etc. from Newbridge to Cardiff. He requested they would present those Roads, adding that if they could not comply with that request he should himself, upon his own view, present those Roads and Bridges. He then came to the New Gaol and passed considerable Ecomiums on many parts of it, and then pointed out what he wished to be done — Vizt. the purchase of the Bakehouse adjoining, so as to be enabled to lay out more ground for Air and to raise the Walls of the Courts at least four feet higher, to made some small alterations in the Chapel, and to partition off a Passage to prevent the Debtors and Criminals from seeing each other on their way to the Chapel. He then noticed the different Offences in the Calendar, and proceeded to a Political and affecting description of our present calamitous situation, lamenting the Mutinys in the fleets,[121] and said it behoved every one to be on his Guard with respect to their associating with persons who had imbibed the principles of Thomas Pain[122] or in other words inculcated or privately recommended his doctrine. After which he concluded — rather a long but fine address.

September 5th   Old Issue Day. The only Cause of importance this day was one between Miss Roberts of Cowbridge, Plaintiff, and Miss Jenkins of the same place (your Tenant for the Castle land, and to whose Evidence with that of her Father I attribute the loss of the Golledge Cause)[123] Defendant. The Action was tried in part last Sessions, but was referred to Mr. Hopkin Llewellin of Pyle; but his having lately put a period to his Existence, it was obliged to be tried again.

It was brought for Trespass sustained by Miss Roberts in consequence of

Miss Jenkins's having built on her premises. After a hearing of 3 hours a Verdict was given for the Plaintiff of Five Guineas Damages. It will cost Miss Jenkins about £150.

September 6th Gaol Day. The Prisoners were tried according to the Calendar.

September 7th New Issue Day. The Court was much crowded from there being two Special Jury causes to be tried. Most of the Grand Jury was detained with the addition of Mr. Morgan of Ruperra and a few others to form the Special Juries to try those causes

The first was Between the Dowlais Co. of Merthyr, Plaintiffs, and Rd. Crawshay Esq. & Co., Defendants. The Action was brought for damages on account of Mr. Crawshay's refusing to accept a quantity of Pig Iron for which he had contracted with the Dowlais Company. Most of the Iron Masters in the Country were Subpeonaed, and after a Hearing of 4 Hours it was agreed to be referred.

The next was between Rd. Reece Surgeon, Plaintiff, and Rd. Griffiths Surgeon, both of Cardiff, Defendant. This Action was brought by Mr. Reece to recover damages for a breach of the Articles of Partnership by Mr. Griffiths's absenting himself from business and paying more attention to the Canal Concerns than he did to those of the partnership. After a hearing of 7 hours the Jury found a Verdict for Mr. Reece, damages 40s. Many curious circumstances came out on the Trial, such as Mr. Griffiths's being absent for 6 weeks at a time in London attending the Canal Concerns, and his having been at Newmarket on pleasure, and his having been at Cardiff in the Ball Room last Races and not immediately attending a Call. And of Mr. Griffiths's being displeased with Mr. Reece because he talked Politics to the patients, together with many other things which served to entertain the Court. The Judge reprobated the Trial and said it was founded in Malice and brought forward in bitterness.

Eight days previous to Sessions and after I had been several times over the Heath by the desire of Mr. Hollier and Mr. Wood, in order to discover some one person who was likely to stand Trial for one of the Inclosures, it was determined to bring one Writ in the name of Wyndham Lewis Esq. against Edward William, a Mason who lives in a House of Dr. Griffiths's and which comprises an Enclosure of near 2 acres of land. There were some reasons to suppose that Dr. Griffiths would uphold his Tenant, but the Man has suffered Judgement by default, and a Writ of Enquiry will be instituted to estimate Damages, but nothing can be done before next Sessions.

September 8th Judge Hardinge intended going to the Holmes, but the business was not over time enough this day.

September 9th   He asked me to ride with him as a Guide to Mr. Bridges's at Pennarth, which I did and we found the Roads so bad that he is determined to Indict them next Sessions on his own view. He chose to come up in a Boat.

Sunday September 10th   He went to Church this morning and afterwards went to Ruperra where he stops a few days on his way home.

The Justices of the Peace who formed the New Bridge Committee are going to Contract with a person to make a straight cut to divert the water in a direct line from your Arles[124] to the place where the old Bridge stood. This I hope will be carried into Execution as it will prevent the River from incroaching on the Black Friars land.

Old Mr. Hurst was lately arrested by a Mr. Rich, an attorney of London, for, I believe, £500, and was in Gaol 3 days, but gave Bail. David Prichard the attorney has delivered him a Bill for law business to the amount of £800, but that is to be considerably taxed.

The Canal Tolls have lately been put down in the Poors Rates, and are liable to pay Two Hundred pounds per annum, being Rated at £4000 at 1s. in the pound.

The Miss Bassetts[125] have built a New House in Crockherbtown, and that Street is otherwise much improved.

1798

February 24th   Last night about Eight o'Clock, the Reverend Samuel Molyneux Lowder B.D., Vicar of Cardiff, departed this life and will be interred on Tuesday next. His Widow is the first Annuitant on the Cardiff Sympathetic Club and will receive £20 per annum during life, or till she marries again. I paid him some money for Mr. Hollier a few days back and Received of him £1 16s. 0d. for 18 years Burgage Rent which is the time he lived in Cardiff. It is said that his Successor is a Mr. Jones of Builth in Carmarthenshire, who is Brother in law to Dr. Small of Bristol, the living having been promised to Dr. Small some time back. But Mr. Llewellin late of this place having officiated for Mr. Lowder during his illness, a petition from the inhabitants of Cardiff to the Dean and Chapter of Glocester was drawn up for Mr. Llewellin and he set out for Glocester with it yesterday Morning.

The Supplementary Militia business has been carried on with the greatest vigour. I have been writing etc. day and Night since the Act came down, and warrants from the Deputy Lieutenants etc. have been dispatched by me to all the Clerks of Hundreds, Chief Constables and Petty Constables in the County.

The Ballot for the Hundred of Kibbor and this Town took place this day at the Cardiff Arms, and the Ballotts of every Subdivision in the County will take place on Monday next. Circular letters were dispatched to all the Clerks of the Western Hundreds last night to request in your name the attendance of the Deputy Lieutenants and Magistrates at the different Subdivision Meetings on Monday next, and I hope *that all* the Ballotted men will appear [be embodied *crossed through*] here the 5th of March as appointed.

Judge Hardinge having heard of Mr. Lowder's approaching dissolution, he commissioned me, when that event should happen, to apply for his letters to Mr. Lowder — which I have just had from his Son. They were tied up in bundles by the deceased and contain the correspondence of 8 years. I send them by this Mail packed in a Box, and I believe the letters alone will weigh 12 or 14 pounds. But I do not perceive by the dates on the outside of the bundles that they corresponded after the 8th of May 1796.

The Canal is now ready to admit Brigs etc[126] but the Iron is not yet removed to the Canal Wharfs and Bason near the South Gate. That Ruinous House, Barn and fold yard of yours by the South Gate will be an excellent situation for an Inn as it lies on the Margin of the Bason, and some of the Vessels will lie immediately opposite to it.

The people on and near the Heath are enclosing with more impudence than ever.

July 4th   I have attended at Caerphilly twice, and have had every Book and Paper that was in the late Thomas Howells' possession. The Chief Rent Books he had formerly, and which I brought with me, are of little or no use, as the Rentals have been considerably improved and augmented annually during the 21 years since the 11th of May last that I have known them.

A full Account of the opening of the Sea Lock of the Glamorganshire Canal at Cardiff on Thursday last, which appeared in last Monday's Glocester Journal, was transmitted to that Paper by me for the purpose of its meeting your Eye.

The Audits were held last Saturday and Monday at the Cardiff Arms. Lord Plymouth's Audit was also on Monday, and as they have only one day at Cardiff and their Number being [Ninety Eight *crossed through*] large, they were accomodated with the Long Room to dine in, and the Lantrissent Tenants etc. had the largest parlour.

Mr. Davies of Cogan, who was to ride one of your Horses, hinted to me on Monday Evening last that he wished to ask Colonel Capper if he should be permitted to Ride his own Horse, as it would save him the old duty and the assessed Taxes, amounting to £4 16s. 0d. per annum. I encouraged the Idea, knowing there would be no necessity to purchase a Horse for him on your

Account, and the Colonel immediately agreed with him to ride his own Horse, but to be found Clothes and Accoutrements at your Expence. He attended Muster this day, and will regularly attend on Sunday Evenings and Wednesday Mornings. He applied to his Cousin who lives in a small farm of yours at Cogan to come on the same terms, but he has declined it.

One of the Phillpotts of Roath who Rents £60 per annum under you has, within this hour, been with me at Cathays and proposes to Ride and Maintain any Horse of yours during the time this business may continue and return him when it may cease. The Colonel has not agreed with him, but waits to see if any one will offer who would Ride their own Horse, on the like plan with Mr. Davies. A good Horse, fit for the purpose and sound in every respect, has been offered for £12 12s. 0d., and unless some one of your Tenants can be had to serve on Mr. Davies's plan I presume it will be purchased for Mr. Phillpotts, but the Mare that is kept for Mr. Bew's riding would, in my opinion, do for Mr. Phillpotts.

On Sunday Evening last, just as the Troop were going to Exercise, Lieutenant Colonel Sanxter, who is connected with Lord Milford and is raising Six Troops of Cavalry in Pembroke and Carmarthenshire, happened to pass through Town, paid us a Visit, and was good enough to Drill us for three hours, by which means he gave the Troop the first principles of Exercise etc., and met us the next Morning at 5 o'Clock and drill'd the Troop for 4 hours, which has been of infinite Service, as we are in some degree able to go on 'till we get a Drill Sergeant.

Mr. Bacon, late of Landaff, who is now here for the purpose of purchasing the Maindy of Mr. Wyndham Lewis, came into the Ranks this Morning and means to join us in the event of his settling here. He now lives near Newbery[127] and belongs to a Troop there.

Colonel Capper said he should write to Lord Bute tomorrow on the Cavalry business.

The Officers wait for their Commissions.

Wednesday Night 11 o'Clock.

July 30th   The Pocket Rental I finished complete to this time, packed it up with care and directed it 'The Marquess of Bute' etc. etc. etc. - to be left at the Lamb Inn, Stall Street, Bath 'till called for. It was delivered by J. Bird into the hands of Mr. Bradley's Son in Law, the Book-keeper at the Angel, and paid him the Booking on Thursday night the 26th Instant. It was regularly sent from Cardiff, and the most likely thing is that it was put in the Pocket of the Coach from Bristol, and as they do not change Coaches till they come to Thatcham, it is presumed it was carried on there and afterwards returned as directed.

I have been all this Morning over the Heath, and have selected 12 Persons who are the most eligible to be served with declarations in Ejectment, which I shall deliver myself for safety and regularity, as there is no trusting to Sheriff's Officers who have not the Interest of the Plaintiff properly at heart.

The enclosed paper of Lots belonging to Wyndham Lewis Esq.[128] was put up by Auction on Saturday last — and not a single Lot sold. Mr. Crawshay attended but did not bid.

I have been over the Lordship of Senghenith with the New Bailiff and have collected the Chief Rents. I am to meet Mr. Goodrich on an early day to settle that long Account of the Energlyn Estate.

The day before the Collection at Merthyr, Mr. Crawshay invited me to dine with him and was pleased at my having it in my power to explain some things in the Act for Assessed Taxes, and at its having appeared that I had sent that Account to the Glocester Journal relative to the opening of the Sea Lock at Cardiff, which Mr. Crawshay had attributed to Mr. Wood. He behaved much better to me than I had a right to expect. He is building a New House at Merthyr[129] the oposite side of the River but quite in front of the old one.

Mr. Phillpotts of Roath and Young Harris of the Splot are the two Cavalry Men who ride for the Marquess of Bute. Mr. Harris rides his own Horse, and Mr. Phillpotts rides one which I could not sell at Lantrissent a fortnight back when I went there to dispose of Thomas John's Cattle etc. taken in distress [on your Account *crossed through*].

Since the Coach came in to-night I have seen the Way Bill of last Friday to Bristol, and it appears that the parcel was regularly delivered there from its being accounted for on that Way Bill.

The Drill Serjeant arrived here last Saturday. He belongs to the 18th Light Dragoons and is a very decent Man. We have now begun in a regular way. I ride for Colonel Capper but find my own Horse, exclusive of his keep, and Act as Secretary to the Corps without emolument.

August 18th   The Judges came in from Merthyr.

August 19th   At Church as usual. The Selection of Music performed on both days together with the Calendar; as per Enclosures.

August 20th   The Grand Jury were: Thomas Wyndham, Jno Price, Samuel Homfray, Jno Richards of Landaff, Robert Jenner, David Samuel, Wm. Goodrich, Henry Hollier etc. etc. Esquires.

No charge from Judge Hardinge, but Judge Moysey observed that the Calendar was very trifling, for which reason he should not detain them with any charge.

Mr. Williams[130] of the Post Office arrived from London in order to give evidence on the Heath business. I have been over the Heath several times previous to Sessions and made the services of the declarations in Ejectment perfectly complete upon the twelve persons selected. They seemed inclinable to try the Issue.

August 21st No business of consequence.

August 22nd Gaol Day.

August 23rd New Issue day. The Heath Incroachments may now be taken down as soon as your pleasure is known, that is, the twelve ejected as they have suffered judgement to go against them by default. They had employed Mr. Daniel Jones to defend for them but he was too late in applying. A very considerable altercation took place between Councellor Bevan for the Plaintiff and the Attorney General for the Defendants, but the latter was completely over-ruled.

The [Iron Masters *crossed through*] Canal Company brought an Action against the Dowlais Company to compel them to adopt the proper weight of 112lb. to the Cwt. instead of 120lb. which they have used in their Tonage on the Canal. The difference between them is £75. It is left to Reference and the opinion of the Judges.

Judge Hardinge was much pleased with the appearance and progress of the Cardiff Volunteer Cavalry who have all had their Uniform and make a very smart appearance.

Mr. Hollier and Self are going to Swansea etc. to Receive the 3 Instalments of the Assessed Taxes.

Mr. Bew has had his Appointment for Searcher. About a Month back a very capital Seizure was made at Barry Island of more than two hundred Anchors[131] of Brandy from Guernsey and 3 Chests of Silk Handkerchiefs. The whole is worth from 12 to 14 hundred pounds. Government will receive one Moiety and the other will be divided between 4 Officers, Vizt. Alexander Willson, Richard Price, Thomas Hopkins of Sully, and an Officer from Bristol who happened to be at Barry at the time.

October 2nd Last Night the remains of Mrs. Richardson[132], formerly Mrs. Bowen of Merthyr Mawr, were interred at Old Castle, Bridgend. She died of an Appoplectic fit. Mr. Stephen Jones of Swansea refused to let her be interred in the family Vault at Merthyr Mawr. He has taken Possession for himself and Sister of the Merthir Mawr Estate.

One of the Men who rented the Fishery[133] has been here this Morning and offered £14 per annum for the part which Mrs. Richardson rented at £8. This comprises the fishing of 4 days out of 8 in Ogmore River, and the whole fishery in Ewenny River from the Bridge to the Sea. Mr. Hollier has not yet agreed with him [but told him he must wait your determination *crossed through*].

Colonel Capper and Dr. Williams were sworn in for Bailiffs on Saturday last. The Dinner at the Angel was a very good one and well attended.

Mr. Wood has had a Lease from the Company of Cordwainers[134] for 90 Years at £1 2s. 6d. per annum of the Shoemakers Hall,[135] which is to be rebuilt and converted into Offices, with a proper Place for the Company to Meet and hold their aniversary of Saint Crispin[136] etc.

The Account of all the Land Tax[137] on the Old and New Estates will be sent in two or three days — some of the most distant is the cause of the delay — as also Colonel Capper's Plan of the School of Industry which he gave me this Morning to Copy and at the same time desired me to give him my opinion of it. Therefore, with submission to the Colonel, I mean to inform him that very few, if any, Children will be found in the Town or Vicinity who can work on the Turnpike Roads, dig in fields or Gardens etc. without Shoes and Stockings, that being very different from simply walking Barefooted.

Admiral Knight of Landaff died on Sunday night last.

The Chief Topic now is the intended Dram Road from Merthyr to Newport, which the Projectors, Messrs. Taitt, Homfray and Hill, pretend to say will be made to Convey Iron at 4s. per Ton less than is now done by the Canal. Dr. Griffiths told me this Morning that it never will take place, as neither of the parties have any money to spare out of their business, and before that can be accomplished the Tonage on the Canal will be lowered. It is said that Mr. Saml. Homfray is gone to London with Sir Charles Morgan on that business, whilst others say it is only a scheme to force the Canal Proprietors to let those Iron Masters carry the long weight of 120lb. to the Cwt. instead of 112lb.

On Mr. Wood's return from the Quarter Sessions I am to deliver Notices to those persons on the Heath to Abandon their Enclosures, previous to the Sheriff's levying possession.

Lord Landaff, Earl of Ossery etc.

1799

January 31st   The enclosed Paper contains a part of the Lots to be sold by Auction the 19th & 20th days of February next at Cardiff. And a Sale of near 40 Lots will take place at Cowbridge the same days, a Copy of which shall be transmitted as soon as printed.

Colonel Aubrey[138] Reviewed the Cardiff Troop of Volunteer Cavalry Yesterday, and the Weather being frosty and the Ground hard the Review took place in the Castle. A great many Genteel people attended as spectators Vizt. Mr. & Mrs. Leigh of Pontypool, Mrs. Hurst, the Pearsons[139] of Landaff, Mr. Jenner, Mr. Wrixon etc. etc., with some hundred of different descriptions. When all the Evolutions were performed the Colonel expressed his approbation [by thanking the Captain and Troop for the pleasure they had given him *crossed through*] in the following words 'Gentlemen, you have performed your exercise extremely well, and I am much obliged to the Captain and you for the pleasure of so good a Review. Gentlemen, I wish you a good Morning'. He then rode to the Gate, gave his Horse to his Servant, and immediately joined some Ladies on the Terrace. He was attended by two of the Troop during the Review. When we were dismissed, Captain Wood requested our attendance at the Angel for five minutes, the purport of which was to explain the limits of the addition to the Severn District which is now extended to the Counties of North Wales, Lancashire and Cheshire, and to ask us if we meant to extend our Services so far, which would secure us from being ballotted for in the Supplementary Militia. It was immediately agreed by the Troop to extend their Services to the limits of the District.

I have written the Circular letters to the Deputy Lieutenants and Commanders of Volunteer Corps on the above subject, and the Meeting for that purpose is to be held at Pyle on Monday next, the 4th of February.

[I hope *crossed through*] Mr. Crawshay's Address and Mr. Taitt's answer were [received as I caused them to be *crossed through*] transmitted the day they were Printed, which was Quarter Session week at Cardiff, but no business of consequence.

A Great fall of Snow all this day, and it is ex... [*Entry ends abruptly*]

Cardiff March 23rd   The Great Sessions began this Evening. A very respectable company attended Mr. Sheriff Goodrich on the occasion. He took his Carriage and four to meet the Judge, and at Roath Bridge Mr. Hardinge quitted his Horse and got in. They then set off by the desire of the Under Sheriff, Mr. Williams (Son of Rowland Williams of Gwernllwyn) as fast as the Horses could Trot and at that rate came into Town.

March 24th Easter Day   A Selection of Sacred Music as usual.

March 25th Easter Monday   The Sheriff's Chaplain was the Reverend Mr. Davies of Wenvoe[140] who gave a more Political discourse than I ever heard before. His Subject was from Romans 13 Verse 1 'Let every Soul be subject to the higher Powers, for there is no power but of God, the powers that be are ordained of God'.

The Grand Jury were very respectable, being 17 in number and consisted of Thomas Wyndham, John Price, Robert Jenner, John Richards of Cardiff, John

A
SHORT ACCOUNT
OF THE
TRIAL
OF
JOHN WEBBORN,

Who was found Guilty, at the late Great Seſſions
for the County of Glamorgan,

OF THE

𝕸𝖚𝖗𝖉𝖊𝖗

OF

WM. THOMAS, HIS SERVANT;

And who was executed, in Purſuance of his Sentence,
on Friday, March 29, 1799, at Cardiff,

AND ALSO,

THE JUDGE's
Excellent Address to the Convict,
𝕺𝖓 𝖕𝖆ſſ𝖎𝖓𝖌 𝕾𝖊𝖓𝖙𝖊𝖓𝖈𝖊 𝖔𝖋 𝕯𝖊𝖆𝖙𝖍.

ANNEXED IS

AN ADDRESS TO ALL INHUMAN MASTERS
AND MISTRESSES.

" Whatever ye would that men ſhould do to *you, do ye* even ſo
to *them.*"—Mat. vii. 12.
" Whoſo ſheddeth man's blood, by *man* ſhall *his* blood *be
ſhed.*"—Gen. ix. 6.
" Whoſo killeth any perſon, the *murderer* ſhall *ſurely be put
to death.* Ye ſhall take *no ſatiſfaction* for the *life* of a
murderer, who is guilty of death, but he ſhall *ſurely be put
to death.*"—Numb. xxxv. 30, 31.

CARDIFF:

PRINTED BY JOHN BIRD;

AND SOLD BY BULGIN AND SHEPPARD, BRISTOL;
AND BY ALL THE BOOKSELLERS IN
SOUTH-WALES.

—

1799.

Title-page of the printed account of John Webborn's trial. *By courtesy of South Glamorgan County Libraries.*

Richards of Landaff, Jere. Homfray, Samuel Homfray, Rd. Crawshay, Wm. Taitt, Rowland Williams, Thomas Thomas, Wm. Goodrich Esq. etc. etc.

In addressing the Grand Jury His Lordship founded his Remarks upon the aspect of Public Affairs at the present alarming crisis. He took notice of that Glorious achievement, the Battle of the Nile,[141] and paid the highest compliment to Lord Nelson. He observed that our Navy was in so formidable a state that no united power of the Enemy could contend with it for years to come, but that WE must not sleep but be on our Guard against internal commotions etc. etc.

He thanked the Grand Jury for their having paid such attention to the Gaol, and observed that that place of confinement was now in a good State. He then noticed the Calendar, and expatiated largely on the Crime committed by John Webborn,[142] but reprobated in strong terms the irregularity of the Magistrate in wording the Commitment, and said that he should certainly be under the necessity of interfereing if he continued to be so shamefully irregular, as it was not the first time, by many, that he had met with such jumbles of nonsense from that quarter that were in fact a disgrace to the Commission.

The other Offences were slightly noticed, and some further remarks made on them, when the Morning Court was adjourned.

March 26th Easter Tuesday   Old Issue day. The only Trial of consequence was between the Proprietors of the Canal and the Penydarran and Dowlais Companies, but being obliged to prepare the three Commissions for Messrs. Jones, Geering and Grailand could not attend till the Evening, but understood the Verdict was left to the Opinion of the Court when, after near an Hour's explanation by Judge Hardinge, a Verdict was given for the Defendants Messrs. Homfray & Co. and Lewis & Co. The Action was brought for Ninety seven pounds, being freight claimed by the Proprietors of the Canal for the difference between the long and Short Ton for a certain period.

Wednesday March 27th   The Prisoners tried as per Calendar.

Thursday March 28th   Several Trials this day, but the most entertaining was brought by Mary Jenkins of Cowbridge (the Woman who has the Castle and fields at Lanblethian, and whose evidence was of such consequence on the Gollege Cause), against Miss Roberts her next Neighbour for incroaching on a wall. Mary Jenkins was nonsuited in consequence of a Mistake at Mr Wood's Office in laying the declaration for a Dwelling House instead of an Out House. Judge Hardinge left his Brother Moysey to complete the business of this day, and the Court in the Judges Chambers tomorrow morning, and went with Mr. Sheriff Goodrich to Energlyn to dinner, and from thence to Brecon.

Friday March 29th   Mr. Theophilus Jones of Brecon, the Marshall of the Court, drew up an Account of the Trial and Conduct of John Webborn for the purpose of being Printed.[143]

Saturday March 30th   The Dearest Market at Cardiff ever remembered.

Sunday March 31st   The Cardiff Cavalry had their Feathers.

Monday April 1st   At a Parish Meeting held at the Workhouse this day it was agreed to displace the present Master, Geo. Harrington, and to put the House on a better footing, for which a committee was appointed consisting of Dr. Williams, Mr. Wood, Mr. Richards, Mr. Hollier, Mr. Hussey and Mr. Allen, who are to visit the House once a Week in rotation.

The Castle is very clean and in good order.

The Plantation on the Hill next the Friars and onwards to Cathays will soon have a very pleasing effect.

June 11th   This morning was fixed upon by Mr. Wood and Mr. Williams the Deputy Sheriff for taking down the 12 Cots and enclosures on the Great and Little Heaths which had suffered Judgment.

Considerable resistance was made for more than two hours, and the consequences were very disagreeable, 'till I was dispatched to Town by the under Sheriff for the Assistance of the Cavalry. Upon whose appearance, headed by Mr. Wyndham Lewis, Mr. Powell Edwards and Captain Wood, after taking one of the Ringleaders into Custody, the Hostile part of the Mob began to disperse. But as the Undersheriff was apprehensive that a greater body would assemble in the Evening, I was dispatched express to Caerphilly and Energlyn for the Assistance of their Volunteers. Mr. Goodrich, as Sheriff, immediately returned with me and directed his Son and the other Officers to be as expeditious as possible in bringing down the Volunteers, who immediately Mustered. When we got to the Hill above New House I discovered that the Cot where the resistance was made had been set on fire as the most effectual method of destroying it. And when we came to the 3rd Mile Stone from Cardiff [I] found that the appearance of the Cavalry had entirely dispersed the whole of the hostile part of the Mob and that the Undersheriff and his Bailiffs, with Mr. Bew and your Workmen, had been joined by a competent number of Stout fellows from Cardiff who were desirous of giving all the assistance in their power, and that the Caerphilly Volunteers were not wanted, as the Cottagers were all suing for pardon and time to remove their Goods etc. One Month has been granted them for that purpose, when the 12 who have been ejected are to be abandoned. Dr. Griffiths's House will come down, being one of the number, and Possession has been given to you by the Sheriff of the remaining Eleven which are only standing on sufferance for one Month.

The Women for some time acted the part of Amazonians, having armed themselves with Pitchforks, etc. etc.

[Mr. Hollier is gone to Bath to bring back Mrs. H. Hollier who has been very ill but is now much better *crossed through*.]

Tuesday July 30th 1799   The High Sheriff Mr. Goodrich and his Deputy Mr. Williams, with Mr. Vaughan Attorney, Mr. Bew, the Workmen, Horses, Chains and Implements for pulling down etc. etc. went to the Heaths for the purpose of destroying the 4 Cottages of those who had not signed the Petition for leave to remain till the 29th of October next. I attended to Identify the Premises, and the four who had not signed were very glad to come into the same terms with the others. The best part of a Hedge and Bank was destroyed and Burnt in the presence of the Sheriff etc., which had been Errected by a Man not included in the 12 but who had, on several Occasions, behaved with insolence.

Saturday August 3rd   The Great Sessions Commenced this Afternoon. Judge Hardinge in coming from Brecon dined at Energlyn, but the Sheriff attended his Dinner at the Cardiff Arms. The Judge was attended by Mr. William Goodrich, and was Met at the 2nd Mile Stone by a respectable Cavalcade of Gentlemen etc. with the Sheriff.

Sunday August 4th   Judge Hardinge attended Divine Service as usual this day and Monday, and the Selection of Sacred Music was well performed by Mr. Cook[144] the new Organist with proper assistants.

Judge Moysey stoped at Tredegar as usual.

Monday August 5th   The Gentlemen of the Grand Jury were: John Llewellyn of Penllergare, John Morris, Edward Morgan, Edward Thomas of Tregroes, John Price, Robert Jenner, Robert Jones, and John Richards of Landaff, Esquires, with 6 others, in all 14.

The Judge in addressing them began in nearly the following words:

'Gentlemen of the Grand Jury'

'I was in hopes I should have been able to have congratulated you upon the Success of another important victory, but we have lately been so rich in Conquests that we can afford to wait that desirable event. But I congratulate you on the Events of the little Six Months last past which have opened a Scene on the Continent to which no page in History bears the least Similitude'.

He then paid the highest Compliment to the prompt exertions made in this County as to its internal defence, and in the warmest language applauded the behaviour of the Militia who had, unsolicited even to a Man, offered their Services in the Sister Kingdom. Colonel Aubrey came into Court just in time to hear the Charge, and seemed to feel the Effect of that part which so much related to his Corps. He then noticed the Calendar which he was happy to say was so very trifling that he had not even brought it with him, and expatiated largely upon the nature of procuring Confession from Culprits, and pointed out what ought and what ought not to be the mode pursued in those Cases.

Tuesday August 6th This being Old Issue day, and no Cause to be tried, it was noticed by several in my hearing that no such Circumstance had ever happened in their recollection.

A Young Man of the name of Curtis, whose Father is a Timber Merchant at Swansea, was liberated from Confinement under a most illegal and unparalled Commitment by Mr. Snead[145] and Mr. Gabriel Powell, the latter of whom had acted as Judge in his own Cause.

Wednesday August 7th There was but one Prisoner tried, which was only petty Larceny against Mary Thomas who was sentenced to 6 Months Solitary Confinement. Several Affidavits being read touching the Conduct of Mr. Snead and Mr. Powell, a rule was granted against them to shew cause, and the very Person whom they committed went off to Swansea to serve them with that Rule, by which they were compelled to appear at the next Evening Court. They were so much alarmed at these proceedings that they travelled all night and got to Cardiff in the Morning of Thursday when they were allowed to file Affidavits of their late Conduct to Curtis at the Court then sitting – object to – struck off Rolls and sue for false Imprisonment.

Thursday August 8th Thirteen Causes entered. The first, which took up 8 Hours, was between Rd. Hill Esq., Plaintiff, and the Company of Proprietors of the Glamorganshire Canal Navigation, Defendants. It was brought by Mr. Hill to recover damages for the loss he had sustained in being deprived of the Water belonging to his Works, and which it was proved amounted to £500. Six of the Jury were obliged to go with the deputy Sheriff the day before to view the Acqueduct etc. at Cyfarthfa, and after an hour's deliberation found a verdict for [the] Plaintiff, damages £300. Mr. Crawshay was in Court the greatest part of the time and could hardly be restrained from speaking. At one time he got up and asked the Witness then under examination 'Do we choak the River, or do the River Choak us'?, which threw the Court into a burst of laughter. He was Cautioned not to speak but by his Council, and which with difficulty he complied with. The other Causes, altho' trifling in themselves, were not finished till Dinner time on

Friday August 9th.
Lady Plymouth and her Brother in Law Major Crespigny[146] are here, and

gave a Dinner to 220 of the Tenants at the Cardiff Arms. Mr. Key[147] the late Agent is dismissed and the Tenants had Notice not to pay him. [The Gentleman's name I have not heard, but have been informed he is a Colonel in the Army *crossed through*.]

I conducted them thro' the Castle and shewed them the Pictures etc. with which they seemed very much pleased.

I got a friend in London to make enquiry of the value of the late Lord Plymouth's[148] Coach Horses in order that Mr. Hollier might ascertain what sum he should name for the Heriots due at his Death in Miskin and Senghenith, but the Answer was that Lady Plymouth had sold the Coach Horses and had taken [the] Job Horses with her to Hewel Grange[149] [previous to her coming here *crossed through*].

Mr. Jones of Fonmon passed fines[150] on a great part of the Estate in order to his being enabled to dispose of as much wood as would pay off the incumbrance thereon.

Went to Bristol Sunday 11th after writing the foregoing Account. Mr. H[ollier] and wife went to Swansea.

August 31st Lady Plymouth is still here and a Gentleman of the Law with her. They have been much engaged in riding over the Estate and attending to business, as Mr. Key has left the Country and his accounts are in a very deranged state. It is said he is a defaulter to the amount of many thousand pounds.

Caerphilly Castle. Watercolour by Thomas Hornor, 1819. *By courtesy of the Glamorgan Archive Service.*

Mr. Hollier being at Swansea I waited on her Ladyship last Thursday and pointed out the different Chief Rents etc. that were in Arrears.

The Heriots were also mentioned, and she told me that the new Agent, a Mr. Webb[151] who is shortly expected down, should settle the whole.

Mr. Richards of Landaff has sold the nine Acres of land adjoining the Spittle to Dr. Williams for £570.

Monday October 21st   Went with Mr. Hollier to Gellygaer, 6 Miles across the Hills from Quakers Yard, to see a small farm of Mrs. Price of Pontypandy which, with other things, was to be Sold by Auction and which adjoins Rosser John's farm of £10 per annum. The Rent of it £6 6s. 0d. and would be very convenient to annex to Rosser John's, and as there is on the average every fourteenth year 200 Cords[152] of Wood cut thereon at 10s. per Cord it must be a desirable thing, and not withstanding it is in a very wild Country. The two united would let at £28 per annum and the wood to be kept up.

The Sale was at Caerphilly on Thursday the 24th, being the day on which the Court Leet[153] was held, but not an Article was sold.

Thursday October 24th   Went with Mr. Martin of Lansamlet,[154] a Gentlemen extremely conversant in Collieries, Mines etc., to shew him Caerphilly and Rudry Commons, and am particularly happy that Mr. Hollier desired me to accompany him, as I have now gained a competent knowledge of the situations of the Veins of Coal and Mine on those Commons. I got the Colliers to shew him every thing necessary, and he put his Men to take a level from Caerphilly Common towards that of Rudry through the Dingle which in part is Lord Plymouth's property, and also from Caerphilly Common on the North side to the foot of *Cwm Ywbbwb* (i.e. the Murdering valley) where a Capital level might be driven at a moderate expence, which would drain the whole works on Caerphilly Common and make them of immense value.

The substance of Mr. Martin's report will be 'That by proper management, and pursuing the plan he should project, there would be Coal and Ore enough on Caerphilly Common only to employ an Iron Furnace for one hundred years'. The Veins of Coal are twelve in number, and the Mine Seven, many of which are of considerable thickness, and no Situation in the Kingdom is better adapted for an Iron Furnace and a level 6 feet square both for draining the water and bringing out the Coal and Mine than might be made at the top of *Cwm Ywbbwb*, all within your own property.

The Common of Rudry is equally Rich and wants nothing more than a mutual Agreement with The Representation of the late Earl of Plymouth to make a joint level through both properties, by which means great advantage would arise, and the Country would be supplied with Coal, which is far from being the Case at present. And indeed both Commons have only been skimmed, from the want of a competent level to drain the whole. But Mr. Martin's Report, which he told me should be ready in a few days, will explain the whole and give regular Sections and Elevations and admeasurements, as also particular descriptions of the different Stratas of Coal and Mine.

Friday October 25th   On Account of His Majesty's Accession, The Cardiff Cavalry went to Cowbridge and made a Grand Field day with the Cowbridge Volunteers, and returned home in good order the same Evening at 8 o'Clock.

Saturday October 26th   Captain Walters have had his Sloop, the *Castle of Cardiff*, released on paying £40 and all expences, which together will be about £200.

Sunday October 27th   Wheat sold yesterday in Cardiff Market at 33s. per bushel of 20 Gallons. The weather this last week has been particularly fine, and will save the hilly part of the Country where the major part of the Corn was out.

1800

March 20th, 21st and 22nd   At Lantwit, Cowbridge etc. etc. in settling Chief Rents and accounts preparatory to making general return of arrears etc. etc.

Tuesday March 25th   The Judges came in this afternoon at 6 o'Clock. The appearance with the High Sheriff, Mr. Jenner, was very respectable. The greatest part of his Tenants in this neighbourhood attended and a numerous body of Gentlemen and Yeomanry.

Wednesday March 26th   The Judges at Church as usual, and Mr. Hardinge's selection of Sacred Music was well performed.
    The Gentlemen of the Grand Jury were: John Price Esq., John Richards of Cardiff, John Richards of Landaff, Robert Wrixon, Thomas Thomas, Wm. Taitt, Calvert Jones, Herbert Hurst Esquires, etc. etc. in all Fifteen. The Calendar being heavyer than has been remembered, Judge Hardinge chiefly attended to *that* in Addressing the Grand Jury, and made some few remarks on the scarcity of Corn etc., and doubted not 'but that similar plans would be adopted here to what had been done in other places for the relief of the poor'. Nothing has yet been done either in making Soup or entering into a Subscription.

Thursday March 27th   The Old Issues tried this day were only two in Number, and were too frivolous to be brought before the Court.

1800

Friday March 28th The Prisoners were tried as per Calendar.

Saturday March 29th No Causes of Consequence this day, and I have heard many of the Attorneys say they never remembered less business at Nisi Prius.

Mr. Stephen Jones is in Town and told me he was going to Sue several people for Fishing in Ogmore River, but the dispute has been settled.

Mr. John Key having a Colliery at Duffryn Frood which is now intersected by that rough Field at Craig'r Allt called *Cae Tre'r Dinas* (the Doe's Home), which was let to Mr. Bacon for 21 years from February 1780 at £1 11s. 6d. per annum and which contains 13¾ acres of land, has proposed to pay a Galeage[155] of 1s. 0d. per Ton for all the Coal that can be got there. And as Mr. Key's level is now nearly got to your land, and as it would cost him a considerable sum to go round it to Duffryn Frood land beyond, I have the authority of an Experienced [Engineer *crossed through*] Gentleman, who now has Mr. Tanner's[156] Collieries at Pont y Pool, for saying that it would be well to agree with Mr. Key on those terms, at the same time taking care to tye him to work all the Coal that can be got out of your land before he takes the level quite through, for it is totally impossible to get any Coal out of this spot without a level in one part or other of the Duffryn Frood Estate. Therefore it will be only a mutual accomodation and I am assured that the Quantity of Coal in the 2 veins under your land is imme[n]se. The Person I allude to is related to my wife,[157] and to oblige me he rode with me to Duffryn Frood, and we went into the level with Mr. Key and his Collier to explore the situation of the Work when many improvements were suggested to Mr. Key.

Sunday March 30th The Judges and Officers of the Court at Church as usual.

Went with Mr. Hollier to Swansea etc. to Receive 2 Instalments of the Income bill, which prevented me from sending this Account sooner.

Monday March 31st The Sessions ended and the Judges set off for Brecon.

Tuesday April 1st The Berkshire Cavalry left Cardiff in order to be disbanded. Captain Wood and his Troop attended them to Rumney Turnpike, as did also the Sheriff, Mr. Richards of the Corner House etc. etc.

Friday April 4th Assisting Mr. Hollier to make out statements of Old and New Estates, the probable production as under:

Old Estate	After Deductions	carefully averaged about	£3000 per annum
New Estate	Do.	Do.	£ 900 per annum

The particulars will be sent by Mr. Hollier in a day or two.

Another Troop of Horse is expected do.

Mentioned dearness and scarcity of Provisions.

Monday April 19th   The Address from the Boroughs[158] was sent after me to Lantrissent where I was with Mr. Hollier receiving the Taxes, which over, I got it signed by Mr. Rickards, Mr. Davies and others of the Corporation. Left Lantrissent between 6 and 7 at night and got to Neath by 11, when I waited on the Portreeve,[159] Mr. Edwards, who signed it in bed.

Llantrisant. Engraved by J. Tingle after Henry Gastineau, *c.*1830. *By courtesy of University College Cardiff Library.*

Tuesday April 20th   As I had assured Mr. Hollier that if it were possible to be done I would return to Cardiff in time to send it by this Night's Coach, I got it finished at Neath by 7 this Morning, as most of the Gentlemen signed it in Bed and were much pleased at the promptitude displayed on the Occasion. I then proceeded to Swansea, where every one was anxious to sign, and had the good fortune to get it done thro' the County *this day*, and arrived at Cardiff at 10 o'Clock in time to shew it Mr. Wood, Pack it up and deliver it at the Coach Office, with strict Charges for its dispatch.

Monday April 26th   Began the Week's Collection of Taxes at Bridgend.

Tuesday April 27th   At Neath, where we first heard the Account of the Address from the Boroughs having been presented. But the paper did not mention by whom.

Wednesday April 28th   At Swansea. Mr. Rowland Prichard and Son came to thank Mr. Hollier for his good Offices etc. relative to the Son's being appointed at Neath to the Collectorship of the Customs.

Thursday April 29th   At Swansea. Never found the Collection of Taxes so perplexing, from the irregularity in the Reg[istrar's] Office for the redemption of Land Tax not having sent down the Certificates of Purchases in the different Hundreds so as to enable the Receiver General to make the necessary deductions, as also the Payment of the Eight pences per week to each of the wives and families of the Militia serving in Ireland,[160] from the time of passing that Act to the present.

Friday April 30th   Receiving at Pyle, and it was singular that two years back a County Meeting should be held there on the day the Taxes were received, and that the next County Meeting should also Clash with the Collection.

Mr. Wood and Mr. Taitt came to Pyle in a Post Chaise and got there by 11 o'Clock. We knew there were no Gentlemen coming from Swansea, as Mr. Talbot was gone to Bath to fetch his sister in law Lady Elizabeth, and Mr. Wyndham was at Clearwell.[161] And also from the circumstance of Mr. Hollier's having been requested to sign for Mr. Llewellyn of Penllergare, Mr. Calvert Jones, Mr. King and Mr. Wm. Jeffreys. The only Gentlemen that attended were Mr. Rees of Courtcolman, Mr. Bassett of Bonvilstone, Mr. Edmd. Traherne of Castella, Mr. Griffith Llewellin of Baglan, Mr. Franklen of Pwll y Wrach, Mr. Taitt and Mr. Wood, in all no more than Seven as Mr. Hollier could not attend them. Mr. Wood brought a Copy of the Address with him, and after a few alterations it was agreed to, when Mr. Wood requested [Mr. Hollier to let *crossed through*] me to write it, which was done in the midst of Hurry and bustle or I could have done it much better.

The seven Gentlemen got very merry, and as they drank nothing but Claret the Bill came to one Guinea each.

Mr. Taitt and Mr. Wood stoped at Pyle[162] that Night, and Mr. Hollier and self supped with them and returned in Company with them the next Morning to Cowbridge, where we stoped to Receive, and returned home at Night with near £14,000 in Mr. Hollier's Gig which I lately purchased for him from a relation of my Wife's.

Sunday June 1st   The Cavalry went to Church, and afterwards in the

Castle Mr. Wood produced the County Address, where in true Military Stile it was signed, by as many of the Troop as were present, on the Head of the Bass Drum.

Monday June 2nd   Landaff Fair day. Mr. Wood attended with the Address and got it filled, and at 10 at night I was requested to Clean it and pack it up, which was accordingly done and directed to Robt. Jenner Esq., No. 37 St. James's Street, London.

Mr. Jones of Fonmon's bill for Customary Rents amounting to £80 6s. 2¼d. is to be paid very soon, if he will keep his word.

The Building at Roath Church[163] goes on as fast as possible, and the Hay in the Castle was cut yesterday and today. The Crop is great indeed.

[It is said that Mr. Clutterbuck[164] leaves Cathays in the course of the year, and that in future when the Marquess of Bute visits Cardiff his residence will be there and not at the Cardiff Arms as heretofore *crossed through*.]

Saturday July 25th   The Second Division of the Royal Glamorgan Militia was met by the Cardiff Troop this Morning at 7 o'Clock at Rumney, and were attended into Town amidst a vast concourse of people. Colonel Aubrey is with them, and this Division is to remain here a few days and then proceed to Swansea, where the Regiment is to be reduced to 317 men.

Fonmon Castle. Lithograph after Jeston Homfray, 1828. *By courtesy of University College Cardiff Library.*

Mr. Webb, Lady Plymouth's Steward, and myself devoted 10 hours on Tuesday last to a minute investigation of the Chief Rents due from the Plymouth Estate, and as I had reference to their Surveys I have found out several things that have been in Arrear 45 years, and which could not be collected because the names of the Tenements had been altered since that time. Mr. Webb paid me £88, including £40 for the two Heriots in Miskin and Senghenith. The other Chief Rents due from near 200 Tenements are to be paid by the Tenants, as I have three Letters from Mr. Webb to order the Tenants to pay them to me. One [letter] I shall Give Mr. Davies for Miskin & Pentirch & Clun, the other shall be given to Lewis Edward for Senghenith Supra & Subtus, and the third I shall retain for this neighbourhood.

The Account with John Richards Esq. of Landaff was investigated yesterday with Mr. Thomas, and is in train for settlement. That account is about £80 and Mr. Goodrich will then pay for the 9 years due from the Energlyn Estate. I wish as much could be said for Mr. Jones of Fonmon, but he is quite Refractory and told me 'He'd be D-d if he payed any Chief Rent to Lord Bute or anyone else for that he was Lord of the Manor himself, and would not pay a farthing more than Mr. Franklen should allow of'. He behaved very improperly to Mr. Hollier on Whit Monday last at Mr. Richards's at Landaff, but as Mr. Hollier is to return home to-night I shall propose to him to let me wait on Mr. Franklen next Tuesday at Cowbridge that I may explain to him the 3 Articles which are 43 years in Arrear and [and I make no doubt but that I shall get an Order from him to receive those Chief Rents from the Tenants; some of them have been in Arrear near 50 years *crossed through*.]

[The Mausoleum and Church at Roath will be tiled in by next *crossed through*]

[and] which the late Mr. Jones always resisted from the time he became of age, but which, I hope, we shall be able to prove the payment of when I make the necessary enquiries at Lantwit Major etc. etc., for as Mr. Edwards became Agent in 1758 those articles were then but 2 years in arrear.

The Articles Mr. Jones resists are:	£	s.	d.
No. 38 32 Acres 43 years at 12s.	25	16	0
No. 39 The Western lays 43 years at 12s. 4½d.	26	12	1½
No. 40 Fee farm Rent for Boviarton 43 years at 7s. 3d.	15	11	9
	67	19	10½
Many small articles which Mr. Franklen admits are but few years in Arrear [and can all be proved *crossed through*]	22	5	9¾
	90	5	8¼

Sunday July 27th   The Militia went to Church and in the Evening Paraded in the Castle. A great Number of Ladies and Gentlemen and others were highly gratified by the Officers causing the Glamorgan Band to play for near 2 Hours in Front of the Castle.

Monday July 28th   Received Mr. Mathews's 2 years Rent of £243 8s. 0d. from Mr. Bowen which was immediately paid to Mr. Hollier.

The difference between Colonel Wood and Mr. Mathews is now settled, and the Colonel takes to the whole Estate from Candlemas last.

Tuesday July 29th   Met Mr. Franklen at Cowbridge and delivered him a Copy of the Chief Rent Bill from Mr. Jones. He seemed very reasonable, but said Mr. Jones would certainly litigate the above three articles unless we could prove who paid and received them, and point out the particular lands on which they are chargeable. Every exertion in my power shall be made to accomplish that end.

Saw Mr. Daniel Jones of Lantwit and told him I should call on him shortly to settle his Customary Rents. He said he should be glad to see me.

Colonel Aubrey gave a Dinner at Ash Hall to the Officers etc. etc.

It is publickly said that the Marquis of Bute is shortly to be married to Miss Coutts,[165] who is to receive the same Fortune that Lady Guildford had Vizt. One Hundred thousand Pounds.

Thursday July 31st   Served Wm. John Henry with Notice to Quit his Farm of £25 per annum in Listalybont at Candlemas next. This Farm is to be annexed to that of Thomas John at £16 per annum, and that of Edmund William at £18, but the three will be advanced.

I was told by a Gentleman who dined with Mr. Jenner at Wenvoe Castle lately that he heard him say at Dinner that he intended standing for the County at the next Election, and that he should have the support of the Marquess of Bute and Mr. Talbot.

The Militia left Cardiff this Morning at 5 o'Clock.

Saturday August 23rd   Cardiff Assizes began this Evening. Judge Hardinge dined with Mr. Goodrich at Energlyn, in his way from Brecon, and got to Town by ½ past 7. The Sheriff and his party met the Judge at the Heath.

Sunday August 24th   The Judges went to Church as usual. The Cavalry were also at Church, and afterwards went through the Sword Exercise on foot in the Castle.

Monday August 25th   After Church the Court opened, and the Gentlemen of the Grand Jury were R. Rouse Esq., Bridges, Goodrich, Richardson, Jones,

Miers, Wrixon, etc. etc. Esquires, in all Sixteen, with which Number the Judges were satisfied. It being Judge Moysey's turn to try the Prisoners he as usual spoke but a few words, Vizt. 'Gentlemen of the Grand Jury, there is nothing difficult in the Calendar, but I am sorry to observe that the Offence of House-breaking seems to be rooted in this part of the Country'.

I have attended Mr. Brown[166] to the Heath many times, and have invariably given him every information as to encroachments, boundaries, the Adjoining property etc. etc., and as he boards with me, one or other of my Children daily attends him in Surveying.

Tuesday August 26th Very little business at Sessions, only 3 trifling Causes this day.

Wednesday August 27th The Prisoners tried as per Calendar. The Court was much crowded to hear the Trial of John Guillod, a Native of the Canton of Bern in Switzerland who, it seems, came down from London on purpose to rob his late Master, Mr. Knight of Tythegstone. There were 14 Witnesses and yet not one of them could prove their having seen him on the premises, as he quitted the Coach and lay at Cardiff the night before the Robbery was committed, and took the Coach at Cowbridge at 4 o'Clock in the morning 2 or 3 hours after the Robbery was committed, which was deemed sufficient time for him to walk from Tythegstone to Cowbridge. It was some time after that he was taken by the Bow Street Officers in London, in consequence of Mr. Knight's Journey thither on purpose to lay the information etc. etc.

The Judges paid Mr. Knight a handsome Compliment for his laudable exertions, but lamented in strong terms that the law did not reach the Prisoner as he was not seen on the premises, nor was any part of the property that would be sworn to found on him.

Thursday August 28th Seven Causes tried this day, but nothing of Consequence.

Friday August 29th The Judges left Town at 10 o'Clock.

Saturday August 30th Owing to the dryness of the Season, little or no Trade has been done on the Canal from the want of Water, but the Subscribers to the Aberdare Canal are going to complete the Branch from Aberdare to the Aqueduct. The estimate is about [Ten Thousand pounds *crossed through*] £11,500, and one thousand five Hundred for a Tram Road part of the way.

Saturday September 6th Great part of this Week has been occupied in assisting Mr. Brown on the Heaths etc. A Sketch of the Bill is prepared, and a Meeting of the Proprietors interested will speedily take place. Notices have been given in the different Parishes.

The business at Roath yesterday Morning[167] was conducted with the greatest privacy, and by half past 4 the several Remains were deposited and immediately shut up. Colonel Capper and Mr. Hollier were present, it being at such an hour no persons from Cardiff attended but those necessary. It will take a Month to complete the Chancel.

St Margaret's Church, Roath. Painting by an unknown artist; early 19th century? *By courtesy of the National Museum of Wales.*

1801

January 31st   I have had it much at heart to get in the Arrears of Chief Rents in different Manors, and have delivered many bills. I spent near three days in Cowbridge and the Neighbourhood lately, and got in near £30 of Old Arrears on sundry small things in that Borough, many of which were 40 years standing. But having by accident picked up an Old Burgage Rental for the year 1744, which was made out by Mr. Thomas Lewis the Attorney of Cowbridge, I immediately applied to him, when he instantly recollected the Book, and in the course of conversation assured me that he could prove payment of every Item therein, and that he collected the Burgage Rents that year and for several years afterwards, as it was almost the first thing he did when he was articled to the late Mr. Thomas Williams. Upon the strength of such declaration and the possession of that Old Book, I began enforcing payment of the Oldest Arrears, picked up the above Sum, and have no doubt of receiving the whole, as the properties of Major Edmunds and Mr. Edwin are the most in Arrears. Major Edmondes' Agent, Mr. Morgan of Aburthin, has had the Bill which amounts, with the Customary Rents in Lanblethian, to more than £60, and as that Estate is in Chancery he assured me that on his return from London, where he now is, the whole should be settled. I have discovered that Mr. Edwin's property in Cowbridge is out on Leases, and that the Tenants are to pay the Burgage Rent which amounts to £28, being most of them near 40 years in Arrear. I shall take the same steps to go over all the other Lordships as soon as possible after I have completed Mr. Hollier's Accounts.

I shall be particularly careful in forming the New Books to keep all the Arrears of Chief, Customary and other Rents due Candlemas 1800 separate from the Joint Estate, and make due returns thereof.

Mr. John Richards of Landaff has promised to pay his long bill of Chief and Burgage Rents amounting to [blank] soon as he can sell a part of his Estate, which he is trying to do.

Colonel Capper returned home last Saturday night and on Sunday came into the Castle just as I had returned from Adams Down[168] (where I had been writing) to Dinner. I took the liberty on his speaking to me to enquire after the Marquess, Marchioness etc. when in a very pleasant manner he astonished me by saying 'Lord Bute asked for ye Bird, he says he hears from ye *sometimes*' with a particular emphasis on the latter word. I feel very uneasy, being greatly at a loss for a proper construction on that sentence, [and have] not been able to determine whether it was meant that I should be more communicative than I had been (which was only from the fear of giving offence), or whether I should do right in transmitting a Monthly or weekly Journal of occurrences. The greatest caution and Secrecy have ever been observed [on my part *crossed through*] and I should rejoice at having a line of conduct marked out in that respect, and the most implicit obedience and attention shall be observed therein.

Some time back I was equally at a loss for an Answer to a passage quoted by Colonel Aubrey, who has always been pleased to treat me with great partiallity. It was on his Return home after having seen the Marquess just after the Heath Account had been transmitted. He very jocularly said to me 'So the Women fought like Amazonians — I hope you didn't get your face scratched'. 'That was a famous account of yours' etc. etc.

Old Mr. Hurst of Dynaspowis is both blind and Insane, but Mrs. Hurst has paid a Bill of Fee farm and Burgage Rents which I delivered to her lately, amounting to about £30.

It is said that Mr. Hurst of Gabalva does not mean to return thither, and that the House etc. is to be let.

A Vessell is just Arrived with a thousand Bushells of Barley, and the Subscribers will Issue out Tickets for the supply of the Poor on Saturday next. Colonel Capper has been with me to apportion the number, and each Subscriber of £100 may Issue Tickets for 118 Bushells as it is resolved to Purchase 4800 Bushells etc. On that number the calculation is made.

½ past 12 at night, Saturday

February 14th   I am happy to state that Mr. Daniel Jones of Lantwit, who so long stood out for an Allowance of Land Tax on his Customary Rents, has at length paid the whole of his Arrears without any deduction whatever, and as Mr. Jones is a leading Man in that quarter no others will attempt to Claim it.

I received at Cowbridge last Tuesday £100 from Mr. Taynton for Customary Rents in Lanblethian, and also the Arrears of Fee farm Rent due from Mr. Daniel Jones.

The Accounts of Mr. Lloyd, Mrs. Jones of Fonmon's Father, are the only things that will prove payment of the Articles objected to by Mr. Jones of Fonmon, and I sincerely wish I knew where they could be found, for I believe I am correct in saying that the articles in dispute were paid within a year or two of Mr. Lloyd's death, and when I delivered the Account to Mrs. Jones at Fondygarey I took the liberty to tell her so much, for when Mr. Edwards succeeded Mr. Lloyd as Agent in 1758 those articles were but 2 years in Arrear. Consequently they must have been paid to Mr. Lloyd up to that time, and it is of great importance to ascertain that fact for one of the Articles is a Fee farm Rent on Boviarton, which proves to a demonstration that that property belonged to the Pembroke family and afterwards to the Lords Windsor. I should rejoice greatly in being ordered to search those Old Papers, wherever they may be, which I am certain would elucidate many things before my time. But since the year 1777 when I first went to Mr. Edwards at Landaff, I have invariably endeavoured to treasure up every thing that I conceived would be of service to the Estate.

February 18th   Three days more will complete the Accounts. I am not certain whether Mr. Hollier will go to London immediately after, or whether he will wait 'til Mr. Brown arrives on the Heath business, as Mr. Wood waits for that purpose. All Mr. Hollier's Tax Accounts, Redemption of Land Tax etc. etc. have been made up to the Quarter ending 25th December last.

Mr. Bradley is to have the whole of the Splot Farm for this year and to continue by Lease for 21 years at 300 Guineas per annum. [A Sale of Mrs. Harris's Stock will take place tomorrow *crossed through*.] The Rent is not advanced to what it was 20 years back. The Farm is amazingly cheap. Mr. Bradley's Rents will be great indeed, as he pays the Marquess of Bute £435 18s. 0d. per annum, Vizt. £275 3s. 0d. Old Estate and £160 15s. 0d New. His various Rents [for 1801 *crossed through*] will therefore be about £850 per annum.

Mr. Taitt has bought Captain Walters's Sloops on the Bristol Trade for £1500 and will continue that concern.

Mr. Edward Morgan has had a very long and severe fit of the Gout at the Corner House these 16 weeks, and it is more than probable his place in the Customs may be vacant before Wilson's. I trust that in either case I shall be thought of, as the bringing up my Children [God knows *crossed through*] makes me feel the pressure of the times.

When Mr. Hollier was obliged to give up the Collectorship for the lucrative appointment of Receiver General, he offered to resign the former Office to Rd. Price [who was Clerk to Mr. Traherne *crossed through*] who is now Deputy Comptroller and did the business for the Collector, but as it was incompatible that he should hold both offices, he chose to retain the most advantageous situation. And as Mr. Price was then deemed proper to fill the Office of Collector I may certainly conceive myself adequate, particularly as it does not require so much time as Willson's Office. [Mr. Hollier might have thought of me that time *crossed through*.] Having for many years been in habits of friendship with Mr. Price he told me the circumstance immediately after Mr. Morgan's appointment, and observed 'I realy wondered Mr. Hollier did not think of you instead of Mr. Morgan who did not want it, for as you have been under the Marquess such a number of years his interference would have secured it'.

[Mr. Hollier did not inform me of the late arrangement at the Tax office for the appointment of an Additional Surveyor until it was too late. But I excuse him because he might conceive he would in that case be deprived of my Assistance in the Receiver Generalship, for we are so much accustomed to each other, and I have arranged his Tax Books etc. on such a plan, that we absolutely do twice the business that Mr. Traherne and 3 Assistants used to do. I pray I may not offend by having stated so much *crossed through*.]

Saturday April 4th   Cardiff Great Sessions began this Evening. The Sheriff, Mr. Jones of Fonmon, arrived from London only last night, and considering the short space of time from his appointment, was tolerably well attended.

Sunday April 5th   The Judges were at Church as usual, and Mr. Hardinge's selection of Sacred Music was well performed.

Monday April 6th   The same as yesterday.

The Gentlemen of the Grand Jury were: Llewellin Traherne, John Goodrich, Wm. Goodrich, William Jeffreys, John Williams, Edward Morgan, John Richards of Landaff, Thomas Thomas, Calvert Jones Esquires, and others.

Mr. Hardinge's Charge[169] was extremely well delivered, and the Law rel[ative] to riotous assemblies was clearly laid down and explained.

Tuesday April 7th   Notwithstanding there were 25 Causes on the Prothonotary's Record since last Sessions, not one of them was brought to Trial this day, which is always appropriated for determining the Old Issues. Consequently the morning and Evening Courts were very short.

Wednesday April 8th   Gaol Delivery. The Court was opened at 7 o'Clock and the Trials commenced with that of Samuel Hill, who was considered as the most capital offender when after the most patient investigation he was found Guilty.

The others were brought forward in succession, and occupied the whole of this day and Thursday 9th.

Friday April 10th   The 5 Prisoners Capitally Convicted, as also the whole of the Rioters[170] that had been tried, were brought up, the former to receive sentence and the latter to hear it pronounced.

Mr. Justice Hardinge Address'd the Prisoners[171] in the most affecting and pathetic manner for near three Quarters of an hour previous to passing Sentence, during which time the greatest part of a numerous Court were in Tears, for it is allowed by all who heard him to have been the best, most feeling and most religious of any that ever were delivered in this part of the Kingdom.

There has but one Cause at Nisi Prius been Tried this Assize, and that was for an Assault wherein it was decreed that the Costs of both sides should be equally borne by Plaintiff and Defendant.

Mr. Justice Hardinge sent for me between 8 and 9 at night and kept me employed till 1 in the Morning in taking down the whole of his Address to the Prisoners, which is to be printed.

Saturday April 11th   Mr. Hardinge sent for Mr. Hollier in order that he might ascertain who were proper to be added to the Commission of the Peace and to act in Merthyr and its neighbourhood, for when the Riot commenced there was not a single Magistrate in the place, Mr. Crawshay, Mr. Homfray and Mr. Maber[172] being absent.

Wednesday April 15th   The business Mr. Wood wanted with me at the Quarter Sessions was to give evidence on a Bill of Indictment preferred by Mr. Thomas Guest against Mr. Jere. Homfray for Perjury in his Answer to a Bill in Chancery relative to Mr. Homfray's denying his having had possession of a

House in St. Mary's Parish which he had bought of Mr. Guest. I am almost certain the Jury will find the Bill from what I heard whilst I was examined, as Mr. Homfray had commissioned me to let or dispose of this House for him [which in his Answer he denied having had the possession of *crossed through*.]

The Bench of Justices were numerous, Vizt. Councellor Nicholl,[173] Colonel Aubrey, John Price, Llewellin Traherne, John Goodrich, Thomas Thomas, Saml. Homfray, The Reverend Thomas Davies, Reverend George Williams, David Samuel, Wm. Taitt, Reverend Mr. Maber, and the Reverend Robt. Nicholl.

The first thing done was to qualify Councellor Nicholl to Act as a Magistrate, and the next minute he was requested by Colonel Aubrey and several others to take the Chair, and which after some hesitation he did and Address'd the Jury with a neat and appropriate speech relative to the present situation of things in this Quarter.

The Bench last Night came to a determination to send an exact Copy of the Papers I noticed on Monday Night last to the Duke of Portland,[174] and in the mean time necessary steps will be taken by Colonel Hope to station the Horse in such situations as will, on the first appearance, check the Assembling of those alluded to in the Paper.

The Magistrates meant to adopt some plan to-day relative to the State of Provisions, but as there is no one come from Cowbridge this night I have not heard.

In the event of the bill being found against Mr. Homfray I presume it will be Traversed at Hereford as in the Case of Dr. Griffiths.

Monday April 20th   Receiving the Taxes at Swansea. About 4 o'Clock in the Afternoon a number of poor Women with two Common Girls of the Town at their head assembled and paraded the Streets, and being joined by a number of poor Children whom the Women encouraged to Holloa and Scream, the whole body proceeded to a Corn Warehouse, in which was a large quantity of Barley belonging to Messrs. Grove and Co., and forced open the Door, but did not attempt taking any of it away. On this the Drums beat to Arms, and the Cardigan Militia quartered there were ordered out and repaired to the scene of Action. One of the old Ladies of the Corporation (Mr. W. Jeffreys)[175] read the Riot Act, and in a short time the Women were sent home and one or two of the Ringleaders were taken into Custody and delivered to some of the Swansea Independent Volunteers. But as the Females were of the Cyprean[176] Corps the Independents suffered them to escape.

From this and what had happened on the Saturday before, which was more serious than this day's proceedings, Colonel Morgan[177] (Steward to the Duke of Beaufort and reputed King of Swansea) found himself so intimidated that, notwithstanding he could call out 600 Volunteers of Horse and Foot to his assistance, he immediately sent an Express to Colonel Hope at Cardiff for some of the Iniskillings, as it was rumoured that a large Mob of Miners, Colliers etc. meant to assemble on the next day.

The Cardigan Militia were kept under Arms, with their Band playing at intervals amidst the noise of Men, Women and Children vociferating, screaming etc., until 9 o'Clock when quietness was restored. During the whole of this business, and notwithstanding the greatest Noise was opposite the Mackworth Arms, The Receiver General[178] and myself continued the Collection of Taxes until near 11 at Night.

Tuesday April 21st   About 3 o'Clock in the Afternoon the people passing the Street were heard to say 'The *Scullions* are coming' meaning the Iniskillings, and soon after 20 of them arrived.

Every thing is quiet as present.

Wednesday April 22nd   Went to Neath to Breakfast. Collecting there the whole day and 'till 9 at night when Herbert Evans Esq. of Eaglesbush came in to speak to Mr. Hollier about his Taxes. He had met with some convivial friends and was a little elevated, but I never found the old Welch Proverb so

Neath Town and River. Watercolour by Thomas Hornor, 1819. *By courtesy of the Glamorgan Archive Service.*

completely verified as in that Gentleman's conversation and remarks (Vizt. 'Allwydd y Calon u'r Cwrw' i.e. 'Ale is the Key of the Heart'). He told Mr. Hollier and myself that he was at Swansea last Saturday and was a Witness to the proceedings of the persons who had collected together for the avowed purpose of having Corn sold them at such a rate as to keep them from Starving, and observed that The Marquess of Bute would, in the present conjuncture of affairs, render the County of Glamorgan the most essential service by coming down and convening a Meeting at Pyle for the purpose of taking the sense of the County and acting with the same dignity and consequence which he did when he was last at that place. He was quite warm in his praises of the Marquess, and said he never was so much charmed as with the conduct and deportment of that Nobleman at that County Meeting which was productive of such consequences in putting this County into the defensive state *from foreign foes* as it is at this time. But, said he, the distress of the labouring People is unparraleled. We are without a Head, and being boys all on a par no one will take the lead. There is Mr. Talbot in an insular part of the County doing nothing, and our member Mr. W[yndham] sitting at home and getting drunk, but if the Marquess of Bute was to come down and convene a Meeting it would be the salvation of the Country, and he even went so far as to say that

Dunraven House. Engraved by S. Hooper after Francis Grose, 1776. *By courtesy of University College Cardiff Library.*

it might be the means of preventing a Revolution, for that he had heard many of the lower Order call his Majesty a Dam 'German Butcher, That he delighted in blood, and that they would not be starved under such a *Whelp* i.e. Guelph'. He repeated the same tale many times over and said 'For God's sake Mr. Hollier, do urge the Marquess to come down immediately, there is no time to be lost. I know the sentiments of all the Gentlemen in this part of the County, and By God we will all fly to him at Pyle or any other place in the County when we know we shall have him for a leader, for *his* consequence, *his* experience and abilities are such that the greatest good would result from it' etc. etc. etc.

Mr. Hollier asked what could be done supposing the Marquess was to come down? I took the liberty of observing that I thought the same might be done in this County as was done by Lord Paulet[179] at Illminster in Somersetshire. I was immediately asked what that was? I answered that I had seen in the Bath Paper that Lord Paulet had convened a Meeting, and that the Farmers and Butchers had agreed to sell their provisions at a very reduced rate indeed from the Current prices of the Market etc. Mr. Evans instantly caught the Idea and, insisting that we had no real scarcity, expatiated on it for more than 2 hours with some trifling variation, but always concluding 'That the present conjucture of affairs required the Lord Lieutenant's good offices more than ever' and entreating Mr. Hollier for God's sake to urge it to the Marquess, which Mr. H. promised to do several times. Mr. Evans had talked so much and ate so hearty at Supper that he got quite Sober, when he changed the discourse and observed that the Marquess had a fine property on the Neath Canal, meaning the Mines at Baili Glaes and Hendre Vawr. He said that he had lately surveyed the whole with a Gentleman who would give some thousands for those Mines and beg'd to know what were the Leasing powers etc. etc. Mr. Hollier said he had been offered a Contract with Homfrays, Birch & Co., who are building a furnace at Aberdare, for any Quantity of Mines at 1s. 0d. per Ton, but that he thought it too little etc. etc. Mr. Evans jocularly said 'Oh you Locust, what do you want more than is given in any part of the County and in many places where the Mine is much nearer the Canal than yours?', concluding with beging to know the Leasing Powers, terms etc. etc.

Thursday   Got home at night, but too late to make up this Account.

Friday   No Post day to London.

Saturday Evening   Wrote the above.

Saturday night July 11th   The Pocket Rental came by the Coach last night, and I have devoted the whole of to-day in making the Alterations and Corrections. It is returned by this Mail, and in the Total at Page 30 it will be found that the Old Estate is Increased £244 16s. 0d. and the New at Page 40 Decreased £4 14s. 0d.

No. 147 Ann Miles, an Old Servant of Bailiff Davies's, is kept at £28, but as the Lease is expired I expect it will let for £40 as Mr. William Cook told me he was in treaty for it, but as Mr. Hollier went yesterday Morning to bring back Mrs. H. from Worcestershire I cannot ascertain that fact.

I have lately settled Mr. Taynton's Account of Customary Rents which had not been balanced by him for several years. He paid me £100 and left a balance against himself of £27. I am going to make a Survey of all the Cottage Grants in Lanblethian Lordship, and shall take other Lordships in Rotation.

Travelling about a fortnight back from Crickhowell in Monmouthshire over the Hills to Merthyr, and being near Carno,[180] I determined to make some enquiries respecting that very profitable Tenement to the Dowlais Company who are the Undertenants No. 170.

As there is but one life in being, the Company are raising all the Mines they possibly can on that Tenement, and I may venture to say from the information I obtained that at this moment Carno is worth to the Dowlais Company at least £500 per annum. I have discovered that the only life in the Lease is a Sadler at Abergavenny between 50 and 60 years old, but as it is my intention to see the life in Person before the Marquess arrives in this part of the Country, I hope to be enabled to answer any Question on that head.

Mr. Tynte and daughter, with the Agents Mr. Beiderman Senior and Junior, are now at Kevanmably and will continue for some days.

The Marquess of Bute's Audits were held at the Angel last Saturday and Monday. The Tenants paid full as well as usual.

1802

Saturday January 30th   Mr B[radley] settled his Rent this Morning and has agreed to keep the Moors for the Present year, and if the Marquess of Bute will let him have a House for a Shepherd and some other conveniences on the Moors for Sheltering his Sheep he will agree to pay the usual per Centage for such Buildings. Or, if he shall have a term on the Moors, he will errect such conveniences at his own expence.

Sunday January 31st   Mr. H[ollier] asked me this Evening what had been done with Mrs. Thomas respecting the Post Office, and who a Mrs. Bevan is that is Housekeeper to General Ross. Mr. B[radley] had declined speaking to Mrs. Thomas because he does not leave the Angel this year, but will do so tomorrow morning, and Mr. Hollier's letter immediately after will explain.

Mrs. Bevan is Sister to Dr. Bevan of Cardiff, and to my Brother's Wife, but did not know that I had made any previous application or she would not have done so.

Having some material business with my Booksellers who have omitted to give me Credit for 35 Guineas paid them, and Mr. Hollier having permitted me to be absent for a few days, I purpose being in London on Saturday next with Mr. Brown Junr.

Mrs. John Richards of Cardiff has been in a state of derangement for 10 days Past, insomuch that it is said She is to be conveyed to Dr. Willis.[181]

Tuesday March 23rd   Cardiff Assizes began this day. The Sheriff's party was the smallest I ever saw [cut the most insignificant appearance *crossed through*].

Wednesday March 24th   The Gentlemen of the Grand Jury were: Robert Jenner Esq., John Goodrich, Wm. Taitt, John Lockwood, Richard Hill Senr. [and] Junr., Wyndham Lewis, John Samuel etc. etc.

Mr. Hardinge's Address began with observing that Integrity was the life of Judicial proceedings, and after some observations it turned chiefly on Perjury and the ignorance of the lower Class of People in not understanding the nature of an Oath, and made it appear that if the Clergy were compelled to reside amongst their Parishoners and to explain that most essential article it would in a great measure remedy that dreadful evil. He congratulated the Country on the great good that was likely to result from the Bill now in the hands of Sir John Scott[182] for the above purpose, and after paying the highest compliment to that learned and able Man he concluded a neat and pointed Address.

The Calendar he observed was a mere feather.

Having been at Mr. Hollier's about the Books without the least intermission from the time they were begun, I could see nothing of the business in Court. But I find the most material Cause was between Mr. Traherne of Castella and a Man of Langonoyd about a Sheep Walk of 12 or 13 Acres in the Coedtrehên Estate. The Cause was tried by a Special Jury and took many hours to investigate from the great Chain of Evidence on both sides. The Verdict was against Mr. Traherne and I am told the Expence of this and a former trial would more than purchase the Fee Simple of the Premises 5 times over.

Mrs. Richards Goods Picture etc. etc.

April 1st   Mr. Bradley has by this Post transmitted a Memorial to the Post Master General, of which the enclosed is a Copy.

[The Surveyor of the Roads having been at Cardiff lately and been consulted on this Memorial, Mr. Bradley could not transmit it earlier for certain reasons *crossed through*.]

Mr. Bradley could not transmit it earlier for reasons which shall be explained, and in the course of a Month he means to send in his resignation [but he says that if it is the pleasure of the Marquess of Bute there will be no impropriety in his applying for the nomination in the course of a few days, at the same time taking no notice that Mr. Bradley's resignation will soon follow, but merely stating that he had a person to nominate (applying for the nomination) in the event of such a resignation taking place *crossed through*] previous to which the Marquess of Bute will be apprized thereof. And as I am to pay Mr. Bradley £20 per annum determinable with the life of either him or Mrs. B. for such time as me or my heirs should hold the Office, it is Mr. Bradley's wish to obtain an encrease of Salary for me so as to cover that Sum without taking it out of the present Stipend.

(Copy)

Sir, Please to have 300 of the enclosed Printed off immediately. I will thank you to have some stuck up in the Streets at Cardiff, Lantrissent and Merthyr, and send the remainder to me as soon as possible.

Am Sir
Your Humble Servant
Thos. Wyndham

Dunraven Castle
26 June 1802

(Copy)

To the Gentlemen, Clergy and Freeholders of the County of Glamorgan

Gentlemen,

A Dissolution of Parliament being shortly expected, I am induced by your former kindness again to solicit the honor to represent you in the ensuing Parliament. I have the satisfaction to reflect that ever since you first honored me with your Confidence I have endeavored to discharge my duty Conscientiously and (as I conceived) in support of our most excellent Constitution. If my attendance latterly has not been so constant as I could wish, I rely upon your Candour and liberallity to impute it to the real cause of occasional ill health, and not to any remissness on my part towards a County to which I am so highly indebted. I have the honor to remain with much gratitude

Gentlemen
Your most devoted,
and obliged humble Servant
Thos. Wyndham

Dunraven Castle
26 June 1802

Sunday Evening June 27th   The Bishop of Landaff Ordained 13 Young Clergymen this Morning, Vizt. Seven for Deacons and Six for Priests. He delivered a most Sublime and beautiful Discourse from 3rd Chapter of John, 16th Verse.[183] Mr. Maber to print Sermon.

I have lately spent a day with Mr. Goodrich in convincing him of his Chief Rent being all due. That Account is now in train for settlement. He has been exceedingly circumspect in examining his Conveyances etc. etc. I have taken possession for the Marquess of Bute and the Earl of Windsor of two Cots at Funnon Tave[184] near Pentirch Works, which has been for years in the Family of the Lewis's of Newhouse, but the life having drop'd I got an attornment[185] from the Present Tenant and 10s. 6d. in part of Rent. The old Rent was one Shilling, but in future it is to be £2 12s. 6d. and all Repairs on the Tenant.

Saturday September 4th   Cardiff Assizes ended this Morning. Thursday and Friday there was a great weight of business, but that on Monday, Tuesday and Wednesday was trifling. The Gentlemen of the Grand Jury (of which Mr. Wyndham was Foreman) were the most respectable in the County, as also the three *Special* Jury Causes, which occupied the best part of two days.

It being Judge Moysey's turn to Address the Grand Jury, he only observed 'That there was nothing difficult in the Calendar and on that Account he should not detain them with any charge'.

The Prisoners were tried on Wednesday as in the Calendar.

The first Special Jury Cause was Wm. Lewis Esq. of Pentirch against The Glamorganshire Canal Co. for robbing him of a great Quantity of Water, whereby he sustained Damages in his Works to the Amount as stated in the Declaration of Fifteen Hundred Pounds. The Cause took 9 hours to investigate, and in the Course of the Evidence great Science and ingenuity were displayed, Particularly by Mr. Weldon, an Engineer who had surveyed the Canal and who produced a large and perfect Model of the Triple Locks, Weirs, Skrew Gates etc. where the injury was complained of, and pointed out a mode whereby both parties would have sufficient water without injury to each other. He was highly complimented by the Judge for his Information, Scientific knowledge etc. etc. Mr. Lewis at length obtained a Verdict of £100 damages.

The 2nd Special Jury Cause was Edwd. Bowen, for Robert Rouse Esq., against the Corporation of Cardiff, for taking Toll from a certain Quantity of Barley, the same not having been Pitched in the Market House but delivered at a Storehouse.[186] This Cause afforded great entertainment to a Crowded Court, particularly by Mr. Allen's cross examination of the Evidence, who had been Burgesses, but at the Court of Common Council the day before had been disfranchised Vizt. Wm. Morgan, John Bird Senr.,[187] John Purcell, Wm. Evans, Wm. Prichard and Mr. Wood. Mr. Allen kept the Court on a laugh for some time, and particularly when he observed to the Jury 'Now Gentlemen if it had happened that this Cause had been tried a few Weeks back, and just before the Election, what would have become of Poor Lord Bute when all those Worthy Members of the Corporation' (at the same time referring with much significance to Mr. Wood) 'had been disfranchised?' etc. etc. The Evidence made it appear so plain that the Corporation had a right to 1 Quart of Grain out of every Cardiff Bushell of 20 Gallons that the Judge did not find it necessary to Sum up the Evidence, but directed the Jury to find a Verdict for the Defendants.

The 3rd Special Jury Cause was Between Capel Leigh Esq. and a Man from Baglan, for a Common of some extent. The Verdict was given against Mr. Leigh. There were 20 Witnesses Examined. Mr. Leigh is obliged to take back the Gnoll Estate, Mr. Johnston the late Purchaser not having paid any of the Purchase money. This I got from one of Mr. Leigh's Agents.

Sunday September 5th   The Sale of the late Mr. Edwards's[188] Estates began at 1 o'Clock yesterday, and finished at 8. I attended to state the Chief Rents on the different Lots, and also to be enabled to convey correct information of the Sale, which was as follows:

Mr Rickards of Lantrissent Bought	Acres	Rent		£
Tyr Cwm Frood, Lantwit Vardre	41 Acres	Rent £35	for	710
Rhyd y Llech, Do.	24 Do.	£10 10s. 0d.	for	225
Gellydraws & Coedcae, Coal therein	110 Do.	£25	for	930
Gelly Wyon, Lantrissent, Do.	373 Do.	£105	for	2630
Houses in Do.		£5 5s. 0d.	for	121
		£180 15s. 0d.		£4616

Total bought by Mr. Rickards £4616

Mr. Price of Landaff, 3 Tenements at Coyty and Coychurch £41 15s. 10d. per annum	for £1200
Mr. Jenkins Panty Nowell, 3 Do. Rent £68	for £1905
Mr. Goodrich, Farms in Eglwysilan £83 8s. 0d. per annum	for £2325
Mr. Powell Edwards, Sundry farms near Coedygoras etc £131 1s. 6d. per annum	for £6478
Mr. Traherne Castella, Castella fach 46 acres of wood £14 per annum	for £655

Sundry Persons, Sundry things   £138 3s. 0d. per annum   for   £3066

Total Amount of the Sale   £20,245

Mr. Edwards bought the Tenement adjoining Lord Bute's £7 5s. 0d. in Senghenith.

Lord Henry Stuart[189] and Lady lay at Cardiff on Friday night last and left it on their Journey to Ireland at 7 on Saturday Morning. I had the honor of shewing them the Castle Pictures etc., at which Her Ladyship seemed much pleased.

Mr. Bradley has heard nothing since last Account about the encrease of Salary, but is desirous of my taking The Post Office against the 10th of October next, and as I have 2 Sons who will soon be able to manage the business under my Inspection, I humbly hope The Marquess of Bute will permit me to hold it. His Lordship will be informed a few days previous to Mr. Bradley's resignation.

Complaint against Mr. Snead of Swansea, which caused Judge Hardinge to say 'That if The Lord Lieutenant do not superscede this Man he ought to be supersceded himself'.

1803

Sunday April 3rd   The Accounts are closed and Mr. Hollier will be in Town in a day or two.

The business of the Sessions went of[f] rather flat, as Mr. Hardinge could not attend from illness. Mr. Bold the Marshall, Mr. Maybury the Clerk of the Arraigns and Mr. Theophilus Jones the Cryer of the Court were also unable to attend.

The Grand Jury were very respectable, Vizt. Thomas Wyndham Esq., Colonel Capper, Mr. Lockwood of Swansea, Mr. Goodrich etc. etc. Judge Moysey delivered no Address, and only observed that the Gentlemen of the Grand Jury were fully acquainted with the nature of their Duty and he did not conceive it necessary to make any comments on the Offences in the Calendar.

The Principal Cause at Nisi Prius was between Mr. Hopkin Llewellin of Margam and Mr. Gwynn of Lansannor, for a Mountain lying between their Estates at Ystradyfodwg. There were near 30 Old Witnesses examined on both sides, and the Tryal lasted 9 hours. The Verdict was for Mr. Hopkin Llewellin.

The Influenza etc has carried of[f] many people in this part of the Country, Vizt. Mr. & Mrs. Willis of Gilestone who were both interred yesterday at

Gilestone near St. Athan, [and] Mr. Griffiths Attorney of Merthyr, the most corpulent Man in this County. He died here in full flesh and his remains were this day removed to Merthyr. The Coffin was 3 feet 4 Inches across the Shoulders, and it being impossible to get it down the Stairs the Window Frame of the Room was obliged to be taken out and a Scaffold erected. Mr. Thomas Edwards of Ty newydd, an opulent Tenant of the Marquess of Bute, is also dead, and many others in inferior situations.

The Militia are to have their Clothing tomorrow. Colonel Aubrey lodges with me and says he is very comfortable. None of the Soldiers are suffered to go into the Castle, but the Gates are in a dilapidated state.

Both Rentals are Increased, the Joint Estate about £140 and that belonging to Lord Bute about £40.

Notes to the Text

1. Chief Rents: the rents payable by free-holders of the manor to the lord of the manor. Rent collection was one of Bird's main preoccupations as estate clerk, and references to Burgage Rents (payable by burgesses or freeholders within the boroughs), and Cottage Rents (due from tenants of small dwellings) also figure prominently in the pages of his diaries.

2. John Richards senior of Cardiff. See Biographical Notes.

3. Distress: the seizure of goods or chattels for the recovery of rent arrears.

4. Mary (née Birt), wife of John Richards of the Corner House, Cardiff. See Biographical Notes.

5. i.e. the Glamorganshire Canal. The canal was constructed under the terms of an Act of Parliament, 31 Geo.III c.82.

6. Thomas Thomas of Cardiff, attorney, was under-sheriff in 1774, 1776, 1780, 1781 and 1784. See Appendix D, and Biographical Notes.

7. One of numerous schemes to prevent flooding, particularly on the low-lying moors to the south of the town, and in Cardiff itself, by the construction and maintenance of a series of walls and embankments.

8. Thomas Scandrett of Cardiff, butcher.

9. See Appendix A.

10. The piece of timber cast ashore by the tide had been claimed as wreck on behalf of Lord Bute. Technically all rights of wreck were vested in the Crown, but the everyday flotsam and jetsam of the sea were recognised as the perquisite of the local landowner. As with rights of fishery (note 133) rights of wreck seem to have accrued to the Marquesses of Bute as inheritors of the Herbert family's estates and privileges, rather than as straightforward manorial dues.

11. David Prichard of Cardiff, attorney.

12. The officials of Cardiff Corporation comprised the constable of Cardiff Castle and his deputy, two bailiffs, ten aldermen, the town clerk, two sergeants at mace, two common attorneys, two constables for each ward (East and West wards in 1790), a water-bailiff, a clerk of the cattle market and fairs, a clerk of the shambles, an ale-taster, and the bellman or town crier.

13. Glynronthey *alias* Glynrhondda, one of the manors or lordships inherited by the Marquess of Bute from the Herbert family. The Marquesses of Bute were lords of the following Glamorgan manors: Boviarton and Llantwit, Glynrhondda, Lequeth, Llandough, Cogan, Cosmeston and Walterston, Llanblethian, Llanmaes Bedford and Malefaunt, Llystalybont, Roath Dogfield, Roath Tewkesbury, Spittle, Whitefriars and Kibbor, Ruthin, Miskin with Pentyrch and Clun, Senghennydd, Whitchurch, Rudry and Llanvedw. GRO D/DB E/1,2 Bute estate survey compiled by David Stewart, 1824.

14. One of the principal coaching inns in Cardiff. Situated opposite the Castle, near Cardiff bridge and adjacent to the site of the present-day Angel Hotel, it gave its name to Cardiff Arms Park.

15. i.e. Greyfriars. Part of the estates of the Herbert family from the sixteenth century until the mid-eighteenth century when it passed by inheritance to Hurst of Gabalfa and Jones of Swansea. An Elizabethan mansion was built on the site of the former friary. Remains of the house and friary church survived until 1969 when the Pearl Assurance block was built on the site.

16. Grand Jury: a jury of enquiry not of trial. The Grand Jury, composed of between twelve and twenty-three substantial freeholders of the county, was summoned to attend the court of Great Sessions or Assizes (also the Quarter Sessions) by the sheriff. Its members were instructed in the articles of the charge by the judge, and then received indictments and heard evidence from the prosecution before considering whether there was sufficient cause for the accused to answer the charge. If the Bill of Indictment was found (i.e. was a 'True Bill') the case then went before a Petty Jury or Special Jury for trial.

17. The old county gaol in St Mary Street stood on a site adjoining the Market House. When, in 1832, a new county gaol was erected in Whitmore Lane, on the eastern outskirts of the town, the old gaol continued to be used as the town prison.

18. See Appendix D.

19. Act regulating the tenure of office by sheriffs and their deputies, 23 Hen.VI c.7.

20. See Appendix A.

21. The 'Golledge Cause' in which Mrs Golledge successfully proved her title to the copyhold lands of Davies deceased in the manor of Boviarton and Llantwit. The defendant in the case was Lord Bute as lord of

the manor. NLW Bute Box 86, Manorial R 15. Copyhold: tenure of manorial lands by custom of the manor and copy of court roll. Conveyances of such land were made by Surrender and Admission, the transactions being recorded on the formal record of the manor court, the court roll. Freehold was distinguished from Copyhold tenure by limitations of inheritance and service.

22. John Allen of Clements Inn, attorney; freeman of Cardiff, 1780.

23. Edward Robson of Neath.

24. Petty larceny: minor theft, originally of goods of less than twelve pence in value.

25. The Commission of the Peace: the official document on which are enrolled the names of the county's justices of the peace.

26. Militia: a local defence force raised by ballot from among the able-bodied men of the county between the ages of sixteen and sixty, and called upon in times of emergency to perform military service within their county or district. The Royal Glamorgan Militia was first embodied on 14 January 1761 (GRO D/D Xkn). The Supplementary Militia was recruited among the older men of the county. The activities of the Militia were supplemented by those of the Volunteers. The Volunteer Act of 1794 (34 Geo.III c.31) encouraged voluntary enrolment of 'corps and companies of men for the defence of their Counties, Towns and Coasts, and for the General Defence of the Kingdom.' Troops of Cavalry and Infantry Volunteers were embodied at Cardiff, Cowbridge, Swansea and elsewhere in Glamorgan. For accounts of Militia and Volunteer forces in Glamorgan, see L.V. Evans, 'The Royal Glamorgan Militia', *Glamorgan historian*, 8 (1972), pp. 146-166, and Bryn Owen, *Glamorgan: its gentlemen and yeomanry* (Newport, 1983).

27. Hallingbury Place (Essex), seat of the Archer-Houblon family. Jacob Houblon (1710-99) built up an extensive library which was extended by his descendants, among them John Houblon (1773-1831).

28. Stamp inspector: an official responsible for scrutinising all transactions which were liable for the imposition of stamp duty, a tax imposed on a wide range of legal instruments (deeds, bills of exchange, admissions of burgesses etc).

29. The sergeants at mace, who were also sheriffs of the town, were appointed to attend the mayor and bailiffs of the Corporation and to assist the town clerk.

30. Richard Watson, Bishop of Llandaff, consecrated August 1782. Non-resident for thirty years. See *DNB*.

31. Candlemas: Feast of the Purification of the Virgin Mary, 2 February.

32. Fforest Isaf, Whitchurch.

33. Derry *alias* Deri, Rhiwbina.

34. See Appendix A; also Diary, 26 March 1790.

35. The 1st Marquess of Bute was a subscriber to the Cardiff Races which were run over Cardiff Heath.

36. The conversion of encroachments into tenancies was condoned by the Marquess's agents, to the outrage of other landowners with rights on the commons. Disputes over common rights frequently ended in litigation, e.g. Parishioners of Aberdare *versus* Lord Bute, Great Sessions (Cardiff), 1788.

37. Mary Williams (née Davies), wife of Henry Williams of Llancarfan, clock and watchmaker and farmer.

38. Rev. John Williams, M.A. (d.1794), incumbent of Margam 1757-94. He also held the living of St Mary Church.

39. Since the 1760s the Turnpike Trusts had supplemented the often inadequate activities of parish highway surveyors and local magistrates. In 1790 the South Wales Association for the Improvement of Roads was formed, its main objective being the improvement of the mail road from Milford Haven to the New Passage and thence to London. In the same year the Glamorganshire Canal Act provided for a new artery of communication between the ironworks at Merthyr and the sea at Cardiff.

40. Evidently the judge's earlier complimentary remarks related only to the roads in close proximity to Merthyr.

41. Merthyr was, at the end of the eighteenth century, the largest town in Wales. Its population had exploded as the ironworks of Cyfarthfa, Dowlais and Penydarren were established from the 1750s onwards. By 1801 the inhabitants of Merthyr parish numbered 7,705, those of Cardiff less than 2,000. The lack of adequate numbers of local magistrates exacerbated the complex problems of law enforcement and administration within this volatile community.

42. John Lord Mountstuart, later the 1st Marquess of Bute. See Biographical Notes.

43. Rev. William Paley. See Biographical Notes.

44. Dr Charles Collins of Swansea.

45. Rev. Samuel Molyneux Lowder. See Biographical Notes.

46. A reference to the portraits of members of the Stuart (Bute) family which hung in the Castle.

47. Trover: action brought for the wrongful appropriation or use of another man's possessions.

48. Presumably confirmation of Bird's refusal to print an account of Dr Richard Griffiths's trial at Hereford.

49. Dr Bloom Williams of Cardiff, surgeon. See Biographical Notes.

50. Shambles: the borough market for the sale of meat (and grain). Supervised by the clerks of the market in accordance with the town's byelaws.

51. Captain William Prichard of Cardiff, whose building activities ended in bankruptcy. See also Diary, 1 and 16 April 1793.

52. The medieval keep of Cardiff Castle was refurbished to provide an armoury and munitions store for the Militia. 'It is called the Magazine, having been used for that purpose by the Militia', T.J.Hopkins (ed.), 'Francis Grose's tour in Glamorgan, 1775', *Glamorgan historian*, 1 (1963), p. 161.

53. John, 1st Earl of Portarlington, married Lady Caroline Stuart, sister of the 1st Marquess of Bute.

54. The senior aldermen, from whom Sabine and Hollier were subsequently elected to the influential office of bailiff. William Prichard (not to be confused with the Captain mentioned in note 51) is commemorated by a plaque in St John's church, Cardiff, as 'a most active magistrate of this town for upward of 40 years'. He died in 1839 aged 88.

55. Mary Lewis (née Price), widow of the Rev. Wyndham Lewis.

56. William Morris *alias* Morrice was commissioned by the parish vestry of St John's, Cardiff, to undertake this survey in 1785. See also Biographical Notes.

57. The Hirwaun ironworks were founded by John Maybery and John Wilkins in 1757. In 1780 the works were leased to Anthony Bacon and in 1786 to Samuel Glover. In 1803 the lease was granted to Jeremiah Homfray and others. From 1819 to 1864 Hirwaun was owned by the Crawshay family of Cyfarthfa.

58. Neath Canal Act, 31 Geo.III c.85. The Canal was completed c.1795, and extended in 1799.

59. The previous occupant was the attorney, David Prichard. See Diary, 7 October 1790.

60. Castleton, Monmouthshire.

61. See Appendix A.

62. The Friars estate was sold to the Marquess of Bute. Gabalfa was retained by Herbert Hurst for the prospective benefit of his wife during her widowhood, but after being mortgaged to the Wood family, bankers, it was sold to Sir Robert Lynch-Blosse in 1809. See also Biographical Notes under Hurst.

63. The printing press formerly belonged to Rhys Thomas, the Cowbridge printer. *DWB*; B.Ll.James, 'The Cowbridge printers', *Glamorgan historian*, 4 (1967), pp. 231–244.

64. Baili Glaes *alias* Bailyglas farm, Rhigos.

65. The clerk of the peace. See Biographical Notes.

66. Cardiff Castle provided a convenient store for Bute estate, borough and county records, including those of Quarter Sessions, in the eighteenth and early nineteenth centuries. Bird's diary for 1826 contains several references to the Record Room at the Castle. See also Diary, 27 January 1795.

67. Hereford Assizes, March 1791, case of the Freeholders of Hirwaun *versus* Lord Bute (lord of the manor) for granting away parcels of waste land thereby depriving them of rights of commonage. The verdict was given for the plaintiffs. An account of the case in the *Hereford Journal* for 30 March 1791 states that 'upwards of one thousand acres are said to have been thus parcelled out on a single common, with rents, heriots etc. reserved to the lord . . . '

68. Calendar: the list of prisoners for trial at each Sessions.

69. i.e. Great Sessions.

70. See Appendix E.

71. Thomas Caldecot. See Biographical Notes.

72. William Taitt lived at this house, 19 St Mary Street, from 1792 until his death in 1815.

73. Flat Holm (49 acres) was part of the Cardiff Castle estate and was leased to tenants. The lessee in the 1730s was William Crispe, a Bristol merchant, and it was Crispe, with the support of the Society of Merchant Venturers of Bristol, who petitioned Trinity House for a lighthouse on the island. The lease of the island and the light subsequently came into the possession of the Dickinson family, from whom a quarter share in the light was acquired by Thomas Rothley, a Bristol Customs House official, in 1755. Rothley's association with the light and its management continued until his death in 1798. For a detailed account of the building

and management of the light see
W.R.Chaplin, 'The history of Flat Holm
Lighthouse', *The American Neptune,* 20
(1960), pp. 5–43.

74. Mrs Taylor, a widow, had succeeded
her husband as tenant of Flat Holm and
keeper of the light, and occupied the house
adjacent to the lighthouse. The reference to
the miners appears to relate to Lord
Mountstuart's abortive attempt to re-open
ancient lead workings on the island.
W.R.Chaplin, op.cit.

75. In December 1790 the lighthouse was
struck by lightning. The top of the tower was
extensively damaged and the iron grate which
held the coal-fire light was smashed.
D.B.Hague and Rosemary Christie, *Light-
houses: their architecture, history and archae-
ology* (Llandysul, 1975); W.R.Chaplin, op.cit.

76. Cardiff Great Sessions, September
1791. Suit brought by John Lord Cardiff
against Thomas and Samuel Rees for trespass
on Hirwaun Common.

77. The purchase of the Friars estate by
Lord Bute was completed in 1793. The purchase price was £19,000. See also note 62.

78. For details of John Bird's activities as a
printer, see Ifano Jones, *A history of printing
and printers in Wales* (Cardiff, 1925), pp.
92–9.

79. For an account of the career of Joseph
John, see Roy Denning, 'The Devil had a
share', *Glamorgan historian,* 5 (1968), pp.
110–20.

80. Nisi Prius (unless before): Civil cases
specifically set aside for determination on a
particular day by the assize judges, and which
had been commenced in one of the divisions
of the High Court.

81. Patrick Crichton, 6th Earl of Dumfries.
His daughter Elizabeth ('Lady Eliza') married
John Lord Mountstuart in 1792. The Dumfries title was inherited by the 2nd Marquess
of Bute.

82. George Yates, cartographer and en-
graver. His map of Glamorgan, 1799, was
dedicated to the Marquess of Bute. A facsi-
mile of the map was published by the South
Wales Record Society in 1984.

83. The Bute and Loudoun families each
owned extensive estates in Ayrshire. Flora,
Countess of Loudoun, married the Marquess
of Hastings, and the daughter of that marriage, Sophia, became the wife of the 2nd
Marquess of Bute.

84. Thomas Hughes Vernon of Sandhurst
(Gloucs.) leased a house and land in Dinas

Powys from William Hurst for seven years in
1788. Landlord and tenant were subsequently
involved in disputes concerning their respective obligations (see Diary, 29 March 1792).
Vernon absconded in 1793 leaving his debts
unpaid (see Diary, 22 August 1793).

85. Crib: a wooden frame for strengthening
river banks, etc; a rectangular frame of logs
or beams strongly fastened together and
secured under water to form a pier or dam.

86. Following the death of the 3rd Earl of
Bute (George III's prime minister) in 1792,
his son and grandson assumed the titles of
Earl of Bute and Lord Mountstuart
respectively.

87. Ricket Willett of Cardiff, tailor, with
premises under the town hall steps. Sergeant
at mace, 1786.

88. Phillip Davy of Cardiff, baker and
grocer. See Biographical Notes.

89. Newbridge *alias* Pontypridd.

90. John Wilkes (ed.), *The universal British
directory*, published in parts 1790–8.

91. Heriot: a payment in money or kind
(usually the best beast) due to the lord of the
manor on the death of a tenant.

92. James Parry of Brecon, bridge-builder
and architect. He died in 1832, aged 59, and
was buried in St John's churchyard, Cardiff.

93. The Gordon family lived at Greenmeadow as tenants of the Prices of Park, St
Fagans.

94. Crim.con. (criminal conversation):
adultery.

95. John Bevan (GRO D/D Xkn).

96. Captain-lieutenant John Quin (GRO
D/D Xkn).

97. Republicans and levellers: terms used
by the judge to encompass all those with revolutionary sympathies, i.e. Radicals.

98. Judge William Henry Ashurst. See Biographical Notes.

99. Dedimus: writ empowering a person to
exercise judicial authority (dedimus potes-
tatem — we have given the power).

100. Long Cross was a house on the
boundary of St John's and Roath parishes
which took its name from a medieval boundary stone. The property was demolished in
1844 to make way for the Artillery barracks.

101. Old Franky, the gatekeeper at Cardiff
Castle.

102. The Energlyn estate was inherited by
the Richards family from Roger Powell. See
Biographical Notes.

103. Cathays House was leased to a succession of tenants including Colonel James

Capper (see Biographical Notes), but was also used as an occasional residence by the 1st Marquess and his son. In 1813 the house was demolished and a new mansion built on the same site at the north-west end of Cathays Park.

104. The future 2nd Marquess of Bute.

105. Panels: those empanelled to serve as jurors; jury lists.

106. Replevin: writ empowering a person to take legal action for the recovery of his goods. In this instance, for the recovery of debts from the sureties of the debtor.

107. The Roath estate, including Roath Court mansion house, had descended early in the eighteenth century from Sir George Howels of Bovehill to the Gwynne family of Llanelwedd, Radnorshire, by whom it was burdened with a succession of mortgages. In 1787 the mortgagee was Sir Herbert Mackworth of Gnoll. The property was eventually sold to the Cardiff banker and attorney, John Wood senior.

108. Computed on the basis of an annual rental of approximately £250, the Roath estate comprising 48 acres.

109. Robert Jenner married a daughter of Peter Birt of Wenvoe Castle. See Biographical Notes under Birt.

110. Improvements at the *Cardiff Arms* were carried out at the expense of Lord Bute who stayed there, or at Cathays House, on his visits to Cardiff.

111. Sir Robert Humphrey Mackworth, aged 30. His widow married Capel Hanbury Leigh. See Biographical Notes.

112. Thomas Edwards, clerk of the peace. His daughter Jane married Michael Richards of Cardiff. See Biographical Notes.

113. Lord Bute was ambassador in Madrid, 1794–96.

114. Hundred: an administrative unit within the county that was established as part of the Tudor pattern of government (27 Hen. VIII c.26) and survived into the nineteenth century. Glamorgan was parcelled into the ten hundreds of Caerphilly, Cowbridge, Dinas Powys, Kibbor, Llangyfelach, Miskin, Neath, Newcastle, Ogmore and Swansea.

115. Among the Grant Francis collection of miscellaneous papers at University College, Swansea (formerly at the Royal Institution of South Wales) is the following manuscript: 'Proposals for raising a corps of infantry in the county of Glamorgan, to be called the Glamorgan Rangers and to consist of eight companies of sixty men each at the

least, and to be composed of rifle men or sharp shooters, by Thomas Mansel Talbot Esq., Colonel', *c.*1795.

116. Deodand: the object responsible for the death of any person within a lordship or manor was confiscated by the officials of the manor court for the benefit of the lord.

117. For an account of banking in this period, see R.O.Roberts, in *Glamorgan county history*, vol.V (Cardiff, 1980), chapter VIII.

118. The Brecon Old Bank of Messrs Wilkins.

119. There were two prisons in Swansea at this date, a debtors' prison within the castle and 'a dark room for felons' under the town hall (later transferred to the castle). The former, a private franchise gaol owned by the Duke of Beaufort, continued in use until the mid-nineteenth century. The latter, maintained by the Corporation, was used to house those awaiting trial or transfer to the county gaol at Cardiff. R.L.Brown, 'Swansea debtors' gaol', *Morgannwg*, XVII (1973), pp. 10–24.

120. Richard Gough Aubrey of Ynyscedwyn. See Biographical Notes.

121. Mutinies at Spithead and the Nore (April and May 1797). Four months later the same fleet won a resounding victory against the Dutch at Camperdown.

122. Thomas Paine (1737–1809). He defended the French Revolution in *The rights of man* (1791–2), was accused of treason and fled to France. *DNB*. In 1792 the Corporation of Cardiff burnt an effigy of Paine outside the town hall.

123. See note 21.

124. Arles: meadowland, part of the Heath, in St John's parish.

125. Eleanor, Joan and Anne Bassett of Lanelay, spinsters, inherited the Lanelay estate from their brother, the Rev. Thomas Bassett.

126. The extension of the Glamorganshire Canal to the sea lock and basin was authorised by Act of Parliament, 31 Geo.III c.69.

127. Newbury, Berkshire.

128. The Maendy estate (450 acres) of Wyndham Lewis was sold to the Marquess of Bute in 1804. In 1826 his lands in Aberdare and Llanishen were also acquired by the Bute estate.

129. The second house at Cyfarthfa, replacing an earlier edifice erected by Bacon in 1765. Built by Richard Crawshay, Cyfarthfa House provided the family residence in Mer-

thyr until the 1820s when that most ambitious scheme, Cyfarthfa Castle, was realised by William Crawshay II.

130. William Williams of the General Post Office, London. Burgess of Cardiff, 1779.

131. Anchor (anker): a cask or keg of capacity of $8\frac{1}{2}$ imperial gallons.

132. The wife of John Richardson of Swansea and widow of Charles Bowen (d.1787). She was involved in protracted litigation with her late husband's half brothers and sister, including Stephen Jones, over the settlement of the Merthyr Mawr estate (case in Chancery 1796–1804).

133. The owners of the Merthyr Mawr and Dunraven estates shared the fishing rights in the lower reaches of the Ogmore and Ewenny rivers, but apparently as lessors not owners of those rights, the ultimate ownership being vested in the Marquess of Bute as inheritor of the lands and privileges of the Herbert family. The whole subject of fishing rights requires detailed investigation.

134. Cordwainer: shoemaker, leather worker. The Cordwainers and Glovers were a survival from the medieval craft guilds. See R.Bettridge, 'A Cardiff guild in decline', *Annual report of the Glamorgan archivist*, 1983, pp. 11–14.

135. Situated on the south side of Shoemaker Street, near the junction of High Street and Duke Street. The hall was in a ruinous condition by the 1770s, its maintenance beyond the resources of its dwindling number of members, among them John Bird senior, father of the diarist. The lease to John Wood was followed by the outright sale of the premises to him in 1806.

136. St Crispin, patron saint of shoemakers and leatherworkers. Feast day 25 October.

137. Land Tax: a tax levied annually from 1692 onwards upon each county. It was apportioned among the constituent parishes of each hundred within the county, assessed by local commissioners and collected by the petty constables. The tax was made permanent but redeemable in 1798 (Land Tax Perpetuation Act, 38 Geo.III c.48).

138. Richard Aubrey of Ash Hall. See Biographical Notes.

139. Edward Pearson, notary public, chapter clerk or registrar of Llandaff, 1791–1817.

140. Rev. Thomas Davies, J.P.

141. One of Admiral Lord Nelson's great sea victories against the French, fought on 1 August 1798.

142. See Appendix B.

143. See Appendix B.

144. George Forster Cook of Stroud, Gloucs. Resigned as organist of St John's in 1802.

145. Edward Snead of Swansea, J.P., coroner of Gower.

146. Sir William Champion de Crespigny married the Earl of Plymouth's sister, Sarah, in 1786.

147. Thomas Key of St Fagans. See Biographical Notes.

148. Other Hickman, 5th Earl of Plymouth, died 12 June 1799.

149. The Worcestershire residence of the Earls of Plymouth.

150. Fine: Final Concord. A legal device employed to convey land, used particularly to bar entails upon estates.

151. Francis Webb of Salisbury. Plymouth estate agent at St Fagans 1799–*c*.1808. In 1809 Messrs Webb, Webb and Attwood were the agents.

152. Cord: a measure of cut wood, usually 128 cubic feet.

153. Court Leet and View of Frankpledge: manorial court, presided over by the steward, dealing mainly with the regulation of nuisances. The chief court of the manor, which declared and enforced manorial customs and regulated tenancies, was the Court Baron.

154. Edward Martin, mineral surveyor. See Biographical Notes.

155. Galeage: a royalty paid to the owner of the land in return for a licence to dig for coal, iron or stone.

156. David Tanner of Monmouth. See Biographical Notes under Cockshutt.

157. Sarah Bird (née Vaughan?).

158. The Loyal Address to the King from the boroughs on the occasion of the 'brilliant victories over the French'. Similar sentiments were expressed by the county gentry.

159. Portreeve: chief officer of certain boroughs, equivalent to the mayor or bailiff elsewhere.

160. In 1799 the Royal Glamorgan Militia were sent to Cork and Fermoy.

161. Clearwell Court, near Newland, on the edge of the Forest of Dean, was the Gloucestershire residence of the Wyndham family.

162. The Pyle Inn, built at the expense of Thomas Mansel Talbot of Margam in the 1780s, provided convenient accommodation for meetings and overnight lodgings.

163. The Bute family mausoleum and

vault, constructed at the expense of the 1st Marquess, who was patron of the living of St Margaret's, Roath. The old church survived until 1869 when it was demolished and a new edifice erected on the same site.

164. Robert Clutterbuck, the Hertfordshire historian, stayed at Cathays House with the tenant, James Capper. T.J.Hopkins (ed.), 'Robert Clutterbuck's tour through Glamorgan 1799', *Glamorgan historian*, 3 (1966), pp. 201–219.

165. The Marquess married Fanny Coutts on 17 September 1800, twelve days after the body of his first wife had been re-interred at Roath and nine months after her death.

166. Thomas Brown of Luton, Beds., estate surveyor and enclosure commissioner.

167. The exhumation and re-interment of the bodies of the Marchioness of Bute, her son and daughter-in-law were carried out under a licence from the bishop of London dated 4 August 1800.

168. Adamsdown House and lands were part of the estate of Henry Hollier. In 1811 the property was purchased by the Marquess of Bute.

169. The Charge is printed in George Hardinge, *The miscellaneous works*, (London, 1818), vol.I.

170. A reference to the Merthyr 'grain riots' of September 1800.

171. The address is printed in Hardinge, op.cit.

172. Rev. G.M. Maber. See Biographical Notes.

173. William Nicholl. See Biographical Notes.

174. William Henry Cavendish, 3rd Duke of Portland (1738–1809), Home Secretary 1794–1801. See *DNB*.

175. William Jeffreys, portreeve of Swansea 1804.

176. Cyprean, i.e. Cyprian: a licentious person, a prostitute.

177. Colonel Thomas Morgan.

178. Henry Hollier.

179. John Poulett, 4th Earl Poulett (1756–1819), lord lieutenant of Somerset.

180. Carno lands, leased to the Dowlais Iron Company by Lady Windsor in 1752. See John Davies, 'The Dowlais lease', *Morgannwg*, XII (1968), pp. 37–66.

181. i.e. committed to an asylum. Dr Francis Willis, proprietor of a private 'madhouse' in Lincolnshire, earned national recognition for his attendance on the King during his periodic bouts of 'insanity'.

182. Sir John Scott, 1st Earl of Eldon (1751–1838), lord chancellor. See *DNB*.

183. 3 John 16, 'For God so loved the world, that he gave his only begotten Son ...'.

184. Funnon Tave (= Ffynnon Taf): Taffs Well.

185. Attornment: the legal acknowledgement of a new landlord by a tenant. The need for any formal deed of attornment was abolished by statute in 1705 (4 Anne c.16).

186. An ingenious attempt by Rous to evade the imposition of the toll on corn payable to the clerk of the market and due to the Corporation.

187. Father of the diarist (d.1815).

188. Thomas Edwards of Llandaff. See Biographical Notes.

189. Youngest son of the 1st Marquess of Bute. He married Lady Amelia Mason-Villiers, daughter of the 4th Earl of Grandison.

Biographical Notes

THE FOLLOWING brief notes are intended merely to put individuals who figure regularly or prominently in the Diaries into a family context and to elucidate events and activities described by Bird. They are not intended to be comprehensive biographies, for which the reader is referred to entries in the *Dictionary of National Biography (DNB)*, *Dictionary of Welsh Biography (DWB)*, *Complete Peerage (CP)*, *History of Parliament (Hist. Parl.)*, and other works.

The places mentioned are in Glamorgan unless otherwise stated.

Ashurst, William Henry (1725–1807), Judge of the King's Bench. His charge to the Grand Jury of Middlesex, 10 Nov. 1792, was delivered soon after the September massacres in France. In it he attacked the doctrines of the French Revolutionaries and their supporters, praised the English system of government and counselled support of that system. The Charge was printed by the Society for Preserving Liberty and Property against Republicans and Levellers. *DNB*.

Aubrey, Richard (1744–1808), of Ash Hall. The youngest son of Sir Thomas Aubrey, 5th baronet, of Llantrithyd, he was lieutenant-colonel of the Glamorgan Militia (cavalry) and a deputy-lieutenant of the county. Through his wife, Frances Digby, he was related to Herbert Mackworth of Gnoll (q.v.). His eldest brother, Sir John Aubrey M.P. (1739–1826), was a lawyer, a Radical and member of the notorious Hellfire Club. Richard Aubrey was buried at Llantrithyd.

Aubrey family of Ynyscedwyn, Breconshire. Richard Gough of Ynyscedwyn, a descendant of the Awbrey *alias* Aubrey family, was a captain in the Glamorgan Militia in 1793. The son of William Gough of Ynyscedwyn, he assumed the additional surname of Aubrey and in 1797, under that name, was commissioned a brevet major in the 'Royal Glamorganshire Battalion of Militia'. He was a deputy-lieutenant of Glamorgan, and sheriff of Breconshire in 1807. Both his uncle, the Rev. James Gough Aubrey (who married Eleanor Williams of Aberpergwm), and his brother, the Rev. Fleming Gough (Aubrey), served as rector of Ystradgynlais, Breconshire.

Bacon, Anthony (d. 1827), of Cyfarthfa and Aberaman. The eldest son of Anthony Bacon (d. 1786), the founder of the Cyfarthfa, Plymouth and Hirwaun ironworks. He relinquished Cyfarthfa to Richard Crawshay (q.v.), and his share in the Hirwaun Works to his brother Thomas. In 1794 he was living at Llandaff Court, and in 1806 purchased the Aberaman estate from the Mathew family. He died at Aberaman and was buried at Speen, Berkshire. His brother Thomas disposed of the Plymouth Works to Richard Hill (q.v.). *DWB*.

Bevan family of Neath. Several generations of this family practised as doctors and surgeons in Neath, including John Bevan, the son of Morgan Bevan of Abergavenny a supervisor of excise, and Richard Bevan, both of whom were in practice in the 1780s. Dr Richard Bevan junior of Gelligaled, Neath, pioneered a tramroad from Dinas to the Neath Canal in 1799, his brother John being associated with him in this enterprise. Both brothers were magistrates, and Richard was a deputy-lieutenant of the county.

Bew, William. Freeman of Cardiff (1789), Sergeant at Mace of the Corporation (1792 and 1795), and a churchwarden at St John's, Cardiff. Bew's multifarious appointments included those of bailiff of Kibbor, searcher at the Cardiff Custom House and supervisor of workmen on the Cardiff Castle estate in the 1790s.

Biedermann, John William (1767–1831), land surveyor and cartographer, of Tetbury, Gloucs. The son of H.A. Biedermann of Blankenburg am Hartz, he became a naturalised British subject in 1804. He and his son, John Edward Biedermann, worked extensively in England. In South Wales they are known for their valuation of the Merthyr Mawr estate and as agents to the Kemeys Tynte family of Cefn Mabli (q.v.).

Birt family of Wenvoe Castle. Peter Birt of Armin, Yorkshire, purchased Wenvoe Castle from the Thomas family in 1775, and rebuilt the mansion house. He died in June 1791 and was buried at Wenvoe, having been predeceased by his wife (1787), his son Peter (1788) and his daughter Mary, the wife of John Richards of Cardiff (1790). Of Peter Birt's surviving daughters, Ann married Robert Jenner of Doctors' Commons (q.v.), Jane married John Price of Llandaff and Llandough-juxta-Cowbridge (q.v.), and Judy married Sir John Nicholl of Merthyr Mawr.

Blannin, John . Cardiff Street Commissioner (1785) and a freeman of Cardiff (1787). Blannin was associated with William Prichard in a scheme for rebuilding a ruinous house near the quay, and was proprietor of a yard in Cardiff for the storage of iron brought down from the Merthyr ironworks. He was also the owner of vessels engaged in the shipment of iron.

Bradley, John . Bradley was an innholder and mail contractor, and was John Bird's predecessor as postmaster of Cardiff. Proprietor of the *Angel Hotel*, where he ran livery stables, and later of the *Cardiff Arms Inn* which became Cardiff's main posting inn and hostelry, he was also a substantial tenant of the Bute estate, leasing Splott farm, Adamsdown and Whitmore farms and land at Cathays. Bradley's Lane (off Park Place) derived its name from the family's Crockherbtown residence.

Bute (Stuart) family.

John, 1st Marquess of Bute (1744–1814). The son of the 3rd Earl of Bute (George III's prime minister), he was known during his father's lifetime as Lord Mountstuart. He was granted the title of Baron Cardiff in 1776, and on his father's death in 1792 he became 4th Earl of Bute. On 21 March 1796 he was granted a marquessate enjoying the titles of Viscount Mountjoy, Earl of Windsor and Marquess of the County of Bute. He was lord lieutenant of

Glamorgan 1772–93 and 1794–1814. His first wife was Charlotte Windsor, daughter and co-heiress of Herbert Lord Windsor, inheritor of the estates of the powerful Herbert family. His second wife was Fanny Coutts, daughter of the wealthy banker Thomas Coutts. Despite political aspirations, he never achieved prominence in politics, and his diplomatic career, occasioned by financial difficulties, was undistinguished. He died at Geneva in November 1814, aged 70, and was buried in the family vault at Roath alongside his first wife.

John, Lord Mountstuart (1767–1794). The eldest son of the 1st Marquess, he was known as Lord Mountstuart from 1792 until his death. He represented the Glamorgan boroughs in Parliament 1790–94 and was lord lieutenant of Glamorgan 1793–94. He married Lady Elizabeth Crichton in 1792 and died two years later leaving an infant son, John, and a pregnant wife who gave birth to a second son (Lord James Stuart) a few months after her husband's death. Lord Mountstuart's brothers, Evelyn James Stuart and William Stuart, succeeded him in the representation of the Glamorgan boroughs.

John, 2nd Marquess of Bute (1793–1848). He was brought up by his paternal grandfather the 1st Marquess, his widowed mother having died in 1797 and his grandmother in 1800, and was known by the title Earl of Windsor until he succeeded his grandfather in 1814. This Lord Bute is often referred to as 'the Creator of modern Cardiff'. He married first Lady Maria North (d. 1841) and secondly Lady Sophia Hastings. The son of the second marriage became the 3rd Marquess of Bute.

CP; *DWB*; John Davies, *Cardiff and the marquesses of Bute*.

Caldecott *(alias* **Caldecot**), 'Counsellor' Thomas (1744–1833), lawyer. A prominent member of the Oxford and South Wales circuits, he was Attorney General of the Brecknock Circuit 1789–1827. Caldecott was a book collector and Shakespearian student, and published two volumes of reports of cases concerning the office and duty of a justice of the peace. *DNB*.

Capper, Colonel James (1743–1825). After retiring from military service with the East India Company, Capper settled in Glamorgan where he pursued interests in meteorology and agriculture. He lived at Cathays House, where he was host to his son-in-law Robert Clutterbuck, the Hertfordshire historian, during the latter's tour of Glamorgan in 1799, and later moved to the Knap, Barry. He was active in local affairs as a capital burgess of Cardiff (1793), bailiff (1795), trustee of the Cardiff Turnpike District, and as a magistrate and deputy-lieutenant of Glamorgan. His various improvement schemes included proposals for the establishment of a school of industry for the poor children of Cardiff. Capper purchased lands under the terms of the Heath Enclosure Act, and also acquired lands at Fairoak from Henry Hollier which he later sold to the Marquess of Bute. He moved to Norfolk from South Wales and died there. His published works include a volume of *Meteorological and miscellaneous tracts*, printed and sold by J.D. Bird of Cardiff (1808), and *Observations on the* *cultivation of waste lands addressed to the gentlemen and farmers of Glamorganshire* (London, 1805). *DNB*.

Choiseul, Jean Baptiste, Marquis de. Choiseul was a French émigré and naturalised British subject who claimed kinship with Louis XV's minister, the Duc de Choiseul. He married Mary Dawkins the heiress of Kilvrough (Gower), and a minor, at Swansea in 1790. The marriage was later dissolved and in 1806 the Kilvrough estate was sold to Thomas Penrice.

Cockshutt, James, of Cyfarthfa, engineer. He was associated with David Tanner of Monmouth and others in the Cyfarthfa works 1784–86 but, when Tanner disposed of the works to Richard Crawshay, Cockshutt remained at Cyfarthfa. In December 1791 the partnership of Crawshay, Cockshutt and Stevens was dissolved, the entire shareholding being assigned to Crawshay. Cockshutt was also a shareholder in the Glamorganshire Canal.

Coffin, Walter (1784–1867), of Bridgend and Llandaff Court, coalowner. A descendant of the Price family of Tynton, Llangeinor, he was the son of Walter Coffin of Bridgend who invested the profits of his tannery business in land. Coffin was an industrial pioneer and coalowner who successfully marketed and exported Rhondda coal. He connected his colliery at Dinas to the tramroad and canal built by Dr Richard Griffiths (q.v.). He was M.P. for Cardiff 1852–57. *DWB*.

Crawshay family of Cyfarthfa, ironmasters. Three generations of the Crawshay family were alive in the years covered by John Bird's diaries:

Richard Crawshay (1739–1810). One of the chief promoters of the Glamorganshire Canal, he took control of the Cyfarthfa Works in 1794, and built a new residence 'Cyfarthfa House' near the Works in 1798. His nephews Joseph and Crawshay Bailey were actively involved in the management of Cyfarthfa. A deputy-lieutenant of the county. He was buried at Llandaff Cathedral.

William Crawshay I (1764–1834). Little involved in the management of Cyfarthfa, he left the running of the Works to his son, William II, and directed the business from London. He died at Stoke Newington, Middlesex.

William Crawshay II (1788–1867), the 'Iron King'. Sheriff of Glamorgan in 1829. He managed the Cyfarthfa and Hirwaun Works, and acquired additional Works at Treforest and elsewhere. He built Cyfarthfa Castle and also erected a mansion on his Caversham Park estate, Oxfordshire. He and his brother Richard married two sisters, Elizabeth and Mary Homfray. *DWB*; J.P. Addis, *The Crawshay dynasty* (Cardiff, 1957); M.S. Taylor, *The Crawshays of Cyfarthfa Castle* (London, 1967).

Dadford family, engineers. Thomas Dadford and his sons were engineers and surveyors for the Glamorganshire and other Canal projects in South Wales. Charles Hadfield, *The Canals of South Wales and the Border* (Cardiff, 1960).

Davy, Phillip, of Cardiff, baker and grocer. Constable of Cardiff in 1786. Lessee of a house adjoining the Castle wall in Shoemaker Street. He and Jonathan Davy, grocer, were declared bankrupts in 1792.

Deere, Reynold Thomas (*c*.1749–1815), of Penllyne Court. A barrister at law and a deputy-lieutenant of the county. The son of James Thomas of Garth, he assumed the surname of Deere on succeeding to the Penllyne Court estate under the will of his great uncle and godfather, Reynold Deere (d. 1764).

Edmondes family of Cowbridge, St Hilary and Llandough. They were in origin attorneys and estate stewards to the Aubrey family of Llantrithyd. Colonel Thomas Edmondes of the 1st Regiment of Footguards was the younger son of Thomas Edmondes who had purchased the St. Hilary (Beaupre) estate in 1755. Col. Thomas Edmondes was a deputy-lieutenant of the county. He and his brother John (d. 1778), both lived at Llandough Castle as tenants of the Margam estate.

Edwards, Thomas (1716–1794), of Llandaff House. Lawyer. Clerk of the Peace for Glamorgan 1763–94. Steward to the Cardiff Castle (Windsor, later Bute) estate for thirty years, *c*.1758–88. He was the son of William Edwards of Monmouth Castle, solicitor, and grandson of Gabriel Powell of Swansea (q.v.). His first wife was Elizabeth Richards of the Corner House, Cardiff, and his second Mary (née Powell) the widow of Thomas Roberts of Llandaff. He inherited the Llandaff estate from his second wife and rebuilt Llandaff House. He had two sons, William (b. 1744), who died young, and Powell who took holy orders and became rector of Neath. His daughter Jane married William Richards of Cardiff (q.v.) and provided the eventual heirs to her father's estates. A keen antiquarian, Thomas Edwards compiled a history of Glamorgan and genealogies of the county families.

Edwin *see* Wyndham.

Evans, Herbert (1750–1830), of Eaglesbush, Briton Ferry. A descendant of Walter Evans of Eaglesbush who married Mary Evans of Gnoll in 1666. He was a deputy-lieutenant of Glamorgan, a magistrate of the county and a burgess of Neath.

Franklen, John (1734–1824). He came to the Vale of Glamorgan in the 1760s from the Swansea area as steward to the Llanmihangel estate, an office he filled for over fifty years. He was a founder, first treasurer and secretary of the Glamorganshire Agricultural Society (1772), and was active in societies for the promotion of new turnpike roads. He married Susan Durel, daughter of the headmaster of Cowbridge School. In 1766 he purchased the Candleston estate for himself and his heirs. His son, Thomas Franklen, married Ann Crawshay of Cyfarthfa and his grandson married into the Mansel Talbot family of Margam.

Glascott family of Cardiff. Thomas Glascott of Cardiff (will 1780), a saddler, was part owner of the sloop 'Nancy' trading with the West Country. His eldest son, William, a currier, was a burgess of Cardiff (1780) and a churchwarden of St John's. William Glascott married Sarah Malcott (d. 1762), daughter of a Bristol brass founder. Several members of the family are commemorated by memorial tablets in St John's church, Cardiff. In 1830 a Mrs Mary Glascott was associated with her sons in establishing the Cambrian Copper Works at Llanelli.

Goodrich family of Energlyn, Caerphilly. The Goodriches were members of a family which returned to England from Virginia on the secession of the American colonies in 1775 and settled in Devonshire. John Goodrich purchased the Energlyn estate from the descendants of Roger Powell (q.v.) in 1775 for £7,000, and was sheriff of Glamorgan in 1799. By his will dated 28 November 1815 John Goodrich, who was then living in Bristol, left his estate to his sons William Goodrich of Wootton House (Gloucestershire) and the Rev. Bartlett Goodrich of Great Saling, Essex. John Goodrich and his sons all served as deputy lieutenants of Glamorgan.

Gough *see* Aubrey.

Gould, Sir Charles (afterwards Morgan) (1726–1806), Judge Advocate General. M.P. for Brecon borough and county. He married Jane Morgan, heiress of Tredegar, Monmouthshire, and on being created a baronet in 1792 assumed the surname and arms of Morgan. His eldest son, Sir Charles Morgan (1760–1846) succeeded to the baronetcy. One of his daughters, Jane, married Samuel Homfray of Penydarren (q.v.). *DNB; Hist. Parl.*

Griffiths, Dr Richard (1756–1826), surgeon and man-midwife. The son of William Griffiths of Gellifendigaid, Llanwonno. He practised medicine in Cardiff with his partner, Dr Richard Reece (q.v.), and was also coroner of Cardiff. As an industrial speculator he acquired a considerable mineral estate in Llanwonno, Llantrisant and Ystradyfodwg, and he constructed the 'Doctor's Canal' and tramroad from Hafod to Treforest, thereby providing an outlet for the emergent coal industry. Contentious by nature, he was involved in numerous lawsuits (see Appendix A). After his death the bulk of his estate passed to his nephews, Thomas and George Thomas of Llanbradach and Ystrad Mynach (q.v.). *DWB.*

Guest family of Dowlais. Thomas Guest (d. 1807) succeeded his father John Guest (d. 1787) as manager of the Dowlais Ironworks and as a shareholder in the Company. His son, Sir Josiah John Guest (1785–1852) took over the management in 1807 and by inheritance and purchase acquired the entire shareholding of the Company. Thomas Guest's sister Sarah married William Taitt (q.v.). *DWB.*

Gwinnet, Miss Emilia (d. 1807), of Cottrell. She inherited the Cottrell estate from her brother, the Rev. Samuel Gwinnet (d. 1792), curate of St Nicholas, and was bequeathed the Penllyne estate by her friend, Lady Vernon (d. 1786).

Hardinge, George (1743–1816), judge. Solicitor General (1782), Attorney General to Queen Charlotte (1794) and Tory M.P. for Sarum. Hardinge succeeded John Williams as senior judge of the Brecknock Circuit of the Great Sessions and made his first appearance as judge at the August Sessions held at Cowbridge in 1787. He was the 'waggish Welsh judge' of Byron's *Don Juan*. An Author, F.S.A. and F.R.S., his collected works were published in three volumes in 1818. *DNB.*

Harford, James, of Melingriffith (Whitchurch) and Bristol. One of a group of Quaker ironmasters from Bristol who leased the Melingriffith Works from Lady Windsor in 1770. In addition to the iron and tinplate works at Melingriffith, Harford, Partridge and Co. were also associated with the Monmouthshire ironworks at Nantyglo and Ebbw Vale, and with the Caerphilly furnace.

Hill, Richard (d. 1806), of Merthyr Tydfil, ironmaster. Hill was manager of the Plymouth Ironworks for Anthony Bacon (d. 1786), and was in possession of the Works by 1803. He was elected a burgess of Cardiff in 1784. He was involved in litigation with the Glamorganshire Canal Company in 1794 over water taken from the river Taff, and was awarded damages. His eldest son, Richard (1773–1844) moved to Llandaff in 1818, and his daughter, Mary, married John Nathaniel Miers of Cadoxton Lodge (sheriff 1808). *DWB.*

Hollier, Henry (d. 1830), Bute estate steward. Hollier was chief steward of the Bute estate from 1784 until his dismissal from office in 1815. He was also an alderman and bailiff of Cardiff, town clerk of Cardiff 1786–89 and collector of customs for the port of Cardiff. As Receiver General of Taxes for Glamorgan he was accused of defaulting in his payments and was prosecuted by the Crown. He served as Clerk of the Peace for Glamorgan 1795–97 and was clerk of the General Meeting in 1802. Hollier lived at Cathays and later at Adamsdown House. In 1811 Adamsdown House and lands were purchased by the Marquess of Bute.

Homfray family of Penydarren.

Sir Jeremiah Homfray (1759–1833) was proprietor, with his brother Samuel, of the Penydarren Ironworks at Merthyr, but gave up his share in the management of the Works in 1789. He married Mary, daughter of John Richards of Llandaff (q.v.), and lived at Llandaff House. He was sheriff of Glamorgan in 1809, and was a deputy-lieutenant of the county.

Samuel Homfray (1763–1822) was proprietor, with his brother Jeremiah, of the Penydarren Ironworks. He was one of the chief promoters of the Glamorganshire Canal and of the tramroad from Penydarren to Navigation. He married Jane, daughter of Sir Charles Gould Morgan of Tredegar Park, Monmouthshire (q.v.), and in 1800 became a partner in the Tredegar Ironworks. He brought a suit against Dr Richard Griffiths at the Hereford Assizes in 1791 for alleged fraud at cards (see Appendix A). His son, John, was sheriff of Glamorgan in 1843 and purchased the Penllyne Castle estate in 1847. *DWB.*

Howell, Thomas, of Caerphilly. A Bute estate bailiff and minor official in the manor of Senghennydd.

Hurst family of Gabalfa and Dinas Powys. William Hurst, sheriff of Glamorgan in 1776, married one of the heiresses of the Herbert family of the Friars and thereby acquired a moiety of that family's estates in Cardiff and Swansea. The other moiety was inherited by his cousin Calvert Richard Jones of Swansea (q.v.) through his wife. William Hurst was the 'Old Mr. Hurst of

Dynaspowis' described as blind and insane by Bird in 1801. His son Herbert Hurst, 'Mr. Hurst junior', married Mary Ann Wrixon daughter of Robert Wrixon of Corntown, Llandaff and Penarth. The Hursts disposed of their interest in the Friars estate to their cousin C.R. Jones, but retained Gabalfa as a prospective residence for Mary Ann Hurst during her widowhood. In 1805 Gabalfa passed into the hands of the Wood family (q.v.) and in 1809 it was sold to Sir Robert Lynch-Blosse. The Dinas Powys estate remained in the possession of the Hurst family until 1822 when, on the death of Herbert Hurst without issue, it descended to the Lee family.

Hussey, John, of Cardiff (fl. 1790s). A boot and shoemaker by trade, he served as Master in the Guild of Cordwainers and Glovers and was also an alderman and bailiff of Cardiff, and a churchwarden of St John's.

Jeffreys family of Swansea and Brecon. The Jeffreys were bankers, lawyers and businessmen. Gabriel, William and John Jeffreys were all aldermen and portreeves of Swansea in the 1780s and 1790s. Gabriel Jeffreys was county treasurer of Glamorgan (discharged in 1785). Gabriel Jeffreys of Brecon assisted in the management of the Ynysygerwn estate during the minority of John Llewelyn (q.v.) in the 1750s. Walter Jeffreys of Brecon, banker, was associated with the Wilkins family of Brecon. (q.v.).

Jenkins family of Pantynawel (Llangeinor) and Llanharan. Richard Jenkins of Pantynawel was sheriff of Glamorgan in 1788. His son Richard Hoare Jenkins purchased part of the estate of Thomas Edwards deceased in 1802, and in 1806 bought Llanharan House and lands from the daughters of the Rev. Gervase Powell.

Jenner, Robert (1743–1810), of Wenvoe, Sheriff of Glamorgan in 1800. A lawyer and advocate of Doctors' Commons, he married Ann Birt of Wenvoe Castle. He was the son of the Venerable Charles Jenner, prebend of Lincoln.

John, Joseph, of Llantrisant, carrier. Joseph John was a prominent figure in Llantrisant parish affairs from the 1770s to the 1790s. He was agent for the Rev. Gervase Powell of Llanharan, a major landowner in Llantrisant. He was frequently in conflict with the Rev. Robert Rickards (q.v.), by whom he was accused of attempted violence. He and his supporters accused Rickards of persecution. As treasurer of the parish workhouse he was accused of embezzlement. In 1792 John was convicted at Great Sessions for assault and perjury, sentenced to transportation and imprisoned in Cardiff gaol. Roy Denning, 'The devil had a share: the destruction of Joseph John', *Glamorgan Historian,* vol. 5 (1968), pp.110-120.

Jones, Calvert Richard, of Veranda, Swansea. The son of Calvert Jones senior and his wife Elizabeth, one of the heiresses of the Friars estate of the Herbert family, he was a cousin of Herbert Hurst of Gabalfa (q.v.) from whom he purchased the Friars estate in 1791. In 1793 the heavily mortgaged Friars estate was sold to the Marquess of Bute for £19,000. He was involved in colliery enterprises at Swansea.

Jones, John, of Bristol and Cardiff, merchant. The owner of Long Cross, Cardiff, in 1793. His daughter married Henry Cunniff 'a West Indian merchant' about 1794. He is tentatively identified as a descendant (possibly a son) of John Jones of Bristol, ironmaster, one of the original partners in the Dowlais Iron Company.

Jones, Robert (1738–93) of Fonmon spent considerable sums on the alteration and embellishment of Fonmon Castle. He took refuge from his creditors in France in 1784. In 1792 severe financial difficulties compelled him to sell some of his properties, the purchasers including the Marquess of Bute and Robert Rous (q.v.). Robert Jones married first Jane Seys, the heiress of Boverton, and secondly Joanna Lloyd, daughter of a Cardiff attorney. He was a deputy-lieutenant of the county. On his death the Fonmon estate passed to his eldest son:

Robert Jones (1773–1834). Sheriff of Glamorgan in 1801 (in place of Llewelyn Traherne of St. Hilary who was excused). He died unmarried and is remembered particularly for his interest in horses and horse-racing. His sister Diana married John Richards of Energlyn and Cardiff (q.v.).

Jones, Stephen, of Swansea and Merthyr Mawr. The inheritor, with his brother Thomas and sister Ann, of the Merthyr Mawr estate of their half-brother Charles Bowen (d. 1787). In 1802, after protracted litigation with his brother's widow, Catherine Richardson, over his inheritance, he sold the Merthyr Mawr estate to Sir John Nicholl, one of the trustees.

Kemeys family of Newport (Monmouthshire) and Ynysarwed. William Kemeys (d. 1807 aged 76) was sheriff of Glamorgan in 1783. His first wife Catherine was the widow of John Llewelyn of Ynysygerwn. The family was distantly related to the Kemeys-Tynte family of Cefn Mabli. *DWB.*

Key family of St Fagans and Cardiff. Thomas Key, agent for the St Fagans estate of the Earl of Plymouth 1784–99, lived at Pentrebane, St Fagans. He failed to render an account of his stewardship to the estate trustees on the death of the Earl in 1799, was dismissed from office and absconded leaving outstanding debts of £7,000. His brother John Key, who leased property in Ely and Cardiff from the Plymouth estate, surrendered his leaseholds in part satisfaction of his brother's debts in 1799. Members of the Key family were involved in a variety of business enterprises. Thomas Key was a haulier with waggons transporting goods between Cardiff and Merthyr. John Key was associated with a coal level at Duffryn Ffrwd.

Knight, Colonel Henry (d. 1825), of Tythegston. Sheriff of Glamorgan in 1794, a deputy-lieutenant of the county, and a colonel in the Glamorgan Militia. He died without issue, and was succeeded by his nephew, the Rev. Robert Knight, rector of Newton Nottage.

Knight, John, of Barnstaple (Devonshire) and Duffryn (Aberdare). He married Margaret Bruce of Llanblethian and Duffryn, and was trustee for his son

John Bruce Knight (later Bruce Pryce), of the Duffryn Aberdare estate which the latter inherited from his uncle, the Rev. Thomas Bruce (d. 1790). Hilary M. Thomas, 'Duffryn Aberdare', *Morgannwg,* XXI (1977), pp. 9-41.

Landeg family of Swansea and Carmarthenshire. Colonel Roger Landeg, businessman and shipowner, was one of the founders of the Glamorganshire Bank in 1771. Lieutenant-colonel John Landeg commanded the Swansea Royal Volunteers in 1797.

Leigh, Capel Hanbury (1776–1861), of Pontypool, Monmouthshire. The son of John Hanbury of Pontypool, he assumed the additional surname of Leigh in 1797. He married Molly Ann (née Miers) the widow of Sir Robert Mackworth of Gnoll (q.v.). Capel Hanbury Leigh was an industrialist and a landowner.

Lewis family of Newhouse, Llanishen and Greenmeadow.

William Lewis of the Pentyrch Forge (d. 1810) was the son of Thomas Lewis of Newhouse (sheriff of Glamorgan 1757), one of the original partners in the Dowlais Iron Company and the founder, with Nicholas Price (q.v.) of the Pentyrch Works. He was also a partner, with William Taitt (q.v.), in the Dowlais Company. William Lewis was sheriff of Glamorgan in 1790. His brother, the Rev. Wyndham Lewis of Newhouse, married Mary Price of Tynton. His sister, Eleanor, married Dr Bloom Williams of Cardiff (q.v.).

Henry Lewis of Greenmeadow (1774–1838) was the son of the Rev. Wyndham Lewis and Mary Price. He was an army officer. His elder brother Thomas married into the Goodrich family of Energlyn (q.v.). His younger brother Wyndham, M.P. for Cardiff and Maidstone, married Mary Ann Evans, later Viscountess Beaconsfield.

Wyndham Lewis of Llanishen (1752–1835), lawyer and industrialist, was the son of Thomas Lewis (sheriff of Glamorgan in 1745) and a cousin to the Lewises of Newhouse. He was sheriff of Glamorgan in 1795, a deputy-lieutenant of the county and a captain in the Glamorgan Militia. Wyndham Lewis sold his Maendy estate to the 1st Marquess of Bute in 1804, and his estates in Llanishen and Aberdare to the 2nd Marquess in 1826.

Llewellin (Llewelyn) family of Penllergaer and Ynysygerwn. John Llewellin of Ynysygerwn, sheriff of Glamorgan in 1792, inherited the Penllergaer estate from Griffith Price, a distant cousin. His daughter Mary married Lewis Weston Dillwyn, the Swansea businessman, naturalist and owner of the Cambrian Pottery. He commanded the Glamorgan Militia (infantry), and was involved in disputes with Colonel Aubrey (q.v.) over the respective merits of cavalry and infantry forces. He was a deputy-lieutenant of the county.

Llewellin, John, of Great House, Welsh St Donats. Sheriff of Glamorgan in 1789. He was the son of Thomas Llewellin and nephew of John Llewellin of Coedriglan. His sister, who married Edmund Traherne of Castellau (q.v.) collector and deputy comptroller of customs at Cardiff, inherited Coedriglan from her uncle.

Llewellyn family of Margam and Baglan. Hopkin Llewellyn senior

(1724–1811) was steward to the Margam estate of the Mansel Talbot family for over thirty years. He was father of Hopkin Llewellyn junior, attorney, who committed suicide in 1797, and of Griffith Llewellyn (1767–1822), attorney and Margam estate steward from 1798 until his death. Hopkin Llewellyn senior was coroner of the county with Dr Richard Griffiths (q.v.). Hilary M. Thomas, 'Margam estate management', *Glamorgan historian*, vol. 6 (1969), pp. 127-147.

Lockwood, Thomas, of Lower Forest and Danygraig, Swansea. A businessman and industrialist, he was co-partner with the Rev. Edward Lockwood, John Morris of Clasemont (q.v.) and others in the Forest Copper Works, Llangyfelach.

Lord, Major Hugh, of Bideford (Devonshire), Aberaman and Llandaff. He acquired part of the Aberaman estate by his marriage with Eleanor Mathew, daughter and co-heiress of Edward Mathew of Aberaman, and was related by marriage to the Gwynne family of Buckland, Breconshire.

Lowder, Rev. Samuel Molyneux (d. 1798), Vicar of Cardiff. Son of Thomas Lowder of Bristol. He studied at St John's College, Oxford, acquiring the degrees of B.A. (1759), M.A. (1763) and B.D. (1768). He became vicar of Cardiff in 1777. Lowder was the first president of the Cardiff Sympathetic Society, of which his widow was the first annuitant. He was involved in a dispute with his parishioners over the refurbishment of St John's church in 1791. He corresponded with Judge George Hardinge (q.v.), and one of his letters on the state of the gaol in Cardiff was published in 1789.

Maber, Rev. George Martin (d. 1844), Rector of Merthyr Tydfil. A magistrate and deputy-lieutenant of Glamorgan. He was appointed to the living of Merthyr in 1795 by the Marquess of Bute. His relationship to Thomas Maber the Neath printer has not been established.

Mackworth, Sir Herbert (1732–1791), of Gnoll. Industrialist, banker and agricultural improver. F.R.S. Steward of Cardiff Corporation 1759, Constable of Cardiff Castle 1766. He represented the Glamorgan boroughs in Parliament from 1766 to 1790 when he was displaced by the Cardiff Castle nominee. He was a lieutenant-colonel in the Glamorgan Militia, and a deputy-lieutenant of the county. His death from blood-poisoning is recorded by John Bird. His son, Sir Robert Humphrey Mackworth, survived his father by only three years. Sir Robert's widow married Capel Hanbury Leigh (q.v.). *DWB; Hist. Parl.*

Martin, Edward, of Llansamlet and Morriston, mineral engineer and surveyor. His 'Description of the mineral basin in the counties of Glamorgan, Monmouth, Brecknock, Carmarthen and Pembroke' was published in the *Philosophical transactions of the Royal Society* in 1806. He worked on canal projects in South Wales including those of Swansea, Penclawdd, Kidwelly and Llanelli.

Mathew, Anthony (d. 1825), of Leckwith and Whitchurch. The son of Thomas Mathew of Leckwith, a descendant of the Mathew family of Radyr and Llandaff, he acted as estate steward for his kinsman, the Earl of Llandaff. After his marriage to Anne Morgan, widow, in 1801, he lived at Ty Mawr, Whitchurch, and was overseer of the poor, highway surveyor and land tax assessor for Whitchurch parish.

Mathews, Thomas, of Llandaff Court. Sheriff of Glamorgan in 1769. A grandson of Admiral Thomas Mathews who built Llandaff Court *c*.1759, he married Diana Jones of Fonmon. *DWB.*

Morgan family of Tredegar (Monmouthshire) and Ruperra. With the death of John Morgan of the Dderw (Breconshire) in 1792 the male line of this family became extinct. The heiress of Tredegar was Jane Morgan who married Sir Charles Gould (q.v.). The son of this marriage was Sir Charles Morgan, M.P. (1760–1846). The Morgan family had acquired Ruperra at the end of the seventeenth century and the house provided a residence for younger sons in succeeding centuries. *DWB.*

Morgan, William (d.1791, aged 77), of Pengam, Roath. The son of Edward Morgan of Pentwyn, Whitchurch, he was pre-deceased by his wife Jane and six children. After the death of his only surviving daughter in 1819 his kinsman Henry Morgan, and others of the same family, continued the tenancy of Pengam.

Morrice, William and Thomas, surveyors. These surveyors and cartographers, who worked extensively in Glamorgan and Monmouthshire from the 1760s to the 1790s, were probably brothers. Among the Glamorgan estates mapped by them were Llanbradach, Wenvoe Castle and Penllyne. In 1785 William Morrice was commissioned to survey the limits of the parishes of St John and St Mary, Cardiff.

Morris, John (1745–1819), of Clasemont and Sketty Park. Sheriff of Glamorgan in 1803. The son of the industrialist Robert Morris (d.1768) who developed the copperworks at Landore, he was responsible with his father for the erection of Morris Castle to house their workpeople and for the development of Morriston. He was associated with the Lockwoods (q.v.) in the Forest Copperworks. John Morris was created a baronet in 1806. His elder brother, Robert (1743–93), a barrister who pleaded on the South Wales circuit, was a prominent Radical in London in the 1760s and 1770s. Robert Morris's career was punctuated by a series of scandals, including elopement with his young ward and involvement in duels, and by frequent exiles abroad. *DNB;* J.E. Ross (ed.), *Radical adventurer: the diaries of Robert Morris 1772–1774* (Bath, 1971); Wyn Jones, 'Robert Morris, the Swansea friend of John Wilkes', *Glamorgan historian,* vol. 11 (1975), pp. 126-136.

Moysey, Abel (1743–1831), judge. Moysey was the second judge of the Brecknock circuit, 1777–1819, a commissioner of bankrupts, 1771–74, and Tory M.P. for Bath, 1774–90. He was also an official of the Court of Exchequer. *DNB; Hist. Parl.*

Nicholl, 'Counsellor' William (1751–1828). Barrister at law and a bencher of the Middle Temple. He was the son of Whitlock Nicholl of Ham, Llantwit Major, the brother of Edward Nicholl of Llanblethian and a cousin of Sir John Nicholl of Merthyr Mawr, the eminent lawyer. He succeeded Sir Herbert Mackworth (q.v.) as steward of Cardiff Corporation and was mayor of Cowbridge. He was buried, with his wife Frances, in Cowbridge churchyard.

Paley, Rev. William (1743–1805), Archdeacon of Carlisle. A prominent churchman who played an active role in the anti-slavery movement and published a number of pamphlets on that subject. He wrote numerous works on morality and is best remembered for his *Evidences of Christianity* (1794). *DNB.*

Plummer, 'Counsellor' Sir Thomas (1753–1824). He was called to the bar in 1778 and enjoyed a distinguished legal career. A member of the Oxford and South Wales circuits, he was appointed a judge on the Anglesey circuit in 1805, and later became Solicitor General and Master of the Rolls. *DNB.*

Plymouth, Earl of. Other Hickman Windsor, 5th Earl of Plymouth (1751–99), married the Hon. Sarah Archer (d.1838). The only son of the marriage was Other Archer, 6th Earl (1789–1833). *CP.*

Portland, Duke of. William Henry Cavendish Bentinck, 3rd Duke of Portland (1738–1809), a prominent statesman; Home Secretary 1794–1801. *DNB; CP.*

Powell, Gabriel (1710–89), of Swansea. The son of Gabriel Powell (1676–1735), whom he succeeded as steward to the Beaufort estate at Swansea. He was a lawyer, magistrate, burgess, alderman and portreeve of Swansea. He was also recorder and solicitor to the Corporation of Swansea, and a deputy-lieutenant of the county. He wielded great power as steward of the borough, and was known as 'King of Swansea'. His third son, Gabriel, lived at Heathfield Lodge, Swansea. Tom Ridd, 'Gabriel Powell; the uncrowned king of Swansea', *Glamorgan historian,* vol. 5 (1968), pp. 152-160.

Powell family of Energlyn. Roger Powell, sheriff of Glamorgan in 1707, and his son (d.1751) were the last male representatives of this family. On the latter's death Energlyn was inherited by William Richards (son of William Richards of Cardiff (q.v.), and his wife Jane Powell) who assumed the name of Powell. Jane's sister Ann married Lewis Morgan of Whitchurch, and the son of that marriage, Edward Morgan, was a claimant to his cousin's estate. After litigation Energlyn was secured to Captain John Richards of Cardiff (q.v.), brother-in-law and cousin of W.P. Richards. Captain Richards sold the estate to John Goodrich (q.v.).

Price family of Pontypandy, Caerphilly. Nicholas Price of Pontypandy (d.1757), proprietor of Pentyrch Ironworks, was the father of Nicholas Price of Pontypandy and Porset (d.1764), William Price (d.1788), and others. William's son, William Price of Ivy House, Tongwynlais, died unmarried in 1821 aged 56.

Price family of Tynton (Llangeinor), Park (St Fagans) and of Llandaff Court and Llandough Castle. John Price (d.1818) was the son of Samuel Price of Tynton and his wife Catherine Williams of Park, and nephew of the philosopher, Dr Richard Price. He married Jane Birt of Wenvoe Castle. His sister and eventual heiress, Mary Price, married the Rev. Wyndham Lewis of Newhouse (q.v.). He lived at Llandaff Court and subsequently at Llandough Castle, near Cowbridge, which he leased from the Margam estate. Whilst resident at Llandough he expended large sums in extending and improving the property. He was a colonel in the Glamorgan Volunteers and a deputy-lieutenant of the county.

Price family of Watford and Pwllypant, Caerphilly. William Price (d. 1800) was an army captain and a magistrate. The son of Thomas Price, one of the original partners in the Dowlais Iron Company, he married Grace Lewis of Newhouse. He died at Pwllypant, having sold the Watford estate soon after his father's death. The Prices of Watford were a branch of the Pontypandy family of the same name and were also related to the Prices of Tynton.

Reece, Dr Richard (1772–1850), of Cardiff. A native of Usk (Monmouthshire) he became a surgeon, apothecary and man-midwife in partnership with Dr Richard Griffiths (q.v.) in Cardiff. He later became an alderman of Cardiff, and was mayor in 1840 and 1846. He was a keen book collector and an F.S.A. His wife was Elizabeth Llewellin of Stockland, St Fagans, who is commemorated with her husband on a memorial in St John's church, Cardiff. J.A. Bradney, *A history of Monmouthshire,* Vol. III, p. 36.

Richards family of Cardiff and Llandaff — Cardiff's leading gentry family in the late eighteenth century.

John Richards, senior, known as Captain Richards (d.1793 aged 60) was of Cardiff and Llandaff Court, and also of Energlyn which he inherited from his wife's brother. He was a descendant of Michael Richards (1672–1729), clerk of the peace for Glamorgan and town clerk of Cardiff. He was sheriff of Glamorgan in 1784, and was also a bailiff of Cardiff and a captain in the Glamorgan Militia. He married first his cousin, Jane Richards, and secondly Elizabeth Priest of Cardiff. Among his children were John Richards junior, Edward Priest Richards (see below) and Mary Anne Richards, who married Sir Jeremiah Homfray (q.v.). He died after a long illness described as 'lingering gout'.

John Richards, junior, (*c*.1768–1819), of Llandaff Court, was living with his father in Cardiff in 1790 (see Appendix A), in which year he is also described as 'of Energlyn'. He married Catherine Diana Jones of Fonmon, and was devisee under the terms of the will of his cousin, William Richards Powell (see Powell family of Energlyn).

Edward Priest Richards (1792–1867), solicitor, took over the law practice of Wyndham Lewis (q.v.). An opponent of the entrenched power of the Wood family (q.v.), he became county treasurer and agent to the Cardiff Castle estate.

John Richards (1746–1824), of Corner House (No 1 St Mary Street), Cardiff, was a descendant of William Richards (brother of Michael Richards, clerk of the peace). He was sheriff of Glamorgan in 1791. He married Mary Birt (d.1790) of Wenvoe Castle, and their daughter Anna Maria married John Homfray of Penllyne. He was buried in St John's church, Cardiff. The elder brother of John Richards of Corner House was William Richards who died in 1780 aged 34. Their aunt, Elizabeth Richards, married Thomas Edwards of Llandaff, clerk of the peace (q.v.).

Richardson, Samuel (*c*.1738–1824), of Hensol Castle. Sheriff of Glamorgan in 1798. Richardson purchased the Hensol Castle estate from Earl Talbot in 1789, and sold it to Benjamin Hall in 1815. He was the founder of a bank in Cardiff and was a noted agricultural improver. He came originally from Newent in Gloucestershire.

Rickards, Rev. Robert (d. 1810), Vicar of Llantrisant. Rickards was vicar of Llantrisant from 1767 until his death. During his incumbency two distinct interests formed in the parish, the one headed by Rickards and Edmund Traherne of Castellau (q.v.), the other by the Rev. Gervase Powell of Llanharan and John Popkin of Talygarn. He was involved in a long feud with Joseph John (q.v.) whose activities brought him and the parish frequently before the justices. The Rickards family was the mainstay of Bute influence in Llantrisant. Richard Fowler Rickards was a deputy-lieutenant of the county in 1798. Roy Denning, 'The devil had a share', *Glamorgan historian,* vol. 5 (1968), pp. 110-120.

Rothley, Thomas (d.1798), of Bristol. A clerk and collector of dues on shipping at the Bristol Custom House. He acquired a quarter share in the Flat Holm lighthouse, of which he was already collector of dues, in 1755, and was actively involved in the management of the light until his death. He was buried at St Augustine's church Bristol. W.R. Chaplin, 'The history of Flat Holm lighthouse', *The American Neptune,* vol. 29 (1960).

Rous, Robert, of Cwrtyrala, Michaelston le Pit. Sheriff of Glamorgan in 1797. He purchased Cwrtyrala from Robert Jones of Fonmon (q.v.). He was the son of Thomas Rous of Piercefield (Monmouthshire) and brother of George Rous, M.P., barrister and Prothonotary for the Carmarthenshire circuit of Great Sessions.

Samuel, David (d.1829 aged 88), of Bonvilston. A landowner and magistrate. He married Jane, daughter of Morgan Williams of Pendoylan and Mary Thomas of Dyffryn Ffrwd, and was the father of John Samuel (1777–1845).

Stuart *see* Bute.

Taitt, William (1745–1815), ironmaster. Taitt was a partner in the Dowlais Iron Company and manager of the Works. He was the son-in-law of Thomas Guest (d.1787) and uncle of Sir Josiah John Guest (1785–1852). He was also associated with the Wood family (q.v.) in a banking enterprise at Cardiff and lived in Cardiff from 1791 until his death. Elizabeth Havill, 'William Taitt and the Dowlais Ironworks' *Transactions of the Hon. Society of Cymmrodorion,*

1983, pp. 97-114.

Talbot, Thomas Mansel (1747–1813), of Penrice and Margam. He initiated ambitious building schemes on his estates between 1770 and 1800, including a new mansion house at Penrice, an orangery at Margam (where the old house was demolished) and a coaching inn at Pyle. He was a collector and patron of the arts, a founder member of the Glamorganshire Agricultural Society, and was sheriff of the county in 1782. He married Lady Mary Lucy Fox-Strangways, daughter of the Earl of Ilchester. (Her second husband was Sir Christopher Cole, M.P.) His cousin William Davenport Talbot of Lacock, Wiltshire, married Lady Elizabeth Fox-Strangways. J. Vivian Hughes, 'Thomas Mansel Talbot of Margam and Penrice' *Gower,* Vol. XXVI (1975), pp. 71-79.

Thomas family of Llanbradach and Ystrad Mynach. William Thomas (1734–94), the eldest son of Thomas Thomas by his wife, Ann Williams of Penallta, was twice married. His first wife was Mary Jones of Fonmon, his second a Miss Rankin of Barry. He died childless and was buried at Llandaff. The Llanbradach estate was inherited by his younger brother, Thomas Thomas (d.1807) who married Jane Griffiths of Llanwonno, sister and heiress of Dr Richard Griffiths (q.v.). Hilary M. Thomas, 'The Thomas family of Llanbradach and Ystrad Mynach', *Glamorgan historian,* vol. 10 (1974), pp. 127-47.

Thomas family of Tregroes. The Thomases of Tregroes and Pwllywrach were descendants of the Thomas family of Llanmihangel. Edward Thomas of Tregroes was sheriff of Glamorgan in 1772. David Thomas of Pwllywrach was sheriff in 1777.

Thomas, Thomas (d.1786), attorney of Cardiff. Town clerk of Cardiff 1766–86, an alderman and capital burgess of Cardiff, deputy clerk of the peace 1768–81 and an under-sheriff of the county. He supervised the Cardiff Castle estate, *c.*1778–84. He was a member of the Thomas family of Eglwysnunnydd, Margam. One of his brothers, Lewis Thomas of Baglan, was agent to Lord Vernon (the Briton Ferry estate). Another brother, Edward Thomas, was the land surveyor and cartographer.

Traherne, Edmund (1734–95), of Castellau, Llantrisant. The son of Llewellin Traherne, a customs official at Cardiff, he became collector and deputy comptroller of customs in the port of Cardiff. He married first Mary Llewellin, who inherited Coedriglan from her uncle, and secondly Frances Popkin of Coytrahen. The eldest son of the first marriage was Llewellin Traherne (1766–1841), of Coedriglan and Castellau, who declined the office of sheriff in 1801. The eldest son of the second marriage was Edmund Traherne (1776–1807).

Tynte *see* Kemeys.

Vaughan, Joseph (d.1796 aged 60), of Melingriffith. He was the agent and manager at Melingriffith Iron and Tinplate Works, and was a member of a large family connected with the iron industry. His father Joseph was associated with Melingriffith, and his brother Thomas was the ironmaster of the Pentyrch Works.

Vernon, Lord (1735–1813). George Venables Vernon married in 1757 Louisa Mansel, daughter and heiress of Bussy, 4th and last Lord Mansel of Margam and Briton Ferry. He was M.P. for Glamorgan from 1768 until 1780 when he became the 2nd Lord Vernon. On his death in 1813 the Briton Ferry estate passed to the Earl of Jersey. *CP; Hist. Parl.*

Webborn, John *see* Appendix B.

White, Stephen, of Miskin. A Bristol merchant, later of Bath. He married Cecil Bassett of Miskin, and served as sheriff of Glamorgan in 1785.

Wilkins family of Brecon and of Maesllwch (Radnorshire) formerly of Llanblethian. The Wilkinses were proprietors of the Brecon Old Bank (founded 1778), an institution which provided much of the capital for the industrial development of South Wales. They were also shareholders in the Aberdare, Neath and other South Wales canal companies.

John Wilkins (1713–84) married Sybil Jeffreys, niece and heiress of the banker Walter Jeffreys, and thereby laid the foundation for the establishment of the Brecon Bank. Three of his sons, Walter, who amassed a fortune in India, Thomas and Jeffreys, were associated with the banking enterprise, Walter (d.1828) being its main promoter. Another son, William, was Prothonotary of the Brecknock circuit of Great Sessions. The only daughter, Anne, married John Maybery, son of the industrialist Thomas Maybery and proprietor with John Wilkins of the Hirwaun Ironworks. Descendants of Walter Wilkins assumed the name 'de Winton'. *DWB.*

Williams, Dr Bloom (d.1802), of Cardiff, surgeon. He was coroner of Cardiff, and a bailiff of the town (1792). As doctor and surgeon he was paid a salary by the court of Quarter Sessions for attending the county gaol. His wife was Eleanor Lewis of Newhouse, Llanishen.

Willson (*alias* Wilson), **Alexander** (d.1824), of Cardiff. A customs official - deputy comptroller (1788) and surveyor of customs (1796), a freeman of Cardiff and a capital burgess. He was the son of John Willson and Mary Purcell and nephew of the Cardiff goldsmith Alexander Purcell (d.1768). William Willson, probably the son of Alexander, was a watch and clock maker who worked on the town hall and church clocks in Cardiff in the 1790s.

Wood family of Cardiff. Attorneys and bankers, solicitors to the 1st Marquess of Bute, the Wood family controlled most of the key offices of Cardiff Corporation and the county of Glamorgan. After accusations of mismanagement of Corporation affairs in 1817, they were dismissed from Bute employment and then headed an anti-Bute faction within Cardiff Corporation.

John Wood, senior (1755–1817), of Roath Court, attorney and banker. He was associated with William Taitt (q.v.) in an early banking enterprise in Cardiff, and was a partner in the Cardiff Bank of Wood Evans and Co., later

Wood Wood and Co. He was treasurer of Glamorgan 1785–1802, town clerk of Cardiff 1789–1804, clerk of the peace for Glamorgan 1798–1815, clerk of the general meeting, clerk to the Glamorganshire Canal Company, treasurer to the Cardiff Turnpike Trust, and was also a magistrate, deputy-lieutenant and under-sheriff. He was a captain in the Cardiff Volunteer Cavalry. John Wood married Mary Nicholl of Llanvithyn, by whom he had seven children, among whom was:

John Wood, junior (1781–1846), attorney and banker. He was clerk of the peace for Glamorgan 1815–36, county treasurer 1802–15 and town clerk of Cardiff 1804–15, an office in which he was succeeded by his younger brother Nicholl Wood. He terminated his legal partnership with his brother to concentrate on the banking business, but was declared bankrupt in 1823. John Wood junior was a lieutenant in the Cardiff Volunteer Cavalry, and a deputy-lieutenant and under-sheriff. He married, as his second wife, the widow Mary Ann Hurst (née Wrixon).

Wyndham, Thomas (c.1763–1814), of Dunraven and Clearwell (Gloucestershire). The son of Charles Edwin of Dunraven, who represented Glamorgan in Parliament from 1780 to 1789 as the Beaufort nominee, and a descendant of the Edwin family of Llanmihangel, he resumed the name of Wyndham which his father had renounced. He represented the county in Parliament from 1789 to 1814, thereby frustrating the Bute family's aspirations to impose their nominee on the county seat, but his long parliamentary career was undistinguished. *DWB* (Edwin); *Hist. Parl.*

Appendix A

The Trial of Dr Richard Griffiths at the Hereford Assizes, 1790

This case concerned a game of cards* played at the house of Robert Wrixon in Cardiff on the night of 6 October 1789, the participants being John Blannin, John Richards junior, Robert Wrixon, Samuel Homfray and Dr Richard Griffiths. Wine had evidently flowed at the dinner which preceded the card-playing, Homfray lost £250 to the Doctor, refused to settle his debt and loudly accused his opponent of marking the cards. What began as a drunken quarrel ended in the Assize courts.

At the spring Sessions in Cardiff, 1790, Samuel Homfray of Merthyr Tydfil, ironmaster, brought charges against Richard Griffiths of Cardiff, surgeon, for alleged fraud at cards, the Grand Jury indicted the Doctor and the case was set for trial at the next Sessions. Outraged by the turn of events, Griffiths made some very indiscreet remarks about 'packed juries' which brought him a swift rebuke from the sheriff.

The following July the Doctor, with a small band of supporters, among them Herbert Hurst of Gabalfa, Thomas Bridges, John Richards of the Corner House and Wyndham Lewis of Llanishen, travelled to Hereford for the trial. The indictment was laid on two charges, that Griffiths had won more than £10 at one sitting, contrary to the Statute of 1711 regulating gaming, and that he had committed fraud. The hearing of the evidence and the examination of witnesses occupied the court for more than half a day, but it was a triumphant Richard Griffiths who returned to Cardiff cleared of the charges and determined to publicise the news of his acquittal.

It is clear from entries in Bird's diary that Griffiths offered him the commission of printing an account of the trial but that he considered it politic to refuse for fear of offending the influential Richards family of Cardiff. John Richards junior had been one of the participants in the game of cards, and had proved an embarrassingly unreliable witness for the prosecution. His sister Mary was married to Samuel Homfray's brother. Their father, Captain John Richards, had long been a supporter of the Cardiff Castle interest and Bird had no wish to cause embarrassment to the Richards family or offence to the Marquess.

Thwarted but undaunted by Bird's refusal, the Doctor sought a printer elsewhere, and in 1791 an account of the proceedings was printed in Bristol and freely circulated. The substantial booklet, comprising over a hundred pages, is entitled: *The traverse of an indictment at Hereford before Mr. Baron Perryn and a special jury on Saturday July the 31st 1790, between Mr. Samuel Homfray of Merthir Tidvil in the county of Glamorgan, ironmaster and Mr. Richard Griffiths of Cardiff... surgeon.* Taken in short-hand by William Blanchard short-hand writer, Clifford's Inn, London. Printed in the year 1791. A copy of the booklet can be consulted at the Cardiff Central Library's Reference Department.

* Lazarus: a game of chance. In essence the game involved the dealer dealing the pack into any number of piles and the players placing sums of money on any one or two of those piles. The bottom card of each pile was then turned up. If the player's card was higher than that of the dealer he won the stake, if lower he paid the banker. Blanchard's description of the trial includes a detailed account of the rules of the game.

Appendix B

The Trial of John Webborn at Cardiff Great Sessions, 1799

John Webborn, a Rhossili farmer, was indicted at Great Sessions for the murder of his servant William Thomas, a child of eight or nine years of age, by depriving him of adequate food, clothing and accommodation. Webborn pleaded not guilty to the charge of murder, but was convicted on the evidence of eye-witnesses to his inhuman treatment of the boy, and sentenced to death. Shortly after the trial John Bird printed an account of the proceedings, entitled: *A short account of the trial of John Webborn who was found guilty at the late Great Sessions for the county of Glamorgan of the murder of Wm. Thomas his servant and who was executed in pursuance of his sentence on Friday March 26th at Cardiff*. The booklet also includes Judge Hardinge's address to the court on passing sentence of death and 'An address to all inhuman masters and mistresses'. Bird dedicated the work to Judge Hardinge, Sheriff Goodrich and the gentlemen of the county who had composed the Grand Jury. A copy of the booklet can be consulted at the Cardiff Central Library's Reference Department.

Appendix C

The Court of Great Sessions and the Assize Courts

The Court of Great Sessions for Wales was established in 1543 (27 Hen.VIII cap.26). Twelve of the thirteen counties of Wales were organised into four circuits, with Glamorgan forming part of the Brecknock circuit of Brecon, Radnor and Glamorgan. The courts were held twice a year in each county, usually in the county towns.

The Court of Great Sessions had the power to exercise all jurisdiction exercisable by the central courts of King's Bench and Common Pleas, and also had equitable jurisdication. It therefore dealt with a great variety of criminal and civil cases ranging from murder and assault to trespass and disputes over personal property.

Its officials included the Attorney General, a senior and a second judge, the Prothonotary (principal notary or chief clerk, responsible for the record of the court), the Chamberlain and Chancellor, the court marshall and the court crier.

Great Sessions for Glamorgan were held in March and August. For twenty years (1768-88) they were held not in Cardiff but in Cowbridge, where the amenities of the *Bear Inn,* the facilities of the House of Correction and the more central location of the town all recommended themselves to the judges. But in 1788 the Sessions returned to Cardiff where they continued to be held, in the Town Hall and other appointed premises, until their abolition in 1830.

It was customary for the judges to be met on the outskirts of the town and conducted to their lodgings by the sheriff of the county (an official nominated by the judges), while the sheriff, justices and other county officials would attend church with the judges at the outset of the Sessions to hear a sermon preached by the sheriff's chaplain.

The Court of Great Sessions was abolished by Act of Parliament in 1830 (1 Wm.IV cap.70), and thereafter the Welsh counties were integrated into the Assize circuits of England. John Bird in his diary uses the terms Great Sessions and Assizes interchangeably, a confusion the more understandable when it is remembered that many legal cases originating in Cardiff or Glamorgan in the eighteenth century were brought not before the Great Sessions but before the Assize Courts at Hereford, Gloucester and elsewhere (e.g. the case of Homfray *versus* Griffiths in 1790).

Officials of the Brecknock Circuit in the late Eighteenth Century: Thomas Caldecott, Attorney General 1789-1827 (Deputy: Henry Allen). William Williams, Deputy Prothonotary 1784-99, Prothonotary 1799-1805. Sir Charles Gould, Chamberlain and Chancellor 1799-1807. George Hardinge and Abel Moysey, Judges.

For further details of the working of the court and lists of officials, see W.R.Williams *The history of the Great Sessions in Wales 1542–1830* (Brecknock, 1899).

Appendix D

Sheriffs and Under-Sheriffs of Glamorgan, 1790-1810

	Sheriff	*Under-Sheriff*
1790	William Lewis of Pentyrch	Hopkin Llewellyn of Margam
1791	John Richards of the Corner House	John Wood senior of Cardiff
1792	John Llewelyn of Ynysygerwyn	Hopkin Llewellyn of Margam
1793	John Lucas of Stouthall (Reynoldston)	Rees Davies of Swansea
1794	Henry Knight of Tythegston	John Thomas of Cowbridge
1795	Wyndham Lewis of Llanishen	John Wood senior of Cardiff
1796	Herbert Hurst of Gabalfa	Ditto
1797	Robert Rous of Cwrtyrala (Michaelston le Pit)	Ditto
1798	Samuel Richardson of Hensol	John Williams of Cardiff
1799	John Goodrich of Energlyn (Caerphilly)	John Wood senior of Cardiff
1800	Robert Jenner of Wenvoe Castle	Ditto
1801	Robert Jones of Fonmon	William Vaughan of Swansea
1802	Richard Mansel Phillips of Sketty Hall	John Jeffreys of Swansea
1803	John Morris of Clasemont	William Vaughan of Swansea
1804	Richard Turberville Picton of Ewenny	Ditto
1805	Thomas Markham of Nash Manor	Edward Powell of Llantwit
1806	Anthony Bacon of Cyfarthfa	John Wood senior of Cardiff
1807	George Winch of Clemenston	Edward Powell of Llantwit
1808	John Nathaniel Miers of Cadoxton	Griffith Llewellyn of Baglan
1809	Jeremiah Homfray of Llandaff House	Wyndham Lewis of Llanishen
1810	Thomas Lockwood of Dan-y-Graig (Swansea)	John Jeffreys of Swansea

A list of sheriffs and their deputies will be found in Thomas Nicholas, *The history of antiquities of Glamorgan* (London, 1874), pp. 139–46. For a complete list of the sheriffs of Glamorgan, 1541–1966, with biographical notes on selected families, see *A list of the names and residences of the high sheriffs of the county of Glamorgan* (1966).

170

Appendix E

A Tour in Wales, 1787, by John Byng, Viscount Torrington.

The two diaries filled by John Byng on his tour of Wales provide a few glimpses of Cardiff that complement the writings of John Bird.

Byng arrived in Cardiff on 31 July 1787 and left three days later. He describes Cardiff as 'a newly paved town', and deplores the number of dogs allowed to roam the streets: 'There are more Dogs in Welsh Towns than I ever met with in other Places, who are eternally fighting, or kick'd and whip'd about. Surely every person must join in a wish for a Dog Tax to remove so dangerous a Nuisance' (see Bird, 9 April 1791).

Byng and his travelling companion stayed at the *Cardiff Arms,* the inn patronised by Lord Mountstuart on his brief visits to Cardiff. On their first evening Henry Hollier called on them and took them around the Castle 'which has lately been repaired, adorned etc. etc. by his Lordship'. Byng was unimpressed by Lord Mountstuart's improvements '(he) has now stop'd works as he cannot purchase the Houses and Land in front: which he had better have bargained for before he expended so much money with so much ill taste on the Reparations of his Castle'. Even Mr Hollier, wrote Byng, seemed ashamed of his lordship's bad taste and folly!

Byng also mentions 'a mean cottage built under the castle walls, near the gate house' from which an old woman (Old Franky, see Bird, 18 April 1793) crept forth to open the castle door.

Among those who dined with Byng at the *Cardiff Arms* was 'Mr.Traherne, Mr. Osborn's first Deputy, a Gentleman of this County' — that is Edmund Traherne of Castellau who makes several appearances in the pages of Bird's diary. During their visit to Caerphilly Byng and his companions were conducted around the castle by 'Mr.Howells, a foolish old man' — that is Thomas Howell(s), the bailiff of Senghennydd, mentioned by Bird.

As he left Cardiff, en route for Cowbridge and Neath, Byng visited Wenvoe where he was met by Peter Birt and was conducted around his newly-built mansion, and also passed Coedriglan, 'Young Mr. Traherne's house' - i.e. Llewellin Traherne, eldest son of Edmund Traherne of Castellau.

Byng's Diaries of 1787 are Cardiff Central Library MSS 3.237. The text is published in John Byng, *The Torrington diaries,* ed. C.B.Andrews, vol.1 (London, 1934).

Appendix F

Brief Notes on the Diary of William Thomas.

The diary of the schoolmaster, William Thomas of Michaelston super Ely, covers the years 1762 to 1795 and contains a diversity of local intelligence on personalities, events and scandals in Glamorgan. By the 1790s, when the diary overlaps with that of John Bird, the entries are little more than catalogues of deaths and burials, with only the occasional leavening of biographical details or social comment. But, covering as they do a critical period of social change and industrial development in Glamorgan, both diaries provide valuable insights into the history of town and county in the late eighteenth century.

Events such as the meetings of the Court of Great Sessions, the progress of the Glamorganshire Canal, the borough elections of 1790 and 1794 are recorded by both diarists. Both make reference to the death and burial of members of Glamorgan's gentry and aristocracy, such as Mrs John Richards (née Mary Birt) in 1790 and Lord Mountstuart in 1794. But, with his penchant for recording current scandal and gossip, William Thomas elaborates on some of the more sober recitals found in John Bird's diary. It is doubtful that Bird would have considered the peccadillos of Peter Birt junior, and his liaison with his mistress Anna Plumber, fit or relevant information to be relayed to the Marquess of Bute, information provided by William Thomas when recording the death of Birt in November 1788. Where Bird records with factual brevity the proceedings of the October Sessions in Cardiff in 1791 and the sentencing of two prisoners to death for burglary, William Thomas's diary provides biographical notes on the prisoners and comments on the execution.

Bird's prime concern in compiling his diary was to chronicle events of relevance to the Cardiff Castle estate. While there are occasional references to Bute interests at Cowbridge, Merthyr or Caerphilly the diary is almost exclusively concerned with people and events in Cardiff. William Thomas cast his net wider, gathering news from all over Glamorgan, yet it is strange that it is he, Thomas, who records outbreaks of smallpox and other diseases raging in Cardiff in the 1790s, local 'news' which Bird ignores entirely in his writings.

Where Bird's diary entries are spasmodic William Thomas's compilation runs in unbroken sequence. Between August 1793 and September 1794 when Bird's diary is empty, William Thomas records the death of Lord Mountstuart and the election of his brother Lord Evelyn Stuart to succeed him as M.P. for the Glamorgan boroughs, and the deaths of Walter Williams the Neath attorney, Thomas Williams attorney of Cowbridge 'an honest man and one of the oldest lawyers in Glamorgan', and William Thomas of Llanbradach 'a civil quiet gentleman who died from a lingering dropsy', all of whom were among Bird's acquaintances.

John Bird's entries are those of a busy estate official and man of business, factual compilations for communication to his employer. William Thomas is the commentator, moralist, antiquarian and tittle-tattler, who jots down any newsworthy items brought to his attention and castigates any whisper of immorality. Where Bird is selective and discreet Thomas is the 'snapper-up of unconsidered trifles'.

Bird's position as an official of the Cardiff Castle estate and his own activities as a businessman and civic dignitary gave him a wide range of acquaintances and a diversity of social obligations. William Thomas the school master moved in more circumscribed circles, his acquaintances being the small farmers and labouring families of South Glamorgan to whom he acted not only as pedagogue but also as unofficial legal adviser and secretary. But between the two there is common ground and both provide rich sources for understanding the society of which they were members.

William Thomas's Diary is in the Cardiff Central Library.

Index

Persons whose names are set in bold type have an entry in the Biographical Notes. All place-names are in Glamorgan unless otherwise noted.

his family, 119, 121, 125, 129, 136, 140
his house, 65
his income, 62, 137, 140
his will, 43, 44, 49
as bookseller, 13, 37, 68, 73, 77, 90
as musician, 27, 84
as printer, 13, 36, 37, 41, 58, 59, 88, 137, 144, 145, 167, 168
as Volunteer, 27, 107
Bird family, *pedigree*, 8, 9
Anne, daughter of J.B., 43
Hannah (née Davies), wife of J.B., 35
Jemima, niece of J.B., 44, 46
John senior, father of J.B., 14, 138, 147, 148
John Davies, son of J.B., 37, 41
John Godwin, nephew of J.B., 44
Sarah (née ?Vaughan), wife of J.B., 119, 147
William, kinsman of J.B., 37
birds, J.B. likened to, 39
Birt, Sarah, maidservant, 72
Birt family, of Wenvoe Castle, notes on, 150
Jane, 150, 162
Mary, 51, 142, 150, 163, 171
Peter junior, 150, 172
Peter senior, 53, 69, 146, 150, 171
Blackfriars, Cardiff, 76, 77, 104
Blackweir (Black Wears), Cardiff, 80
Blanchard, William, shorthand writer, 167, 168
Blannin, John, of Cardiff, 53, 57, 69, 70, 86, 167; notes on, 150
Blosse, Sir Robert Lynch, 144, 156
Blue Anchor see under inns
Bold, Mr, marshall in Great Sessions, 90, 140
Bonvilston (Bonvilstone), 79, 121, 163
books and pamphlets, 77, 90, 91
boroughs *see* Cardiff Borough; Glamorgan Boroughs
Boverton, 157
Boviarton and Llantwit, manor of, 123, 129, 142
Golledge lawsuit concerning lands in, 53, 54, 102, 112, 142
Bow Street Runners, 125
Bowen, Mr, 124
Charles, 157
Edward, attorney, 138
Bradley, John, of Cardiff, 37, 62, 85, 86, 106, 128, 129, 135, 136, 137, 140; notes on, 150
Mrs, wife of, 137
Brecon, 59, 75, 91, 112, 114, 119, 124, 156, 165
Bridgend, 44, 53, 108, 120, 152

Bridges, Mr, 62
Mr, of Penarth, 104
Thomas, 57, 167; listed as grand juror, 67, 89, 124
bridges, 102
see also Cardiff; Roath; Rumney
Bridgewater, Mr, exciseman, 85
Bristol, 13, 30, 34, 65, 66, 73, 85, 96, 98, 100, 101, 106, 107, 108, 116, 144, 153, 154, 155, 157, 163, 165, 167
theatre, 41
trade with, 13, 61–2, 129
Bristol Channel, 31
Briton Ferry estate, 164, 165
see also Eaglesbush
Brown, Mr junior, 136
Thomas, of Luton, Beds, 26, 125, 128, 148
Bruce, Margaret, of Llanblethian, 157
Rev. Thomas, of Duffryn, 158
Bruce Pryce, John, 158
Buckland *see* Gwynne
burials, 21, 51, 80, 85, 86, 126
Bute *see* Stuart
Byng, John, Viscount Torrington, 171

Cadoxton Lodge, Neath, 155
Caercady, Welsh St Donats, 67
Caerphilly (Carphilly), Eglwysilan, 51, 73, 77, 105, 113, 155, 171, 172
common, 26, 63, 117
furnace, 155
mountain, 24, 117
see also Pontypandy; Watford
Caerphilly Volunteers *see* Volunteers
Caldecott, Thomas, attorney general, 68, 69, 82, 89, 108, 144, 169; notes on 151
Cambrian see under newspapers
canals, 34–5, 48, 103, 104, 154, 159, 165
see also Aberdare Canal; Glamorganshire Canal; Neath Canal
Candleston estate, 153
Capper, Colonel James, 18, 26, 66, 90, 99, 100, 105, 106, 107, 109, 126, 127, 128, 140, 145, 146, 148; notes on, 151
Cardiff, bridge, 25, 76, 78, 80, 83, 85, 86, 93, 95, 104
castle *see* Cardiff Castle
gaol *see under that heading*
Heath *see* Cardiff Heath
markets, 30, 61, 78, 83, 113, 118, 138, 142, 144, 148
moors, 57, 63, 73, 91, 135, 142
parish boundaries, 63, 160
parish meetings, 100, 113, 144
post office, 37, 135, 136, 137, 140, 150
races, 35, 143

175

Jane, of Llanwonno, 164

Dr Richard, 32, 34, 35, 68, 76, 82, 84, 89, 91, 103, 109, 113, 152, 158, 162, 164; notes on, 154

his trial at Hereford, 34, 52, 53, 57, 58, 61, 65, 131, 144, 155; notes on 167–8

William, of Llanwonno, 154

Grove [Thomas] & Co., of Swansea, 131

Guernsey, Channel Islands, 108

Guest family, of Dowlais, notes on, 154

John, 154

Sir Josiah John, 154, 163

Sarah, 154

Thomas, 59, 130, 131, 163

Guildford, Lady, 124

Guillod, John, of Switzerland, 125

Gwernllwynchwith (Gwernllwyn), Llansamlet, 59, 110

Gwinnet, Emilia, of Cottrell, 78, 89, 90; notes on, 154

Rev. Samuel, 78, 154

Gwyn (Gwynn, Gwynne), Mr, of Buckland, 64; references to Gwynne family of Buckland, Brecon, and Llanelwedd, Radnor, 146, 159

Mr, of Llansannor, 140

Mathew, 72

Hall, Benjamin, 163

Hallingbury Place, Essex, 55, 143

Hanbury, John, of Pontypool, Mon, 158

Hardinge, Judge George, 25, 29, 32, 34, 35, 53, 61, 73, 75, 82, 83, 85, 88, 90, 92, 93, 95, 101, 103, 104, 107, 108, 110, 124, 140, 159, 169; notes on, 154, 155

his addresses to grand juries, 30, 52, 59, 67, 72, 81, 91, 95, 96, 97, 102, 112, 114, 118, 129, 130, 136, 148

his addresses to prisoners, 130, 168

his correspondence 32, 48, 61, 105

Harford, James, of Melingriffith, 62, 78; notes on, 155

Harford, Partridge and Co., 155

Harrington, George, master of Cardiff workhouse, 113

Harris, Mr, of the Splot, 107

Mrs, of the Splot, 128

Hastings, Lady Sophia, 151

hay, 55, 77, 122

Hayes, The, Cardiff, 43

Heathfield Lodge, Swansea, 161

Hendre Fawr (Hendra Fawr), Hirwaun, 58, 64, 69, 70, 134

Henry, William John, 57, 124

Hensol, 35, 102, 163

Herbert family, references to, 142, 147, 155, 156

Hereford Assizes *see* Assizes

Hereford Journal see under newspapers

heriots, 18, 78, 90, 94, 96, 116, 117, 123, 145

Hewell Grange, Worcs, 18, 116, 147

Hill, Richard, of Merthyr, 51, 59, 61, 109, 115, 136, 149; notes on, 155

Richard junior, 136, 155

Samuel, 130

Hirwaun (Hirwain), 64, 80, 88

common, enclosures on, 24, 57–8, 63, 64, 66, 69–70, 144

see also Baili Glaes; Carn y Gust; Hendre Fawr; Twyn y Bryn; Ty Newydd; Tyr Jenkin David Hafard

Hirwaun ironworks, 64, 69, 144, 149, 152, 165

Hollier, Henry, 14–37 *passim*, 57, 60, 63, 65, 66, 70, 71, 72, 73, 75, 77, 78, 83, 86, 88, 89, 90, 91, 93, 94, 95, 96, 98, 99, 100, 101, 102, 104, 107, 108, 113, 116, 117, 119, 120, 121, 123, 124, 126, 127, 128, 129, 130, 132, 133, 134, 135, 136, 140, 148, 171; notes on, 155

Mrs, wife of, 101, 114, 116, 135

Holywell, Oxford, 90

Homfray, Birch & Co., 134

Homfray family, of Penydarren, notes on, 155

Elizabeth, 152

Jeremiah, 97, 112, 130, 131, 144, 155, 162

John, of Penllyne, 163

Mary, 152

Samuel, 34 51, 53, 57, 63, 109, 130, 131, 154, 155, 167

see also Penydarren ironworks

Hope, Colonel, 131, 132

Hopkin, Margaret, 82

Rees, 72

Hopkins, Mr, of Neath, 53

Hezekiah, 62

John, 67

Thomas, 81

Thomas, of Sully, 108

horse racing, 35, 57, 70, 103, 157

horses *see under* animals

Houblon, Jacob and John, 143

Howdon, Mr, 93

Howell (Howells), Margaret, 61, 62

Thomas, of Caerphilly, 19, 51, 77, 96, 105, 171; notes on, 155

Howels, Sir George, of Bovehill, 146

hundreds of Glamorgan, 96, 98, 99, 104, 105, 146

Hurst family, of Gabalfa, notes on 155, 156

Herbert, 56, 57, 65, 156; listed as grand juror, 67, 85, 118, 128, 144

180

Mrs [Mary Ann], 110, 127, 156, 166
William, 20, 70, 75, 76, 89, 93, 104, 127,
  145, 155, 156
Hussey, John, of Cardiff, 86, 113; notes on,
  156

Ilminster, Som, 134
illnesses, 140
  apoplectic fit, 108
  blindness, 127, 156
  blood poisoning, 75, 159
  derangement, 136
  dropsy, 172
  gout, 129, 162
  headache, 65
  infection from catbite, 63
  influenza, 140, 141
  insanity, 127, 148, 156
  lumbago, 41
  obesity, 141
  rheumatism, 41
  smallpox, 172
India, 165
Inniskillins, 132
inns, *Angel*, Cardiff, 55, 56, 63, 78, 80, 84,
  88, 100, 106, 109, 110, 135, 150
  Bear, Cowbridge, 169
  Blue Anchor, Cardiff, 55
  Cardiff Arms, Cardiff, 52, 55, 56, 68, 80,
    83, 84, 91, 93, 96, 105, 114, 116, 122,
    142, 146, 150, 171
  Griffin, Cardiff, 55
  Lamb, Bath, 106
  Lamb, Cardiff, 55
  Mackworth Arms, Swansea, 132
  Pyle Inn, Pyle, 121, 147, 164
  Red Lion, Cardiff, 55
  Rose and Crown, Cardiff, 55
  Ship and Dolphin, Cardiff, 55
inquest, coroner's, 80
Ireland, 83, 121, 140, 147
iron ore, 64, 117, 119, 134, 135
ironworks *see under names of individual*
  works

James, Henry, 72
Jeffreys, family, of Swansea and Brecon,
  notes on, 156
  Gabriel, 156
  John, 156
  Sybil, 165
  Walter, 156, 165
  William, 30, 102, 130, 131, 148, 156
Jenkin, Hopkin, 57
Jenkins, Elias, of Neath, attorney, 76, 83,
  84, 85
  Lewis, of Caercady, 67

Major, 55
Miss Mary, of Cowbridge and Llanbleth-
  ian, 93, 102, 103, 112
Jenkins family, of Pantynawel, notes on,
  156
  Richard, 139, 156
  Richard Hoare, 156
Jenner, Rev. Charles, 156
Jenner, Robert, of Wenvoe, 20, 93, 110, 118,
  122, 124, 146; listed as grand juror,
  107, 110, 114, 136, 150; notes on, 156
  Ann (née Birt), wife of, 150, 156
Jersey, Earl of, 165
John, David, 66
  David, of Ty yn y Wern, 93
  Joseph, of Llantrisant, 72, 76, 82, 145,
    163; notes on 156
  Rosser, of Gelligaer, 117
  Thomas, felon, 60
  Thomas, tenant, 124
  Thomas, of Llantrisant, 54, 107
Johnes, Thomas, [of Hafod], land revenue
  official, 91
Johnston, Mr, 139
Jones, Mr, attorney, 112
  Mr, of Clytha, 94
  Rev. Mr, of Builth, 104
  Calvert Richard, of Swansea, 20, 65, 84,
    121; listed as grand juror, 91, 97, 118,
    130, 155; notes on, 156
  Calvert senior, 156
  Daniel, of Llantwit Major, 108, 124, 128
  Henry, of Penmark, 90
  John, merchant of Cardiff and Bristol,
    91, 93; notes on 157
  John, of Bristol [?John senior], 157
  Robert (d. 1793), of Fonmon, 58, 80, 83,
    90, 123, 163; notes on 157
  Jane (née Seys), wife of, 157
  [Joanna née Lloyd], wife of, 128
  Mary, sister of, 164
  Robert (d. 1834), of Fonmon, 116, 122,
    123, ?124, 128, 129; notes on, 157
  Diana, sister of, 95, 157, 160
  Stephen, of Swansea and Merthyr Mawr,
    108, 119, 147; notes on family of, 157
  Theophilus, of Brecon, 113, 140
  Thomas, constable of Llantrisant, 72
  William, grand juror, 67, 85
jurors *see* Great Sessions

Kemeys family, of Newport, notes on, 157;
  Mr, 57
  William, 157
Kemeys-Tynte family, 150, 157
  Mr and Miss, 135
Key family, of St Fagans, notes on, 157

181

Pendoylon

St.Georges

Michaelsto

Mill

Sup.r Ely Red Hous

Drope

Mill

Warren House

Tre yr hedin

Culver House

Sweldon

Green Way

Bonvilston

Rev. Gwynnet Cottrell

Coedrhyglan

Llwellyn Treharne Esq.

6

Rhiwau

St. Nicholas

Alps

Y N A S

St. Lythans Down

P O W

Darrac

Walstan

Micl

J.n Anbrey Bar.t

Grimon

St. Lythans

Wrinch stone Castle

Wenvoe

Lanvithen

Carnllwyd

Dyffryn House
Pryce Esq.r

Dyffryn

Wenvoe Castle
Rob.t Jenner Esq.r

Crofsdun

Walterstown

Hamston Vowr

Old Wallas

New Wallas

St. Andrews

H

Lancarvan

idmoor

U N D

R

Molton

Cadox

Penning

Penmark

Merthyrdovan

Rob.t ones Esq.r

onmon Castle

Walters Farm

Holton

New Mill

Treduchan

Hill

rthaw

Fontigary

Roos

Castle

N N E

Porthkery

Barry

BARRY ISLE

RTHAW HARB.

N N E